Professional Competence and Education: The ASSET Pro

Dedication

To the ASSET Programme candidates
whose successful struggles with educational innovation,
often in adverse circumstances,
have been a continual source of inspiration

Professional Competence and Higher Education:
The ASSET Programme

Richard Winter and
Maire Maisch

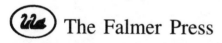 The Falmer Press

(A member of the Taylor & Francis Group)
London • Washington D.C.

UK	The Falmer Press, 1 Gunpowder Square, London, EC4A 3DE
USA	The Falmer Press, Taylor & Francis Inc., 1900 Frost Road, Suite 101, Bristol, PA 19007

First published in 1996

A catalogue record for this book is available from the British Library

Library of Congress Cataloging-in-Publication Data are available on request

ISBN 0 7507 0556 6 cased
ISBN 0 7507 0557 4 paper

Jacket design by Caroline Archer

Typeset in 10/12pt Times by
Graphicraft Typesetters Ltd., Hong Kong.

Printed in Great Britain by Biddles Ltd, Guildford and King's Lynn on paper which has a specified pH value on final paper manufacture of not less than 7.5 and is therefore 'acid free'.

Contents

Contents

List of Documents

Preface

For the past six years Anglia Polytechnic University has been working in partnership with Essex Social Services Department and (for three years) with Ford Motor Company in developing and establishing programmes of work-based, competence-referenced professional education, one in the area of social work and the other in engineering. These two programmes constitute the ASSET project (see Chapter 2) and were funded and supported by the Further and Higher Education Branch of the former Department of Employment of the UK government.

Richard Winter worked jointly with Samantha Guise (a former Ford engineer and currently director of the Learning From Experience Trust) in developing the pilot phase of the Ford (Engineering) ASSET Programme, and with Maire Maisch in developing the Social Work ASSET Programme. The ASSET 'model' of professional education (see Chapter 2) was originally developed in the Social Work Programme, which is currently fully established as the basis for post qualifying professional education in Essex Social Services department, with nearly 100 practitioners enrolled.

Maire Maisch worked jointly with Richard Winter in developing the social work ASSET Programme, and for the last three years has been the Director, Coordinator, and Lead Tutor, with Richard Winter acting as consultant and occasional tutor for modules for social work 'mentors' and 'practice teachers'.

The book is largely based on the experience and documentation from the Social Work Programme, since it is much more advanced and established than the Engineering Programme, which has only recently moved on from its pilot phase. The text has been jointly authored throughout by Maire Maisch and Richard Winter, with the ideas for each chapter being fully discussed and agreed before one of us drafted a preliminary version which was then extensively revised in the light of the other's comments. There are also contributions from many other people, especially the external examiners, tutors and candidates of the Social Work Programme and members of the Ford ASSET team. These contributions are indicated in the text. A full list of all those who contributed more generally to the development of the project is included as Appendix A. The list is a long one, and we take this opportunity of acknowledging the enormous amount of widespread creative work it represents. Without all those people, the ASSET work would not have taken place.

More specifically, the ASSET project would not have been possible without the support and encouragement of a generally innovative educational culture in Anglia Polytechnic University. The senior managers in the Faculty of Health and Social Work and in the Faculty of Technology had already established strong partnership links with Essex SSD and Ford Motor Company, and the staff of the University Centre for Accreditation and Negotiated Awards were a continual resource: time after time we found that the procedural problems we came up with *could* be solved and had frequently been anticipated. In this respect we would particularly like to express our appreciation of the work of Mick Betts, Lynn Brennan, Chris Harris and Mike Taylor. Especial mention must be made also of the visionary capacities of Professor Anne Hilton and Paul Stanton (both of Anglia Polytechnic University) who envisaged the possibility of the ASSET project in the first place and worked with Peter Rudge and Joyce Brough of Essex SSD to articulate its initial outline.

Our thanks are due in general to Essex Social Services Department and to the Ford Motor Company for their enthusiastic cooperation in developing and implementing the ideas of the project, and to the Employment Department for funding the work. We were also particularly fortunate in that the Employment Department was represented on our steering committees by David Pierce, whose supportive wisdom was a continual source of stimulation. Whenever David said, 'There's something here that I don't quite understand, and perhaps someone can explain it to me', we knew we were about to learn something important.

Thanks also for helpful comments from the following friends and colleagues who kindly found time to read earlier drafts of the book, in whole or in part: George Booker, Clare Gillies, Susan Hart, Mike Holman, Samantha Guise, Vivien Nice, Mike Taylor, and Chris Wood.

Our book is about education as a collaborative partnership, and the writing of the book as well as the work it describes are further examples of its topic. Thank you to all our collaborating partners.

Richard Winter
Maire Maisch
Cambridge, Chelmsford
September 1995

Foreword

Beyond the walls of academic institutions there is a hungry ocean of educational demand that is far removed from our traditional view of universities. It is the ocean of demand for continual professional and management education. Professions that twenty years ago regarded qualification as a once and for all entry ticket to practice are now encouraging and sometimes requiring continuous professional education and development. Science and technology are radically changing. Professions that make use of these developments have to update themselves continually. Even professions that are less technologically based like social work and the law have to adapt constantly to economic and social change. Managers have to update their knowledge and extend their skills. The demand for professional and management education and development is huge. But it must be relevant and effective. That is not easy to establish.

Some years ago I attended a development programme for senior managers. It was costly to launch and costly to run; so a great deal of effort went into evaluating its effectiveness. As one of the earliest participants I was questioned in detail and at length about my experience of the programme, what I had hoped to get out of it and what effect it had had on me. These questions proved extremely difficult to answer. Although I had found the programme stimulating and was sure that I had greatly benefited from it I found it hard to be precise about the concrete benefits or effects despite two visits at an interval of several months from those who were conducting the evaluation. This is not an unusual situation in assessing the value of management or professional education and development.

Richard Winter's and Maire Maisch's book addresses both of the above issues. It is a study of how they and a group of colleagues addressed the need for effective education and development in two different professional groups: social workers and motor engineers. They have drawn on, and combined, three different traditions — the principles of National Vocational Qualifications in defining precise outcomes, the tradition of critical and independent professional practice, and the university tradition of theoretical understanding and rigorous questioning and assessment. They have identified in painstaking detail the particular competences and the more general qualities of analysis, judgment and critical understanding required for effective practice of the professions concerned. They have found ways of developing and assessing these skills and competences in the daily practice of the profession rather than in the less direct forum of the seminar room or lecture hall.

In this country we tend not to value the intellectual demands of experience which takes place outside the formal structures of education. The unique feature of the work described in this book is the linking of professional education and development in the workplace with the rigorous disciplines of analysis and assessment of the university. The strength of the link depends much on recognizing and valuing the learning that takes place in the workplace itself. It gives the method a general applicability and the potential for wider recognition.

Richard Winter and Maire Maisch do not minimize the difficulties. The success of the programmes described in this book depends not just on the practitioners' commitment in undertaking them but also on tutors and assessors who need to apply their knowledge and skills in an unfamiliar environment away from the lecture or tutorial room and on the active support of employers and managers in the workplace. They also describe the problems which a university has in adapting its traditions to new contexts for learning and unfamiliar ways of assessing performance.

It does not come easily. But it is hard to see how universities can make the full contribution to the educational needs of the nation which is expected of them without a close engagement with the particular educational needs of industry, commerce, the professions and the public sector. This is not just a matter of turning out graduates with the right qualities, knowledge and skills in their early 20s. It requires engagement over the lifetime of employment.

Because the work-based learning and degree programmes take place in the workplace they integrate into normal work what might otherwise be off the job training either in the university or in training programmes provided by employers. That does not mean they can be incorporated unnoticed or effortlessly into the normal routine of work. They require a structure and a degree of discipline and supervision which adds to the stresses and relentless demands of the workplace.

The work of Richard Winter and Maire Maisch and their colleagues offers a guide to the enormous and valuable opportunities for the practical and economical development of professional and management education and development. It also signposts a road for universities to meet the aspirations of many managers and professionals who wish to deepen and extend in a disciplined way their knowledge and skills. Although their work focuses on social work and engineering the ideas and methods in this book have potential application in many other fields of management and professional practice, such as health, the law, teaching, and public sector management. Any wider application would need the same detailed analysis of particular competences and general qualities as has been applied in the fields of social work and motor engineering.

But the two most crucial requirements are support in the workplace and acceptance and development by universities of the necessary tutorial and assessment methods. This book stimulates thought about the role and practice of universities in adapting and extending their traditions of theoretically based knowledge and critical understanding to the requirements of professional and management practice in the last decade of this century.

Mike Malone Lee
Vice-Chancellor
Anglia Polytechnic University

1 Introduction: Vocational 'Competences' and the 'Relevance' of University Education

An Ancient Debate

The ASSET project is an attempt to establish an innovative model of post qualifying vocational higher education, based on a radical application of the principle
of work-based (experiential) learning and a competence-based curriculum format
within the values and procedures of a university. Our book is addressed to colleagues in higher education, in vocational education and training, and to all who
have an interest in the presentation and organization of professional education. It
contains a detailed analytical description of the ASSET project, with an account
of its theoretical basis and its general implications. These implications involve an
engagement with a broad and ancient debate, namely how 'education' is (can be/
should be) 'relevant' to practical life experience.

The possibility of a gulf between 'education' and 'life' is widely celebrated
in popular humour: from the physics professor who cannot mend a fuse and the
economist who, faced with the problem of how to open a can of beans on a desert
island, begins: 'Let us assume that we have a can-opener'; to the ghetto youth
asked by his maths teacher how long it will take to fill a bath of given volume when
water is flowing *in* from the taps at a given rate and *out* through the plug-hole at
a different rate: 'Man!' he exclaims, 'I wish I had *your* problems!' On the same
theme, but in a different tone, Pelikan (1992) writing about 'The Idea of the University' begins by reminding us of George Eliot's portrait in the novel *Middlemarch*
of Edward Casaubon, exemplifying the aridity of academic learning divorced from
social effectiveness. And it is equally relevant to our theme that the same novel also
presents, in the figure of Lydgate, a portrayal of a *professional* life, in which a commitment to knowledge is expressed through a commitment to the development of
practice and vice versa. Eliot shows us, by implication, the nature and structure of
the supportive relationships that such a life pattern requires, how easily it can fail
in the absence of such support, and how those with potential for achieving it are
excluded through lack of opportunity — all key themes for the following pages.

George Eliot's novel, with its oblique celebration of the possibility of the
professional life, was published a year earlier than the final text of Newman's
well-known vision of the university as a site of 'liberal' education, where 'liberal' is

contrasted with the 'servile' pursuit of commercial and professional aims (Newman 1982 [1873], pp. 80–1) and where the pursuit of knowledge is 'its own end' (Discourse V), characterized by a 'philosophical' spirit based on the dispassionate grasp of 'underlying' principles (p. 76). The debate between these two conflicting views is both unfinished and ancient. On the one hand Pelikan's recent book is explicitly an attempt to reassert the contemporary relevance of Newman's vision (Pelikan, 1992, pp. 9–10) and on the other hand Cobban argues that *medieval* universities 'were inextricably bound up with utilitarian values. They evolved as institutional responses to the pressure to harness educational forces to the professional, ecclesiastical and governmental requirements of society' (Cobban, 1975, p. 8). Thus, he also reports complaints by thirteenth century scholars (!) that the study of 'humane letters' in the universities was being overtaken by the study for pecuniary motives of law and medicine (op. cit., p. 18).

Our book is a case study, and after 700 years of debate we do not pretend to have found any simple solutions. What we have tried to do, however, in the ASSET project, is to recognize the legitimacy of the educational arguments on both sides of this debate and to bring them into an orderly relationship through a coherent and feasible set of procedures.

The Current Emphasis: Skills and Competences

In recent years educationalists in the UK have experienced an upsurge of government sponsored efforts to reinforce the links between educational curricula and the world of employment. (Significantly, the government departments of 'education' and 'employment' were amalgamated as this chapter was being written.) Initiatives such as the Technical and Vocational Educational Initiative (1983) and the introduction of the Certificate of Pre-Vocational Education (1985) in schools were followed in the late 1980s and early 1990s by the 'Enterprise in Higher Education' movement (reported in Heywood, 1994) and a variety of projects, funded by the government Department of Employment, in which work experience was accommodated within higher education curricula. The brochure describing this work explicitly indicates the emphases which the Government has attempted to encourage in higher education, including: 'employer relevance, employer partnership, high level skills supply, and the development, assessment and accreditation of work-based learning' (Employment Department, 1990, p. 88. ff.). Similar themes have been proclaimed by the Confederation of British Industry (1989), The Council for Industry and Higher Education (1987; 1995), the Institute of Directors (1991) and the Trades Union Congress (1989). There have even been proposals to establish a university specifically for and within the motor industry, based on recent developments in information technology (*Times Higher Education Supplement*, 23 June, 1995, p. 60).

This focus on education linked directly to employment has met with predictable resistance on the part of educators who resent what they see as an attack on the liberal university tradition (Barnett, 1990, 1994), the loss of the 'independence' of educational curricula and their subjection to the demands of industrial and managerial control (Elliott, 1991; Field, 1991). However, on behalf of the new 'work-based' higher education curricula it is claimed that they represent not a narrowing of educational vision but, on the contrary, a broadening of access to educational opportunity (Employment Department, 1990, p. 88, ff.) and a broader conception of the nature and process of education in keeping with the promotion of mass participation in 'lifelong learning' (Ball, 1990; McNair, 1993). This again, is not a new line of argument — see Evans (1981), Houghton and Richardson (1974) and, indeed William Morris:

> Education so begun for the child will continue for the grown man, who will have every opportunity to practice the niceties of his craft if he be so minded, to carry it to the utmost degree of perfection . . . for his own pleasure and honour as a good artist . . . The factory, by cooperation with other industrial groups will provide an education for its own workers, and contribute its share to the education of citizens outside. (Morris, 1994 [1884], pp. 15–17)

At the centre of the current phase of this debate, and of key importance, both in terms of the power of its influence and the specificity of its proposals, is the work of the National Council for Vocational Qualifications (NCVQ), which was set up as a result of government proposals in 1986 and rapidly developed a general model for the formulation of 'national standards' as the basis for an integrated continuum of national vocational qualifications (NVQs) in the UK. The starting point for the NVQ format is the authoritative publication of 'competence statements' (i.e., 'standards') which specify by means of detailed 'performance criteria' what students must be able to *do* in their employment context in order to gain a particular qualification. The NVQ format thus specifies in detail the *outcomes* of learning, rather than any particular educational process, so that the emphasis is on the gathering and presentation of *evidence* by the student (in relation to the specified outcomes) and on the valid assessment of that evidence. Assessment is based on a straightforward 'criterion-referenced' decision ('pass' or 'not-yet-sufficient-evidence') rather than on the conventional 'norm-referenced' grading of candidates in comparison with others (Jessup, 1991, p. 167; NCVQ, 1991, p. 21; NCVQ 1995a, p. 30).

This suggests a radical approach to the design of educational curricula, which has been wholeheartedly endorsed by the UK government (and also by the New Zealand government — see NZQA, 1993) and it currently sets the agenda for thinking about the development of vocational education in UK higher education (see CVCP, 1994). The principles behind the NVQ format emphasize: learning outcomes, rather than teaching processes; the individualized variety of work-based evidence, rather than prescribed assignments; the accreditation of what students can already do (as well as what they learn) so that unnecessary repetition of familiar material can be avoided; open access, and transparent assessment procedures. Such ideas pose an intriguing array of challenges to the 'conventional wisdom' of higher education, and seemed to promise a way forward in exploring ways of increasing both the relevance of learning and the empowerment of the learner. The ASSET project took these ideas as its starting point, and our book is an exploration of how far we were able to realize these promises in practical terms, i.e., how far we have been able to establish a unified process which combines the specification of work-based competences with the processes and values of universities. It is a 'case study' of work in two specific areas (social work and engineering) but the project was intended from the outset to devise principles and procedures which would be generalizable to vocational higher education as a whole. For example, the ASSET model shows how 'general' and 'specific' assessment criteria can be systematically linked (see Chapter 4), and how the accreditation of prior experiential learning can be fully integrated into the assessment of learning from current practice (see Chapter 2).

The National Council for Vocational Qualifications (NCVQ) has also nego-tiated with other curriculum agencies a vocationally oriented system of general qualifications (General National Vocational Qualifications — GNVQs) in which the NVQ format is combined with more conventional academic work in a unified *framework* for educational awards (see NCVQ, BTEC, *et al.*, 1995). The use of a modular framework to 'connect' academic education and vocational experiential learning is not new, but its possibilities have recently been (and are currently being) explored with renewed vigour (see Finegold, *et al.*, 1990) and the elaborate 'Unified Curriculum Project' based in the University of London Institute of Education Post-16 Centre). Thus, the ASSET project included the development of a unified award framework in which students could combine conventionally taught theory-based modules and competence-based modules within a single honours degree pathway. But beyond the issue of a *connecting framework* lies the more complex and contro-versial issue of a single curriculum process which in itself integrates academic and vocational learning and thus requires a radical rethinking of both. It is with this issue that the ASSET curriculum model is mainly concerned (see Chapters 2 and 4).

The work of NCVQ (both the 'purely vocational' NVQs and in the 'mixed' format of GNVQs) also attempts to integrate competence-based vocational training with Newman's notion of 'general' education through an emphasis on 'core trans-ferable skills', relevant to the whole of a student's life experience. These have also been attacked for their narrowness of conception (see Barnett, 1994, Chapters 4 and 5) but — in contrast — Ross *et al.*, 1993) have attempted to forge a link between the 'Enterprise in Higher Education Initiative' and a specifically *philosoph-ical* curriculum, including 'reasoning' and 'reflexivity' as part of the development of 'maturity' (Ross, *et al.*, 1993, pp. 7, 8, iv), which relate closely to the GNVQ 'grading themes' — see Chapter 4 in this volume. Again: the debate with the ghost of Newman continues.[1]

Vocational 'Competence' and 'Higher Education'

The 'practical' case for competence-based vocational education (tied to the spe-cification of detailed learning outcomes 'required in employment') has two linked arguments: (i) the needs of the national economy for a 'skilled' 'workforce' in its fight for survival in a competitive global market, and (ii) the need to ensure that those who provide services may be held 'accountable' to their various clients for the quality of those services. Both arguments are more complex and less educationally restrictive than they first appear. As regards the first argument, the nature of the 'skills required' by a 'competitive' workforce remains a fairly open question, and many would argue that they are highly general and are just as much concerned with creative and critical initiative as with specific prescribed actions (see Chapter 8, on 'learning organizations').

The second argument has a number of implications for educational curricula and processes. If universities are to be 'accountable' to their students and to the future employers of those students once they are educationally 'qualified', this means that universities must ensure the transparency and the justice of their assessment procedures and they must also ensure the *effective* relevance of their curricula, since educationally qualified practitioners (i.e., universities' ex-students) will be accountable to their own clients for the appropriateness, justifiability, and quality of the services they are now 'licensed' to provide. This argument is clearly not only about organizational responsibilities — the control and assurance of 'quality' in a culture of consumer's and service-users' rights (expressed from time to time in published 'charters'). It also poses the challenge of fair and equitable educational assessment (NCVQ, 1995a, pp. 31–2, paragraphs 4.3, 4.3.1) to institutions whose key decisions (the assessments which create 'qualified' students) have long been shrouded in a carefully nurtured, self-protective mystery (see Winter, 1993a). This mystery concerning 'outcome' criteria has meant that access to educational qualifications has been restricted to those able to attend prescribed courses of study, and it has also led to periodic expressions of concern concerning lack of comparability of assessment standards across institutions and across disciplines (see, for example, *Times Higher Education Supplement*, 18 September, 1992, p. 3).

These are significant *educational* considerations, but the educational issues are, of course, much broader than this. The aim of the ASSET project is to establish the possibility of a 'bridge' between the legitimate values and aims of higher education and those of employment, and in this context it is helpful, as an introduction to the purpose of our book, to consider the arguments of a recent influential study of what are presented as the educational limitations of the concept of 'competence' (Barnett, 1994) by a writer for whom the idea of the 'liberal' university remains a significant and current ideal (see Barnett, 1990). Barnett readily concedes the ideological limitations of much of the conventional practice of higher education (Barnett, 1994, pp. 178–9) but he is equally critical of the 'impoverished' notion of 'skills' and 'competences' which underlies the work of NCVQ (op. cit. Chapters 4 and 5):

> *If* higher education is in part the acquisition of skills, we must conclude that a *higher* education must develop [a] double capacity: the ability to frame a situation in a range of possible ways and the capacity to identify the appropriate skills to bring to bear on the situation as defined. (Barnett, 1994, p. 58)

He goes on to present a properly 'enriched' conception of 'skills' appropriate for higher education. Skills, he says, must be complex; they must involve reflection, judgement, values, and *breadth* of understanding (op. cit., pp. 58–61). In Part 3 of his study he describes what he terms the 'lost vocabulary' of higher education: understanding (including self-evaluation) critical thinking, interdisciplinarity, and wisdom (the 'integration of knowing, reflection, and action', p. 147). In a final section he proposes a conception of higher education which is 'beyond competence', namely 'life-world becoming' — a form of 'reflective knowing' which accepts the provisional status of both knowledge and practice and subjects both to 'continuous scrutiny' (pp. 179–80) and he ends with a list of general criteria for a genuinely 'higher' education (p. 185), including:

- Systematic reflection on one's actions . . .
- Reinterpretations of the presenting situations . . .
- Openness to possible forms of analysis . . .

Now, our argument is, precisely, that we sympathize entirely with Barnett's views. The ASSET project is above all an attempt to extend and refine the competence-based curriculum model so that it emphasizes complexity, judgment, and critical understanding, both in what candidates are already accomplishing in their practice and in what they learn through their work for the Programme. Indeed, this was the argument of one of our earliest research papers, presented at the British Educational Research Association conference in 1990, and adapted here in the second section of Chapter 4 and Appendix E. In particular, we think that a *practice-based* curriculum for *professional* education is a genuine educational opportunity for the recovery of Barnett's 'lost vocabulary' (understanding, critique, interdisciplinarity, wisdom) and our book may be read as an attempt to illusrate that claim (although we would be the first to admit that the ASSET Programme as it stands is no more than the indication of a possibility).

The Structure of the Book

In Chapter 2 we outline the ASSET project, the two educational programmes it developed (in social work and in engineering) and — in particular — the ASSET curriculum model, indicating its close links with the NVQ model and also a crucial respect in which it differs, namely the introduction of a second dimension of assessment derived from a *general* conception of intellectual development and professional responsibilities. We also provide a sketch of the educational values which underlie our approach.

In Chapter 3 we describe the method by which we identified the specific competence statements which form one dimension of our assessment criteria. We explain the reasoning behind our adoption of the 'functional analysis' method proposed by NCVQ and we discuss the authoritative 'status' of such statements of competence: how far do they succeed in attaining a recognized validity which genuinely transcends our own preconceptions as curriculum designers?

Chapter 4 describes the second, 'general' assessment dimension in which the ASSET model differs most sharply from the NVQ format. We present the arguments for this departure and the outcomes of the research processes (both theoretical and empirical) which led up to the formulation of a set of Core Assessment Criteria. We explain in detail the use of this 'two-dimensional' assessment procedure and discuss how it differs from approaches such as the NVQ/GNVQ inclusion of 'core skills' units.

In Chapter 5 we discuss the relationship between competence statements and 'underpinning knowledge'. In this chapter the double focus of the ASSET project on both social work and engineering is of particular importance. In our main argument we draw upon a distinction between 'propositional' and 'process' knowledge to argue that if competence statements are properly formulated they ought, in themselves, to entail a grasp of the requisite cognitive, judgmental, and reflective capacities. However, we recognize that the relationship between practice and 'bodies of knowledge' may be different in different disciplines.

In Chapter 6 we describe the assessment issues which arise in an innovatory educational programme, once it is recognized that, even with the specificity of detailed competence statements, assessment is never a simple act of 'objective measurement' but always an act of interpretive judgment, and thus requires the building of a consensus concerning the range of acceptable interpretations. We explain how the ASSET Programme, since it leads to an honours degree award, deals with the problem of grading, given that the UK system of degree classifications renders a fully criterion-referenced assessment process impossible at that level (though not, in principle, at other levels).

Chapter 7 presents examples of ASSET candidates' work, so that readers can make their own judgment as to how far our ideals of competence-referenced 'reflective practice' at honours degree level have actually been realized.

Chapter 8 examines how far the Progamme has been able to establish its other key ideal — the 'educative workplace'. It describes the potential harmony between the practice objectives of employing organizations and the educational objectives of staff development initiatives (such as ASSET) as embodied in theories of 'the learning organization'. It also describes the actual experience of tension between the priorities of education and those of service delivery or production in the harsh financial environments of current employment contexts. We then present the procedures of the 'Peer (Learning) Group' in which the ASSET Progamme attempts to resolve these tensions, and discuss how far such procedures may perhaps be inherently necessary for the effective operation of work-based education.

In Chapter 9 we present an overall evaluation of the ASSET model after five years of operation, based on the analysis of questionnaire responses returned by ASSET candidates on the Social Work Programme and their managers.

In Chapter 10 we briefly indicate the direction of future developments of the model, i.e., towards greater involvement of candidates in formulating competence statements and units of learning and towards the development of a *postgraduate* version of the ASSET model of professional education.

We recognize that our book provokes as many questions as it answers, but we believe that a new set of questions can be a powerful source of educational illumination. It is in this spirit that we present our account of the ASSET Programme.

Note

1   GNVQs are proving to be popular, especially as an alternative to the academic emphasis of UK school examinations (*Times Higher Education Supplement*, 30 June, 1995, p. 1; p. 11) and the latest consultative document (NCVQ, 1995b) stresses a number of features which indicate that the GNVQ format, like the ASSET Programmes, are intended as a 'bridge' between general education and work experience (see our 'conclusion', Chapter 10 this volume). However, the GNVQ format is as yet (September 1995) at an early stage of implementation, and GNVQs at university level are a proposal, rather than a reality. Only time will tell whether its various features (core skills, optional units, traditional teaching and assessment of academic knowledge, project work, and 'reflexive' grading themes) will combine to form a coherent curriculum formulation, and it is hardly surprising that a recent report on the assessment process in GNVQs finds considerable duplication of effort and confusion (see Wolf *et al.*, 1994). How much the GNVQ model and the ASSET model (see Chapter 2) have to learn from one another remains an interesting question to be explored over the next few years.

2 The ASSET Programme: An Outline

A Brief Chronology

Towards the end of 1989, the Higher Education Branch of the Training, Enterprise, and Education Directorate within what was then the Employment Department of the UK government agreed to fund a project, jointly proposed by Anglia Polytechnic University and Essex Social Services Department. The project was to initiate a post qualifying course for social workers, which was rapidly christened 'The ASSET Programme': Accreditation for Social Services Experience and Training.[1]

The general aim of the project was to explore whether the competence-based design for vocational qualifications developed by the National Council for Vocational Qualifications (NCVQ) could be used as the basis for *curriculum* design in the context of 'professional' higher education. More precisely, the aim was to establish an honours degree level *post-qualifying* award in social work, for qualified practitioners, focused on work-based 'competences' (skills, abilities, and knowledge). The award would consist of distinct units, validated both by the university and also by the Regional Social Work Post-qualifying Training Consortium on behalf of the Central Council for Education and training in Social Work (CCETSW). It would be a recognized academic and professional qualification, which would also confer eligibility to proceed to higher degree level studies.

At that time, in 1989, NCVQ had begun to develop a competence-based approach to vocational education in contexts such as catering, social care assistance, hairdressing, and vehicle maintenance, which are not usually associated with the demands and traditions of higher education. In contrast, little had been done to explore the applicability of the emerging notion of 'competence' and the assessment of workplace evidence in the contexts where professional practice is associated with university-based education.

As part of the same general government policy which was driving the work of NCVQ, the Employment Department was making available funds for educational initiatives which would explore the links between educational institutions and employers, such as those pioneered in the UK by the Learning From Experience Trust under the general title of 'Accrediting Work-based Learning'. Anglia Polytechnic University already had such links with a variety of local employers. In particular, there was an existing partnership between The Faculty of Health and Social Work and Essex Social Services, arising from an extensive provision of pre-qualifying, qualifying and post-qualifying social work courses.

Essex Social Services Department training section, for their part, were keen to explore a mode of training provision which would offer a developmental route for qualified staff currently in post and which would attempt to ensure that their high level of investment in post experience training would be reflected in more effect-ive workplace practice. The Department attached especial importance to providing a form of training which would avoid the need for expensive secondments from employment, and could thus also be made available to staff whose training needs had hitherto been relatively neglected. The initial focus of the work was in child care, due to the particular need for practitioners with post-qualifying training in that area of specialism.

At the same time, the professional validating body for social work, the Central Council for Education and Training in Social Work (CCETSW) was seeking to develop a coherent framework for post-qualifying education and training which would provide academic credibility for a profession where the basic qualification was not of graduate status, and at the same time would be responsive to the needs both of employers and of staff. For this reason, CCETSW were interested in a format which could provide both academic and professional qualifications, based on the assessment of evidence from practice. Furthermore, in order to ensure progression within the CCETSW framework of qualifications, it was important to establish that the ASSET Programme was at honours degree level. It needed to be more demand-ing than the Diploma in Social Work (the basic professional qualification) and yet also allow for the separate establishment of the CCETSW 'Advanced Award' as a postgraduate higher degree (MA or MSc) (see CCETSW, 1992 [1990], p. 12). CCETSW were thus involved from the start in planning and negotiating the project with the Employment Department, and the CCETSW officer responsible for post-qualifying training was from the outset a member of the project steering committee (see Appendix A). This in turn meant that the ASSET Programme was intended to enable students to gain simultaneously both academic credit, through Anglia Poly-technic University's modular credit system, and professional credit within the CCETSW 'framework' through the regional 'consortium' for professional awards.

After preliminary planning between the university, Essex Social Services, CCETSW, and the Employment Department, a project team was appointed (see Appendix A) and work began early in 1990. Research work was undertaken to clarify the meaning of 'honours degree level' intellectual achievement and the nature of 'professional' qualities and responsibilities (see Chapter 4) and the detailed 'competences' required in the practice of social work (see Chapter 3). After an initial set of procedures and documents had been tested in a pilot phase, an honours degree in social work (i.e., the ASSET Programme) was validated by the university in March 1992, with competence-based 'modules' in 'core' social work and child care. Further competence-based modules covering most of the other social work specialisms were validated in May 1993, after a further phase of research, also funded by the Employment Department.

This degree programme (The ASSET Programme) is now established as the basis for post-qualifying education and training within Essex Social Services department. Its director was originally a shared appointment between the univer-sity and Essex Social Services. Like all awards at Anglia, its underlying structure is a modularized system of credit accumulation and the overall programme consists of a large number of optional modules. Most of these are in the competence-based format (see Appendix B) but some are based on social services' own 'in-house' courses and others are conventionally taught courses offered within the university.

By 1992, it seemed as though the Social Work Programme had established a workable set of procedures and the question arose as to whether the basic approach could be applied in a different context, i.e., how far it could be put forward as a *general* model for practice-based professional education. A potentially fruitful opportunity to explore this question seemed to be provided by the close relationship between the Ford Motor Company and the Technology Faculty of the University, where there was an established programme providing degrees in automotive engineering through the accreditation of prior experiential learning (APEL) and the accreditation of the Ford Motor Company's own training courses. A project was thus initiated in which our purpose was to use the model devised by the social work ASSET Programme, in order to develop further the opportunity for Ford engineering staff to acquire an honours degree on the basis of the learning acquired through their work experience.

Encouragement for the Ford project derived equally from the university, anxious to explore further an innovatory initiative in an area (collaborative partnerships with employers) which was increasingly being defined as a key aspect of the university's work, and from the Ford Motor company, conscious of a competitive commercial environment, and therefore keen to explore ways of improving simultaneously the academic qualifications and professional skills of its staff.

The Ford project began in September 1992, with further funding from the Employment Department. The new project was called the Ford ASSET Programme (with ASSET now standing for Accreditation and Support for Specified Expertise and Training). Again, the programme team involved staff both from the university and from Ford, and the coordinator appointed to the project by the university was herself a former Ford engineer. As a result of the Ford project questions were raised about some aspects of the original ASSET model, and many of the examples and analyses presented in the ensuing chapters draw significantly (explicitly and implicitly) on the lessons learned from the Ford extension of the ASSET Programme.

In March 1994 the Ford ASSET Automotive Engineering degree was validated by the university. By the end of 1994, the pilot phase of the programme had been completed, with the first cohort of seven engineers having completed a 'planning module' and a number of them nearing completion of their first work-based learning module. By this time approximately sixty Essex social workers were enrolled on the Social Work ASSET Programme, with fourteen of them due to be awarded their degree in 1995.

The ASSET model of Professional Education: The Key Components and How They Are Related

'ASSET' was originally the title of a development project, as outlined above, and is now the title of two degree programmes within Anglia (in social work and in engineering) which are based on a characteristic set of processes and documentation, i.e., those developed by the project. These fundamental processes and the key forms of documentation which support them are referred to as 'The ASSET model of professional education' or 'The ASSET model' for short.

This section provides a rough overall guide to the model, outlining its 'components' in turn and showing their relationship by means of a diagram. The final section of this chapter summarizes briefly the rationale behind these different aspects of the model. Subsequent chapters will subject the various aspects in turn to detailed analysis and evaluation, and provide illustrative examples.

1 **Modules** (i.e., units of learning)

Each module consists of a coherent set of competence statements ('elements of competence') which together form a 'unit of competence' referring to the requirements of a particular aspect of workplace practice. (The term 'module' is used, rather than NCVQ's term 'Unit of Competence', for two reasons: i) it is better known in educational institutions, where 'modular credit' systems are being widely introduced; ii) it signals that the set of competence statements has actually been academically validated as an integral part of a *curriculum* document, i.e., as a unit of learning gaining separate academic credit, whereas NVQ 'Statements of Competence' are, in principle, only intended as *guidance* for curriculum designers.) The competence statements listed in each module were derived through a research process based on the elicitation of employment competences as described by groups of practitioners by means of a 'functional analysis' of their work role. (This process is described in Chapter 3; for examples of 'modules' see Document 2 and Appendices C and D.)

2 **Specifications of underpinning knowledge** (*Ford Programme only*)

These were derived by comparing the competence statements indicating the requirements of the occupational role with the learning outcomes of a relevant academic programme. These specified academic requirements thus become part of the basic module documentation. (This is discussed in Chapter 5.)

3 **Core Assessment Criteria**

In contrast to the *specific* occupational competence statements listed in the 'modules', the Core Assessment Criteria (embodying the *general* requirements of the professional role and of honours degree level work) constitute a 'second dimension' of assessment (see Chapter 4). These general criteria are applied throughout the assessment of each module. They were derived through a research process involving:

- a general theory of the nature of professional occupations, i.e., what they require in terms of ethical responsibilities, knowledge, interpersonal understanding, and continuous learning;
- a study of the conceptual vocabulary used in assessing honours degree level work, in a variety of vocational and academic fields;
- a study of practitioners' rankings of their own lists of personal constructs concerning qualities required by the professional role.

(see Chapter 4 for an explanation of how these Core Assessment Criteria differ from the NCVQ 'Core Skill')

4 A module portfolio of evidence

This is the collection of various types of evidence, concerning past and/or current practice, produced by a candidate to demonstrate the specific workplace competences listed in the 'module' document. This 'evidence' must be at the standard indicated by the Core Assessment Criteria (see Chapter 4), and in the case of the Ford Programme the required 'underpinning' knowledge, see Chapter 5. (Examples of extracts from candidates' portfolios are presented in Chapter 7.)

5 A module action plan

For each module an action plan is negotiated between the candidate, the workplace supervisor, and the tutor. The Module Action Plan interprets the elements of competence in terms of the candidate's particular work context, specifies how the Core Assessment Criteria will be fulfilled, and indicates what documentation will be collected or developed as evidence. It may include reference to relevant previous experience and it will include plans for the observation of the candidate's practice and plans for work needing to be undertaken.

In the case of the Ford ASSET Programme, this planning process is extended to cover an overview of the candidate's work for the programme as a whole, and earns separate academic credit as a '**planning module**'.

6 Tutorial guidance

Tutorial guidance concerning the general operation of the programme procedures and up-do-date specialist professional and academic information, is provided by the tutor, i.e., university staff or training staff of the employing organization.

7 Workplace support

This may take one of two basic forms:

- The candidate's line manager may be the official programme supervisor with responsibility for providing support for the candidate's work and contributing to the negotiation of the Module Action Plan. All supervisors must undertake training modules to prepare them for this support role, and this will also earn credit within the award.
- Alternatively, groups of candidates can form a 'peer group', working and providing support for one another under the guidance of a programme tutor. In this case the workplace supervisor then has the lessor role of supporting candidates' work by enabling them to take the time required and of discussing with them, in a general way, their work for the programme. (see Chapter 8 for a full discussion of these alternatives.)

8 Training support

Negotiating the Module Action Plan (or undertaking the Planning Module) may lead to the identification of training experiences to enable candidates to acquire or demonstrate the specified competences, etc. This experience may include:

- participating in courses arranged by the employing organization, by the university, or elsewhere, which would earn academic credit within the programme;
- undertaking 'structured professional experience', such as visits, consultations with specialist colleagues, and brief placements in relevant work contexts.

9 Assessment

The assessment for each module must include at least one element of competence where the evidence is mostly derived from the observation of practice in the workplace. (The argument for this relatively low proportion of observation evidence is presented in Chapter 6.) Observation is carried out either by a programme supervisor (but *not* the candidate's line manager (see Chapter 8) or by a member of the candidate's peer group (see Chapter 8, Appendix G, and Document 9). The assessment for the other elements of competence, which generally do not involve evidence from workplace observation, is carried out by programme tutors. The work for the module as a whole needs to be graded (A–D) if the candidates choose that their final award will be a ('classified') honours degree (see Chapter 6). If, instead, a candidate chooses the award of a Graduate Diploma of Professional Studies (equivalent to the honours degree in standard, but not classified) then all the assessment is on a 'pass'/'insufficient evidence' basis. The tutor providing support and guidance during the candidate's work submits the portfolio to another tutor for final assessment.

10 Accreditation of prior learning (APL)

Candidates are encouraged initially to submit evidence of relevant prior certificated learning, in order to gain credit within the programme. (A number of existing courses at various universities, including Anglia, have been formally 'recognized' in this way, through Anglia procedures specifically developed for this purpose.) However, candidates may also include in their portfolios documentation of learning derived from past practice just as easily as evidence relating to current practice, in order to demonstrate a specified element of competence. In a sense, therefore, the distinction between 'prior' and 'current' evidence of learning is not of key significance within the ASSET Programme. But it is also important to emphasize that the ASSET model itself constitutes a rigorous APL procedure, since it potentially gives equal status to prior and to current practice, in terms of their relevance for academic and professional credit.

11 Quality assurance

The programme is subject to university quality assurance procedures, as follows:

- All assessments are monitored and guided by external examiners from other universities;

- A detailed annual report on the operation of the programme is written by the programme director, agreed by the programme committee (which must include all tutorial staff and student and employer representatives) and scrutinized by the Faculty Academic Standards Committee.

A Diagram outlining the relationship between these components is presented in Document 1.

Document 1

The ASSET model of Professional Development: Relationships between Components

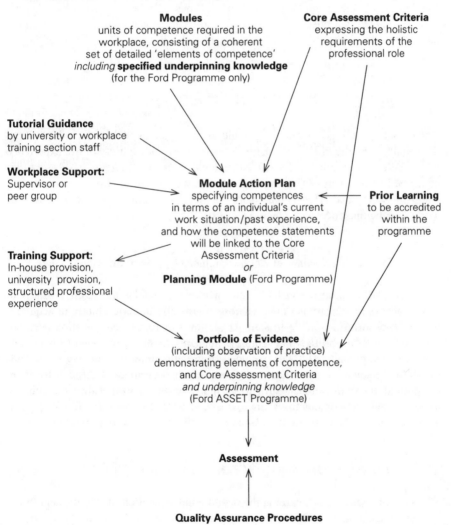

Modules
units of competence required in the workplace, consisting of a coherent set of detailed 'elements of competence' *including* **specified underpinning knowledge** (for the Ford Programme only)

Core Assessment Criteria
expressing the holistic requirements of the professional role

Tutorial Guidance
by university or workplace training section staff

Workplace Support:
Supervisor or peer group

Module Action Plan
specifying competences in terms of an individual's current work situation/past experience, and how the competence statements will be linked to the Core Assessment Criteria
or
Planning Module (Ford Programme)

Prior Learning
to be accredited within the programme

Training Support:
In-house provision, university provision, structured professional experience

Portfolio of Evidence
(including observation of practice) demonstrating elements of competence, and Core Assessment Criteria *and underpinning knowledge* (Ford ASSET Programme)

Assessment

Quality Assurance Procedures

The Educational Values Underlying the ASSET model

From this brief outline of the origins of the ASSET Programmes and the components of the ASSET model, we hope that a picture is beginning to emerge of how the ASSET project attempts to intervene critically yet constructively in the debates surrounding the role of competence-defined curricula and the accreditation of workplace learning in university-based courses of professional education. In Chapter 1 we argued that these debates are long-standing, wide-ranging, and complex, and the purpose of the rest of the book is to elucidate and evaluate the ASSET Programme's attempts to engage with them. In this section, therefore, we merely try to make explicit our starting points, many of which have already been hinted at in Chapter 1 and in the outline presented above. What follows is, in other words, a simple (and perhaps, indeed, simplistic) indication of the basic educational philosophy which motivated our work and created a sense that the issues were matters of urgent concern.

Learning Derived from Experience beyond Formal Schooling

One of our most important starting points is that systems of educational qualifications undervalue the intellectual achievements of the wide variety of life experience which takes place outside formal educational contexts. More precisely, we are concerned to find ways of giving official educational 'credit' for learning derived from the workplace. Hence the focus on units of learning defined in terms of workplace competences.

Extending Educational Access: 'Equal Opportunities'

The focus on learning derived from the workplace enables the ASSET model to extend access to educational qualifications by making the opportunity to acquire a degree level award available to staff whose level of formal qualification does not do justice to their abilities. For example, the programme is intended to help staff who felt (and perhaps still feel) excluded from the culture of academic work, and/ or whose personal circumstances and financial situation made it difficult for them to continue their education, and/or feel (rightly or wrongly) that they are unlikely to be offered secondment from employment in order to undertake further professional development through attendance at a college or university-based course.

'Relevance': The Linking of Theory and Practice

We share the widespread regret at the institutional separation of 'theory' and 'practice' and the defensive attitudes which have grown up to reinforce this dichotomy. In particular, we sympathize with the various voices which lament the apparent failure of academically based post-qualifying courses to contribute to the improvement of professional practice. For this reason, the ASSET model is designed to try to ensure that candidates' work for the programme genuinely documents the quality of current practice and also leads to a raising of the standard of practice, together with an increase in professional understanding. Hence, therefore, the intention that the ASSET Programme procedures should allow the award of academic credit and professional credit to coincide in one assessment process based on a single portfolio of evidence.

The Specification of Assessment Requirements

In order to give candidates maximum autonomy in organizing their work for the programme, the ASSET model attempts to provide an assessment process which should be as 'transparent' as possible. Hence the detailed specification of competences, the Core Assessment Criteria, and (in the Ford Programme) of underpinning knowledge. The ASSET handbook of requirements and guidance aims at a level of detail which would in principle allow candidates to work independently at the preparation of their portfolios of evidence, with the need for tutorial assistance reduced to a minimum. This in turn makes possible a considerable degree of formative peer-assessment and self-assessment.

The 'Holism' of Professional and Educational Processes

The danger of the argument in the previous paragraph is that it can lead to competence statements in a form which leaves candidates working largely from lists of apparently fragmentary 'performance criteria'. In contrast, the ASSET model is specifically concerned to rescue the competence-based approach to curriculum design from common accusations of fragmentation and reductionism (see Callender, 1992, p. 27) and to ensure that it embodies general educational values and criteria (see Chapter 1). For this reason we established from the outset a 'second dimension' of assessment in the form of *general* criteria (the Core Assessment Criteria) which embody a *holistic* specification of educational requirements and professional responsibilities, achievements, and abilities. This is the key difference between the ASSET Programme documentation and conventional NVQs, and gives the ASSET model its uniqueness and (as we see it, in the light of the current debates) its importance. The theoretical basis for this aspect of the model and its various implications are presented in Chapter 4.

Individual Choice, Rather than Prescription

Finally, we are concerned that our attempts to 'be specific' as to required learning outcomes should not lead to documentation of such prescriptiveness that it leaves no space for individual choice or negotiation. Hence, our emphasis on the planning process, in which candidates focus on the need to *interpret* the pre-specified competence statements in relation to their own context. Hence, also, the 'core' requirements are embodied in 'general' criteria, allowing candidates to construct an individualized and developmental sequence of modules appropriate to their particular practice context and career situation from the large array of available possibilities (see Appendix B). Following this logic further, we are now beginning to introduce the option of constructing 'hybrid' and 'personal' modules, as described in Chapter 10.

In the following chapters these general statements will be explained and refined and details will be added to the outline, so that the intentions and aspirations indicated so far can be checked and evaluated in the light of the programme documentation and the experience of its various participants.

Note

1 The point is often made that what is to be given educational credit is not *experience* as such but rather *learning* derived from experience. This distinction is not quite as clear-cut as is sometimes maintained, since it can be argued (and we would wish to do so) that the professional role *requires* learning from practice and that something important is missing if it does not occur (see Chapter 4). Perhaps it might have been better if the acronym had stood for '*expertise* and training', but we came to this conclusion only after several programme documents had been issued with the original wording. We did, however, amend the wording of our title in the acronym for later stages of the project.

3   The Functional Analysis of Competences: An Empirically Based Curriculum?

Background and Rationale

This chapter describes the ASSET Programme experience of defining a vocational curriculum in terms of specific learning outcomes or 'competences'. We present examples of the competence-based units of learning ('modules' — see previous chapter) together with an account of the method of their construction and an evaluation of their format. The general rationale for the approach is given, leading to a discussion of the advantages and limits of the 'functional analysis' method recommended by the National Council for Vocational Qualifications (NCVQ, 1995a, p. 17, paragraph 2.3). This is followed by a presentation of examples from the social work ASSET Programme, an analysis of how and why the ASSET format differs from the NCVQ model, and finally a discussion of the strengths and limitations of specifying competences as an approach to designing a vocational curriculum. This discussion leads directly into the recognition of the need for another dimension in the model, the Core Assessment Criteria, which is the topic of the next chapter.

The competence-based approach to curriculum design is not an invention of the UK government and the NCVQ, nor did it simply spring into being in the late 1980s. Tuxworth (1989) traces it back directly to the USA and the 1960s, where it was a powerful influence on teacher education, and to the 'behavioural objectives' movement in curriculum design in general (p. 11). Norris (1991) makes a similar link, through the work of Ralph Tyler, a central figure in the development of the objectives model of the curriculum whose work also included analysing the 'competencies' of teachers (Norris, p. 338).

The fundamental rationale underlying both the 'competence-based' and the 'objective-based' approaches is straightforward: unless the details of the intended outcomes of the learning process are specified in advance then neither teachers nor learners can estimate whether their efforts are being successful, which means that teachers cannot be held accountable, that learners are vulnerable to intuitive *ad hoc* assessment decisions, and that attempts to improve the effectiveness of learning cannot be properly evaluated. This argument clearly applies to academic education as well as vocational education — see the rationale for a 'learning outcomes' approach to curriculum design in Otter (1992, pp. 2–3). Although the general line of argument has an immediate plausibility, there is an equally strong counter-argument which opposes the emphasis on specifying the details of required learning outcomes in advance of the learning process: according to this argument, learning is essentially a creative individualistic *process*, in which outcomes thus have an inescapable dimension of unpredictability (see Eisner, 1975; Ashworth, 1992). In some respects, the ASSET Programme may be seen as an attempt to achieve a balance between these two counterposed aspects of the learning process.

The starting point for current work on competence-based vocational education in the UK is summed up in Gilbert Jessup's book *Outcomes* (Jessup, 1991). Jessup argues that statements of competence should be derived 'not from an analysis of education and training programmes or the preconceptions of educators and trainers, but from a fresh analysis of present day employment requirements' (p. 18). In other words, he is opposed to the 'proprietory control' exerted by 'educators and trainers over the process of learning'; instead he espouses a 'learner-centred stance': it is individual learners who should 'exercise control over their own learning' (p. 4). This is part of a concern with broadening access to qualifications, irrespective of the availability or otherwise of taught courses (one of the 'criteria' of National Vocational Qualifications, see Jessup, p. 19). This in turn leads to a general curriculum model which is based on publicly specified assessment criteria relating to the 'outputs' of successful learners, rather than on a description of 'inputs' to be provided by educators. Learning will also be more effective, he says, where outcomes are clearly specified (p. 5) and he goes on to argue for 'a new kind of standards that make explicit the outcomes sought in education' (p. 11).

If we accept, for the time being, that there is a rationale for attempting to specify the details of learning outcomes, we nevertheless find ourselves immediately faced with a difficult question: where should such specification come from? This question is described by Macdonald-Ross, in his wide-ranging critique of the objectives curriculum model (Macdonald-Ross, 1975) as 'a serious and deep-seated problem of *origins* [of behavioural objectives] which has never been solved' (p. 355). Jessup's work presents us with this question in an acute form, since he seems to propose two incompatible answers at the same time. On the one hand, his approach is, as we have seen, an attempt to give the individual learner control over her/his learning; on the other hand, it is a search for 'national standards' — in which statements of what learners must do are derived from the needs of the national economy (Jessup, 1991, Chapter 2). To whom, therefore, should we turn in our search for properly authentic learning outcomes/objectives/statements of competence? If we agree that what Jessup calls *educationalists'* 'preconceptions' concerning the content of vocational curricula could benefit from the challenge of additional evidence, do we consult a national professional body, or a trade union, or an employer's association, or a national body who might claim to speak on behalf of the national economy? Or do we consult practitioners, who will give us their own view of the details of practice?

The answer we give to this question is important, because competence statements (like 'behavioural objectives' and 'required learning outcomes') are *prescriptions*, and thus need to be generally accepted by learners as authoritative, i.e., well-founded and realistic. Hence the intractable question about the 'origin' of learning outcomes: the search for authoritative detailed statements about learning outcomes is a search for a certain type of *consensus* among various interested parties. The ASSET Programme has adopted a slightly different route to this consensus from that adopted by NCVQ, even though a key element in both cases is the search for an authentic account of the requirements of workplace practice, in order to ensure that vocational qualifications are 'relevant' to the 'needs' of practitioners and their clients.

The NCVQ search for an authoritative basis for statements of required competence pursues, broadly speaking, the 'corporate route', i.e., it attempts to establish organizations with a nationally representative status, whose conclusions can be promoted bureaucratically as 'national standards' and will be institutionally, even legally binding. To this end a series of Industry Lead Bodies have been established, consisting of training organizations and professional bodies, together with 'employers and employee representatives' (Jessup, p. 41). Since NCVQ is concerned to set up a 'national system' of qualifications with endorsement by the State government this is entirely unsurprising; it is how government works. But there is a question as to how far such 'national' prescriptions will be immediately accepted by either educators or professional practitioners: there is a 'legitimation crisis' (Habermas, 1976) at the heart of modern society which is widely felt by higher education staff, by professional workers, and indeed by many of the population at large, which means that expressions of institutional authority as such are quite likely to meet with some degree of resistance, even if formal compliance is, in the end, forthcoming. Hence the significance of Jessup's argument that the NCVQ model is *learner*-centred, even though it 'also' aims to express the requirements of the national economy.

The ASSET Programme, of course, as a locally based initiative, without the institutional authority of a governmental agency, necessarily takes a slightly different approach to this issue, but the comments at the end of the previous paragraph suggest that this may have advantages. The main purposes of our efforts to devise competence statements were, therefore, as follows:

1 to ensure that our degree programme specifies publicly what learning outcomes will be required, in order to increase candidates' sense of 'ownership' of their learning;
2 to try to ensure that the learning outcomes of the programme are compatible both with the texture of candidates' individual professional experience and with the values and culture of the profession as a whole.

Our efforts, therefore, were in the first instance devoted to establishing competence statements which would seem acceptable to our practitioner candidates, i.e., which would seem challenging but realistic, feasible but 'worthwhile'. In other words, whereas the NCVQ Industry Lead Bodies merely recognized the need to 'consult' with 'employees', for the ASSET Programme the inclusion of the practitioner's voice within the curriculum documentation was our main goal. Of course, this did not remove the problem of the validity or otherwise of our statements of competence. To begin with, in the Social Work Programme we had to ensure that the results of our consultation with practitioners were acceptable to the professional body, The Central Council for Education and Training in Social Work, to the practitioners' Trade Union, and to the local employer, Essex Social Services Department. These three dimensions of acceptability were sought through a form of corporate consultation which is not, in essence, dissimilar to the negotiations of a lead body, albeit on a local scale. Secondly, we needed a method of gathering and analysing the data from groups of practitioners for which some degree of generalizability could be claimed, since all concerned (and especially the university) naturally insisted that the qualification should in principle have national currency. Again, this led us towards processes which are similar in many ways to those undertaken by lead bodies.

To sum up: although it will be seen, in the following sections, that the ASSET Programme has 'borrowed' many of the methods recommended by NCVQ for the formulation of 'national standards', our reason for adopting these methods was not that we wished to carry out the functions of an Industry Lead Body, but because we decided (for reasons to be explained below) that the NCVQ recommendations concerning 'functional analysis' were also appropriate for our own slightly different purposes, namely to construct a curriculum which would be fully informed by practitioners' accounts of their practice. The ASSET Programme is, in other words, a 'social research' route to an empirically based vocational curriculum.

Deriving Competences: The Question of Method

We considered a number of ways of gathering and interpreting data about the detailed texture of social workers' practice: nominal group technique (O'Neil and Jackson, 1983), network analysis (Bliss *et al.*, 1983), focus groups (Morgan, 1988), content analysis (Holsti, 1969, Weber, 1985), personal construct analysis (Kelly, 1955), critical incident analysis (Spencer, 1983), and functional analysis (Fennell, 1989).

In the end we used aspects of various methods, but our basic approach was that of functional analysis (described in detail in the next two sections) which combined various advantages. First, it encourages a large number of practitioners to register the detail of their experience, unlike nominal group technique, where the emphasis is, from quite an early stage, on the gradual elimination of some contributions in order to seek a consensus among group members. Second, functional analysis focuses on what it is that practitioners actually do by means of a sequence of questions which minimizes (though it does not wholly remove) the need for the researchers (i.e., ourselves) to impose an interpretive framework. In this way it has advantages over the focus group method; the latter requires a phase of 'content analysis' (Morgan, 1988, p. 64) which entails either the wholescale imposition of the researcher's concerns (Holsti, 1969, p. 94) or an attempt at a 'general semantic coding' (Weber, 1985, p. 24ff.) which must at best result in excessive abstraction and loss of concrete detail. Network analysis is based on the creation of a 'logical' classification system for a collection of detailed data, which in itself is highly problematic, since there can be no such thing as a 'purely' logical classification without a prior interpretive schema, and here again functional analysis has a distinct advantage: by using a sequence of questions starting from practitioners' perceptions of the 'key purpose' of their role, the practitioners' own ordering of their responses is to some degree 'built in' from the outset.

The personal construct method, as the name suggests, tends to generate respondents' interpretive categories, rather than the actions they carry out, and for this reason it plays an important part in helping to define the Core Assessment Criteria of the ASSET model (the topic of the next chapter) rather than the detailed competence statements with which we are concerned here.

Considerable claims have been made for the value of critical incident analysis, especially as part of the MacBer Company's work on 'Job Competences' (see Elliott, 1991) and so its claims will be examined in more detail in the remainder of this section, before turning to the details of our functional analysis method in the next section. The analysis of 'critical incidents' described by practitioners was used by McBer and Co as an attempt to devise criteria for assessing the competences of USA diplomats. The method is presented in Spencer (1983): 'It asks interviewees to identify the most critical situation they have encountered on their jobs and describe these situations in considerable narrative detail' (p. 2). These narratives were then correlated with the State Department's original categorization of the interviewees as professionally 'superior' or 'average' and subjected to a 'thematic analysis' (p. 7) in order to create a set of 'behavioural patterns and personality characteristics which distinguish superior from average job incumbents' (p. 7).

One of the weaknesses of the approach is that its underlying logic is 'circular': it assumes at the outset what it is trying to investigate. It seeks to use critical incident analysis to create *test criteria* which will *differentiate* 'superior' practitioners from others, but the outcomes of the critical incident analysis phase of the work is entirely dependent on the basis for the original assessment of practitioners (i.e., as being either 'superior' or 'average'). Furthermore, because the correlation between 'superior' practice and the test criterion (e.g., 'accurate empathy' — Spencer, p. 10) is established *statistically*: it *could*, therefore, always be due to another 'intervening' factor, as yet unidentified. In other words, this method, like others mentioned above, depends crucially on the interpretive categories used by the researchers and is thus subject to the disadvantages of 'content analysis' noted above (see Spencer, 1983, p. 7).

In the light of these considerations, therefore, the ASSET Programme followed Alison Wolf (1990) in using the analysis of practitioners' narratives merely as a check upon the validity of the results from the functional analysis, i.e., as a form of methodological 'triangulation'. (The material from this analysis is presented in Winter and Maisch, 1992, pp. 39–46.)

Analysing Competences: Functional Analysis

'Functional analysis' has become well known (through the work of NCVQ) as a method for investigating the content of occupations with a view to clarifying standards for the award of qualifications. It starts with the clarification of a 'key purpose' (i.e., the overall social 'function') for the occupational area, and this is followed by a sequential analysis of details of the required activities, prompted always by the question: 'What needs to happen for this to be achieved?' (Fennell, 1989, p. 4). The method thereby describes a set of occupational activities in terms of a 'structural-functional system', generating a hierarchical pattern in which the detailed elements at one level have the 'function' of making possible the achievement of more general elements at the next level 'up'. Conversely, the general statements at one level are 'disaggregated (see Mansfield, 1989, p. 7) into their constituent details, which at the 'lowest' level of the hierarchy take the form of 'performance criteria'. In principle, therefore, the method aims both at comprehensiveness and clarity of relationships between component activities, although it does present a number of general difficulties.

The first of these concerns the apparent implication that an exhaustive list of 'concrete' performance criteria can be derived from a small number of 'abstract' purposes, simply by means of a 'logical' process of 'disaggregating' wholes into parts. The difficulty here is that in theory the number of observable features of an action is infinite, so that in order to decide on the details at the later stages of the analysis (i.e., the 'performance criteria') some criteria of relevance must be imported from elsewhere. In other words, a functional analysis document, provides an *interpretation* of what is required, not an 'objective description'. This is an important reminder, which serves to counterbalance the persuasive appearance of logical inevitability and comprehensiveness created by the hierarchical format of the analysis. (There is, of course, nothing surprising about this: assessment criteria — in this case the specified competences — always depend for their operational meaning upon the culture within which they are used. Indeed the point is made by one of NCVQ's own consultants: 'the employment value' of the units, elements, and criteria of the functional analysis are 'a political and pragmatic decision' to be taken by the members of an occupation (Miller, 1989, p. 13).)

A second major problem is the emphasis on 'performance criteria' (Fennell, 1989, p. 5). The many-levelled hierarchical format of the NCVQ 'standards' suggests that functional analysis is simply a process of progressively disaggregating general responsibilities into component activities. However, there is an underlying unity to the conception of exercising the responsibilities of a *role* (as indeed the term implies) and to the conception of a *person* engaging in a process of learning. Indeed, functional analysis also has a focus upon 'whole work roles rather than a series of tasks' as the first of its three 'essential features' (Fennell, 1989, p. 3). The social workers participating in our functional analysis groups were therefore not unusual in emphasizing the 'holism' of their practice, i.e., in specifically denying that the characteristic overall ability required can adequately be understood simply as an aggregation of component skills. (see also, for example, Douglas's critique of performance criteria in an article called 'The wholeness of care', 1990, p. 23). The general issue is highlighted by one of NCVQ's key consultants, who stresses the importance of starting with 'a clear functional statement of [sic] the entire occupational area' in order to avoid identifying 'isolated and unconnected tasks' which are 'then aggregated into units' in which 'overarching aspects of the work role and non-task activities and responsibilities' are missing (Mansfield, 1989, p. 5). But this lack of holistic awareness, of course, is precisely the accusation levelled by Douglas at the functional analysis method. The problem is that the process of 'disaggregating' detailed competences from an initial overarching 'holistic' purpose *looks* as though it can with equal plausibility be reversed into a process of assembling a model of professional competence (singular) from a series of discrete competences (plural). And this is what worries professional practitioners and educators alike. (The point was made to us several times by social workers and by engineers during our own functional analysis sessions.)

One might focus this issue by contrasting two different relationships between detail and totality: the 'mechanical and the 'organic'. The mechanical model evokes a complex mechanism which is made up of many components which are all clearly separated from one another, and can be replaced and substituted: one component can fit a number of different mechanisms. The organic model, on the other hand evokes biological forms, in which every cell of a plant or animal bears the DNA code which pre-defines the whole organism, and attempts at substitution between organisms are inherently anomalous, at best difficult, and frequently impossible. It was the organic model which originally underpinned structural functional descriptions of social phenomena: 'The concept of function applied to human societies is based on an analogy between social life and organic life' (Radcliffe-Brown, 1964 [1935], p. 629). In the light of the argument of the previous paragraph, one could argue that it is the organic rather than the mechanical model which should be seen as underlying the functional analysis of employment practices.

There is another way of considering the matter, which is also consistent with the organic model described above. Pat Benner, in her influential study of nurses' professional competences (Benner, 1984) also claims that practical knowledge must be studied holistically (p. 39) and goes on to say that her work 'resembles the study of a text' (p. 39). This echoes her earlier citation of her intellectual debt to the work of Hans-Georg Gadamer (see Benner, p. 8; p. 36). Now Gadamer's method is indeed derived from the study of texts: it involves the well-known 'hermeneutic circle' in which details are given meaning only by the totality of which they are a part, and (competing the 'circle') the 'total' meaning is arrived at only by considering the complex relationships among many details (Gadamer, 1975). Here, then, we have a firm statement concerning the relationship between concrete details and 'overarching' meanings, in which a particular practice (e.g., giving a bed-bath — Benner, p. 40) can *only* be assessed (as indicating competence or incompetence) in the light of the whole professional context.

For this reason, we were not dismayed when social workers participating in the ASSET Programme functional analysis sessions did *not* progress in the course of the discussions towards increasingly concrete behavioural detail (as a simple reading of the hierarchical format might lead one to expect) but frequently returned to earlier general notions (such as 'keeping an open mind as to the possible effects of interventions'). Rather, this confirmed our feeling that the holistic nature of employment roles does not permit an unambiguous behavioural specification of 'competent' practice: the particular detail of practice 'required' at a particular moment (a touch, a tone of voice, a decision) often 'all depends' on the context. And in order to make that judgment of the context (and hence of the detail) practitioners must draw upon the complex totality of their professionalism.

This whole argument has two very important consequences for the format of the ASSET model. First, the specification of *detailed* requirements in the statements of competence is complemented by a second dimension of assessment, the Core Assessment Criteria specifically embodying the 'overarching' aspects of the role (see Chapter 4). Indeed the outline of these general requirements was sketched out *before* we undertook the functional analysis work, and thus provided our interpretive analysis with explicit criteria of relevance. Second, our detailed competence statements avoid the language of 'performance criteria' as tending to imply that precision of judgment can be found *simply* through 'behavioural specification' of detailed activities.

There is also a third, rather different emphasis on which we would like to end this discussion of methodology. Although we originally described our approach as a form of 'social research' (as opposed to a corporate negotiation), this may risk implying that the practitioners played the passive role of simply giving us 'data' to analyse. The account of the process below will, we hope, correct that implication: the practitioners, it will be seen, contributed the elements of the interpretive framework itself; indeed, functional analysis appealed to us as a method largely because (unlike some other approaches) it seemed to encourage and to require a collaborative mode of working and a respect for practitioners' own understandings which underpins the ASSET Programme as a whole (see Chapter 2). How this actually worked out in practice will be seen in the next section.

Functional Analysis: Working with Practitioners

This section describes the functional analysis work with social workers, leading to the development of the competence-based 'core' social work modules. Further work to develop modules in various 'specialist' areas of social work was undertaken separately later.

Altogether twenty-seven social workers took part in this phase of the work, in five groups varying in size between four and eight members. Four of the groups were drawn from different parts of Essex, and one group consisted of a social work team in Greenwich, in central London. Participants were all experienced and professionally qualified workers, whom we had contacted through their line managers.

We used the sequence of questions described by Miller (1989) and outlined in the Training Agency Guidance Note No. 2 (see Fennell, 1989, p. 4), and offered minimal direction, allowing a brainstorming process to operate where possible. The format of the discussions was thus as follows:

1   Establishing the key purpose. This involved two questions:
    • think of one phrase that sums up the focus of the work that you do.
    • what is the key purpose of the work that you do?

2 We then asked: 'What new developments are there in the field?' and 'Do these new developments affect the original summary phase?' (Responses at this point sometimes changed the original summary phase, giving a different emphasis or adding a word, but generally verified the key phrase and key purpose.)

3 The next stage was to establish a framework of tasks and work roles by asking: 'What has to happen for the key purpose to be achieved?' or 'What is involved in doing this?' Three 'prompt categories' were used here:
   - task-oriented: referring to activities/responsibilities which directly fulfil the requirements of the key purpose.
   - organizational: referring to the management of the working environment, e.g., people, records;
   - creative: managing change, innovation, and development.

4 Finally we took each of these statements in turn and developed them further by asking in each case, 'What do *you* have to do to achieve this?'

The sessions lasted approximately two-and-a-half hours. If it appeared that we would not have time to 'disaggregate' all the listed statements and would be left with two or three, we asked the group to choose which of the remaining ones they felt were more important to focus on.

Throughout the sessions, we checked with the group that what was being written on the sheets was an accurate reflection of what was being said. At the end of each session we asked the group how they felt about it, and generally received quite positive comments, such as 'very interesting', 'invigorating', 'it makes you think', and 'I hadn't thought about it like that before'. This was important, since it suggested that our work had been of value to the participants, so that when the time comes for us to update the analysis we shall not feel hesitant in asking busy staff to contribute their time.

After the whole series of meetings had been completed, the material from the discussions was organized into the format of the functional analysis document below. The format of the document follows the structure of a logical hierarchy (in which details are arranged under more general headings) but we chose not to present it in the form of the 'branching tree diagram' characteristic of national standards documents, since we felt that such a format creates an inappropriately mechanistic impression. Instead we chose the more discursive format below as an attempt to achieve a more *readable* and persuasive document which would be more accessible both to the original participants and to the wider social work community, when we circulated the first draft for checking and amendment.

Since our purpose is merely to illustrate the method underlying the ASSET model, only an extract is given here. (see Winter and Maisch, 1992, pp. 31–7, for the full analysis.)

A number of interesting points emerged when we were organizing the practitioners' original statements into the functional analysis document format.

Firstly, it became clear that the order in which the points occurred in the discussion did not always fit the logical framework of the functional analysis. For

Document 2

The Social Work Functional Analysis: Tasks of the Experienced Social Worker

The Key Purpose

The Key Purpose of social workers is:

To identify and provide for the needs of vulnerable groups and/or individuals ('clients').

In order to carry out the Key Purpose, social workers must:

1) Identify and assess clients' needs and entitlements in relation to available and potential resources and services, and legal and statutory provisions;
2) Allocate resources and/or services to fulfil statutory responsibilities in the light of current social policies, while avoiding unnecessary interventions;
3) Assist clients to help themselves to improve their quality of life;
4) Support clients in developing a safe and positive relationship with a personal network and their local community, and work towards preventing avoidable breakdowns in relationships;
5) Mitigate the effects upon vulnerable groups and individuals of oppressively discriminatory judgments;
6) Contribute to sustaining morale among professional colleagues.

These six 'subpurposes' attempt to provide a 'general mapping' of the critical tasks of social work which, together, constitute its characteristic structure. The remainder of the document is divided into six sections, each providing details of one of the main tasks listed above. The third section of the document is given below as an example of the format.

Section 3

3) In order to assist clients to help themselves to improve their quality of life, social workers must:
  3.1) Ensure that clients are aware of the full range of available resources and services, and of the criteria for their provision and therefore:
    3.11) Provide information, publicity, free leaflets, etc. including those from other agencies;
    3.12) Communicate clearly and effectively, using an imaginative variety of styles, modes and media;
    3.13) Advise clients concerning the ways in which legal and statutory provisions will affect their situation.
  3.2) Establish a professional relationship with clients and therefore;
    3.21) Understand the theoretical basis for the social worker's role and practice;
    3.22) Set clear boundaries to the professional relationship;
    3.23) Ensure clients are aware of the scope and the limits of the social worker's role;
    3.24) Combine respect for clients' individuality with attempts to negotiate changes in aspects of their behaviour;
    3.25) Be aware of the differences between clients' perceptions and their own;
    3.26) Understand the relationship between their own experience and clients problems;
    3.27) Establish mutual respect;
    3.28) Acknowledge their power in the relationship, assert it where necessary, and recognize the dangers of its misuse;
    3.29) Deal effectively with the emotional dimensions of the relationship.
  3.3) Help clients come to terms with unavoidable constraints of their situation (such as loss, disability, old age, legal and statutory provisions) and therefore:

      3.31)   Work 'alongside' clients, explaining the advantages and disadvantages of different courses of action;
      3.32)   Accept clients' individuality;
      3.33)   Negotiate client 'ownership' of achievable goals;
      3.34)   Manage meetings so that clients are left with achievable goals;
      3.35)   Work at the client's pace, accepting his/her starting point;
      3.36)   Accept the outcomes of negotiated processes;
      3.37)   Involve clients in effective therapeutic processes.
  3.4)   Develop supportive links between the client, the client's personal network, local organizations, and social work agencies and therefore:
      3.41)   Apply knowledge of clients' specific circumstances to local organizational structures.

example, a number of points were originally made under the heading of 'maintaining enthusiasm', ostensibly derived from earlier concepts such as 'meeting client need' and 'using professional authority', but this link was tenuous, and led on to a number of other comments about 'stress management'. We initially felt that these were not entirely relevant, and tried to divert the group away into other channels, but the group insisted that, on the contrary, these points were of central importance. In the end we introduced the main heading of 'sustaining morale' (Section 6), to provide a logical space of these contributions.

A further example of this occurred when we noted that very little specific mention had been made of the 'anti-discriminatory' dimension of social work practice. We wished to ensure that this should have proper prominence in the analysis, and when we introduced it as a main heading (Section 5) we found that it provided a logical space for many suggestions whose place in the emergent conceptual framework had previously seemed rather 'strained'.

We were thus led to recognize both the strength and the limitations of the functional analysis format as a method for organizing and presenting practitioners' suggestions. Although it makes available the participants' own sense of the links between different aspects of their professional work, it nevertheless requires the investigating team to work at clarifying some of the relationships between participants' contributions. Ideas inevitably occur to participants in a somewhat accidental sequence, as their own reflections on others' contributions accompany the development of the group discussion. In other words, functional analysis is not a mechanical process; on the contrary, the process required us to try to maintain a complex balance between seeking fidelity to the participants' ideas and the need for our own work of interpretation and organization.

The issue of 'good practice' also caused us some concern, given the emphasis in some of the participants' contributions on lack of proper resources or support (see Chapter 8). After some of the sessions we were initially rather worried lest the various accounts of coping without proper resourcing should make the functional analysis document seem like a legitimation of less than acceptable practices. However, this did not turn out to be the case. Sections in the document such as 1.2 ('Improvising new resources and forms of service') and 2.2 ('Managing a complex workload') make a clear and positive emphasis that part of the social worker's role entails managing constructively and imaginatively the gap between perceived need and available resource which the culture of modern society seems to render inescapable.

Checking the First Draft of the Functional Analysis

In order to test its acceptability, the document was distributed (first to the original participants and then more widely) together with an accompanying letter asking recipients to return the document with a response under one of the following three headings:

1 'I find the document as it stands to be an acceptable summary of the general tasks required of an experienced social worker'.
2 'I have amended the document, enclosed, so that it now conforms to my own views'.
3 'I do *not* find the document to be an acceptable summary, but I have no time at present to make the necessary amendments'.
(The inclusion of this last response option was important, so that a positive response was not created by being simply less time-consuming.)

This method of validating the first draft of the analysis may be seen as a form of 'Delphi' technique (Lindeman, 1975; Goodman, 1987).[1] The essence of the process is that it feeds back separately to all members of a group (in this case, the twenty-seven social workers) a statement of members' responses. This means that each member can register assent or dissent free from the face-to-face pressures of the original group process, but in full knowledge of others' views. It can therefore check (and rectify) the dominance of forceful individuals and inaccurate interpretations on the part of investigators.

The results of this 'validation phase' summarized below, were encouraging. Altogether 125 individual responses were received, including the original group of participants and also two members of staff from The Spastics Society. Two collective responses were also submitted, one by the team of five participating practitioners in Greenwich, and the other from a group of four training officers in Kent. Of the individual responses 69 per cent ticked statement 1) 'I find the document as it stands to be an acceptable summary . . .' A further 12 per cent ticked statement 2) 'I have amended the document . . .' but only made very minor suggestions concerning one or two points of phrasing. Thus a total of 81 per cent of responses to the original draft were highly positive.

4 per cent of responses expressed reservations of a more general nature. For example, one respondent said the document was too vague, and two respondents said it was too detailed. Another regretted the lack of reference to the need for an understanding of general social theory, and this was taken into account in the next stage of the work.

13 per cent questioned specific aspects of the document, e.g., why is there no mention of the confidentiality issue? Why no reference to communication or record-keeping skills? and 'some of these points are managers' rather than practitioners' responsibilities'.

Only three respondents ticked statement 3) 'I do *not* find the document to be an acceptable summary, but I have no time at present to make the necessary amendments.'

The collective responses from Greenwich and Kent reflected this overall balance. In general they were very positive, but made one or two general suggestions (e.g., proposing greater emphasis on the social worker's role as 'advocate' on clients' behalf) and three or four suggestions concerning the emphasis and wording of individual statements.

In considering the various changes proposed by the respondents at this stage, we had to bear in mind that there had been a large majority of responses which endorsed the original document, and that we therefore could not make amendments which radically altered its emphasis or content. On the other hand it was possible that those who made suggestions had read the document more carefully than those who merely registered their agreement. Each suggestion was carefully considered, and although some were rejected for one reason or another, most of them led to amendments which clarified or amplified the document.

To sum up, we would claim that the functional analysis document is a description of social work tasks which:

- is derived from social workers' own considered accounts of their professional experience;
- has been found to be acceptable (i.e., realistic and/or illuminating) by over 130 practitioners;
- has been rejected by almost none of the workers consulted; and
- represents a careful synthesis of a large number of suggestions from a variety of sources.

Thus, while it inevitably falls short of universal 'consensus', we were confident that it provided a sound and broadly based framework for specifying units of learning in terms of practitioners' work-based competences.

From Functional Analysis to Units of Learning ('Modules')

A second phase of selection, interpretation, and organization took place when we worked from the functional analysis document in order to draw up a series of units of learning ('modules'). From the university's point of view, modules need to be associated with a specific number of 'credits' within the overall modular system, based roughly on the notional learning time students require in order to complete them successfully. At Anglia Polytechnic University the minimum credit value for a module (unit of learning) at honours degree level is seventy-five hours, and so we sometimes had to re-arrange the subsections of the functional analysis to ensure that the modules were of an appropriate 'size' for the modular system.

The university's conception of units of learning within a modular system was also quite compatible with a number of general statements by NCVQ and the Employment Department, which also guided us in formulating the modules:

a) A unit of competence should 'consist of a coherent group of elements of competence which have meaning and independent value in the area of employment' (NCVQ, 1991, p. 12).

b) Only units of competence which are 'critical' to competence in the occupational area should be included (Training Agency, 1988/9, *Guidance Note, No. 2*, p. 10).

c) Units of competence should be of a length and difficulty which will 'encourage progress'. Units should not therefore be 'too extensive' (Training Agency, 1988/9, *Guidance Note, No. 4*, p. 6).

In general, the module titles are based on sections or subsections of the functional analysis document, and most of the 'elements of competence' are derived from statements in the document (see Winter, and Maisch, 1992, Paper 8). However, a certain amount of rephrasing and reorganization was necessary, as will be seen from a comparison between the module document presented in Document 3 and the section of the functional analysis document presented in Document 2 from which it was derived.

Document 3

Competence-based Social Work Module: Promoting Clients' Potential for Independence

In order to demonstrate this unit of competence, candidates must:

Elements of competence

1 Communicate to clients the full range of relevant resources and services and the criteria for their provision.
2 Advise clients concerning the policies and statutory responsibilities of local authorities and the legal framework within which they operate.
3 Help clients to recognize their own strengths and weaknesses and work with the client in assessing and accepting his/her individual starting point and capabilities.
4 Demonstrate an awareness of the differences between clients' perceptions and feelings and their own, concerning achievable goals, and construct a care plan which accepts the outcomes of negotiated processes.
5 Make effective representations with and on behalf of clients.
6 Develop supportive links between the client, the client's personal network, and relevant local organizations, and social work agencies.
7 Demonstrate a practical understanding of the theoretical basis for the social worker's roles and responsibilities in work with clients.
8 Manage a professional relationship with clients, balancing the exercise of appropriate authority against an understanding of the necessity for client empowerment.
9 Involve clients in discussions and decisions which affect their situation.

Let us, then, briefly summarize the relationship between this example of a competence-based module and the functional analysis document.

- First of all, the title is rephrased in order to clarify the practical focus of the work.
- Most of the elements in the unit of learning, it is apparent, are derived more or less from statements in the Functional Analysis document, sometimes combined together to form a substantial phase of practice. Thus, for example, elements 1 and 2 are taken directly from the functional analysis (see 3.1 and 3.13), element 7 is a combination of 3.21 and 3.22, and element 8 combines 3.2, 3.23, and 3.24.
- Element 4 is based directly on 3.25 but also introduces the 'care plan' (as a familiar category of practice) in order to simplify and make more concrete the notion of 'the outcomes of negotiated processes' (functional analysis document 3.36).
- In element 9 the term 'therapeutic processes' (from 3.37) is simplified and generalized to: 'discussions and situations which affect their situation'.
- Element 3 uses 3.31, 3.32, 3.33, and 3.35 as a starting point but these are rephrased in order to bring out a more unified emphasis.
- Element 5 is introduced from another section of the functional analysis document, following the recommendation from the Greenwich team noted above.

One way or another, therefore, all the statements in the functional analysis are included in the 'elements of competence' of the module, with the following exceptions: 3.41 is omitted as being largely a repetition of 3.4; a statement about dealing effectively with the emotional dimension of the relationship (3.29) and two statements explicitly concerning communication (3.11, 3.12, and 3.27) are omitted because they are embodied in the Core Assessment Criteria (see next chapter).

The work of re-phrasing the competence statements for the unit of learning document involved a general concern to avoid repetition, asking ourselves whether each statement would actually require the candidate to produce different *evidence*. It also involved seeking a terminology which would be both 'enduring' (i.e., avoiding the fashionable 'buzz-words' of professional jargon) and also at the right level of generality, i.e., precise enough to apply to a particular context and yet general enough to apply to a variety of contexts (see NCVQ, 1995a, p. 16).

The example provided here is typical of the fairly close relationship between our functional analysis document and the modules which were derived from them. However, one of the other modules ('Assessing Risk' see Appendix C) was derived by putting together subsections from different parts of the document and the details of the module eventually called 'Anti-oppressive Practices in the Workplace' (see Appendix D) was derived from Section 5 of the Functional Analysis document but involved a lot of rephrasing and elaboration in response to fairly continuous feedback and discussion over a period of three years. It is clear, therefore, that functional analysis as a method is by no means a simple guarantee of the 'objectivity' and general authority of competence statements. We are left, therefore, with the question: what claims can be made for the 'authoritative' status of these statements of competence? Having presented the process by which they were developed, we are now in a position to discuss the nature of their 'validity' (or otherwise).

The Authoritative Status of Competence Statements

Barnett (1994) poses the question sharply:

> Are the practitioners . . . the only authority on best practice? What counts as good practice in social work, the law, medicine and so on are contested goods: the public generally — as potential claimants of the services — and other groups are legitimate voices to be heard in framing the worthwhile competences . . . To any . . . list of competences we are entitled to respond: whose competences are these? (Barnett, 1994, p. 73).

We can begin our response to this challenge by stressing that the competence statements presented in this chapter are only one aspect of the ASSET model of a vocational curriculum. The way in which the ASSET Programme recognized the legitimate involvement of the employers (Essex Social Services Department, answerable to a democratically elected County Council Social Services Committee) is explained later, in Chapter 8. On the national scale of accountability, the involvement of the Central Council for Education and Training in Social Work in the development of the Programme was outlined in Chapter 2.

Concerning Barnett's reference to service users, although clients were not directly involved in framing the competence statements, the ASSET Programme does nevertheless make a point of recognizing the importance of the client's voice. For example, it should be noted that several of the competence statements given above explicitly require the practitioner to work with clients in ways which promote their capacity to voice their own interests; this is indeed the overall theme of the particular module presented. This overall theme is also embodied in the first of the general professional criteria presented in Chapter 4 (see Document 4). Furthermore, the guidance concerning appropriate evidence (see Chapter 6, Document 7) makes a point of encouraging candidates to submit clients' evaluations of their work. Chapter 6 includes an example of such evidence from a candidate's portfolio (Document 8), and there is also a module which focuses directly on this theme — 'Learning from Clients in Order to Develop and Extend Professional Knowledge and Skills' (see Appendix B).

However, our account of the process clearly indicates one major question concerning the competence statements themselves: how far can we really claim to have succeeded in our avowed intention of expressing a curriculum in terms of a set of practice requirements derived 'empirically' from practitioners' own understandings (and thereby to have made a step towards transcending what Jessup calls our 'preconceptions' as educators/trainers (Jessup, 1991, p. 18)? Certainly, this chapter has shown how the competence statements are largely derived from practitioners' descriptions of their professional responsibilities. But equally, it has shown that we, as 'educators' (rather than 'practitioners') have felt the need to rephrase and reorder the practitioners' statements. The functional analysis question sequence does indeed ensure that practitioners contribute both general 'overarching' ideas and also details of required practices, but these do not spontaneously fall into the neat logical hierarchy in which NCVQ present their 'occupational maps' and their 'national standards' expressed in performance criteria. There are various reasons for this. First, the data from the functional analysis sessions is inevitably patterned differently with different groups: the same idea can occur early with one group, as a main heading, and in another group later, as a detail in response to another heading. Furthermore, practitioners contribute ideas following an open-ended 'association of ideas' which does not follow the prescriptive logic of the set question sequence. Nor is this surprising. The widespread popularity of Buzan's work on 'mind-mapping' indicates the limited role which simple classification systems play in human mental processes (see Buzan, 1993).

Clearly, a vocational curriculum will never correspond to anyone's actual 'stream of consciousness-in-practice'. By its nature it is generalized and it is retrospectively selected and ordered. And we, as the developers of the ASSET Programme, had a responsibility to our own understanding of the educational process and to social work theory, values, and 'best practice' which required us to select and order practitioners' contributions with a view to producing competence statements and units of learning that we thought would generally 'work' as practical documents for candidates to use within the programme.

All this may seem to open up our competence statements to two contrasting lines of criticism. If we, as curriculum developers have contributed such a large amount of interpretation and organization of the practitioners' contributions:

- Was it necessary to go expend all the effort involved in involving practitioners at all?
- In what sense can our competence statements have any authority as 'standards of practice' beyond our own personal judgment?

The following paragraphs deal with each of these questions in turn, and in response to the last question we will begin to deal with the relationship between the format of our competence statements and the very different format recommended by NCVQ.

First: was it worthwhile to involve the practitioners? Having now established the format for competence-based units of learning, is it not possible to put together further units simply by deriving the statements of competence from, say, the syllabus and objectives of currently available taught modules, using one's educational and vocational expertise, and thus save a lot of time and effort? Indeed, on two occasions, influenced by this line of thinking, we did try to construct sets of specialist modules using the competence statement format but without involving practitioners in functional analysis discussions. In both cases, we ended up with problems:

in both cases programme tutors found that these competence statements required a lot more explanation, and that, even so, the evidence that candidates submitted in their portfolios seemed to be 'unsatisfactory'.

In one case we drew up a series of modules from a set of very detailed guidelines for an area of practice issued by the professional body (The Central Council for Education and Training in Social Work). These were termed 'competences' but had not been derived through a functional analysis process. Although they were indeed useful as general guidance, candidates found that they could not be explicitly 'demonstrated' from their practice, and we have now reformulated the whole set of modules using the functional analysis method.

In the other case, elements of competence were derived from the assignment guidelines for a taught course. These described a closely-knit sequence of activities, reflecting the sequence of stages in the taught course assignment. On the taught course the candidate was following through a single piece of work (as the assignment requires) so that each stage of the work clarified the others. However, when an aspect of practice (a module) is divided into 'elements of competence', candidates are free to present evidence from different pieces of work for each element. The problem, then, was that because the elements, instead of being independent of one another, were still bound together into the coursework sequence, the evidence for each element in the unit could not be assessed (as representing good practice and full understanding) without reference to work from other elements. But this mutual clarification between the elements did not occur, since the candidates were using evidence from different pieces of work, and thus the tutor felt that an essential form of 'coherence' was missing. Where elements of competence have been derived from a functional analysis, the evidence for each is relatively *independent* of the evidence for the others (this was how we set about avoiding 'repetition' — see above) and so this problem does not arise.

To sum up, in answer to this first criticism, we are inclined to argue that the competence format may *look* deceptively like a mere matter of syntax, a form of *wording*, but in fact the functional analysis does contribute significantly to embedding *each* specified learning outcome in the requirements of professional practice and understanding.

Second, in what sense can our competence statements be thought of as authoritative 'standards' of practice? Let us begin by staking our claims. Our competence statements are derived through a method which was from the outset comprehensively informed by practitioners' definitions and understandings of their role and activities. They were also widely scrutinized and subsequently redrafted, so that we are quite confident of their acceptability within the professional community. For example they have been adopted with very few changes in the very different social context of a large conurbation, Glasgow, by Strathclyde social services department and Glasgow Caledonian University (see Glasgow Caledonian University, 1994; Brodie and Whittaker, 1995). The relevance and helpfulness of the competence statements has also been regularly endorsed by programme candidates. One of them, for example, described them as 'exactly what I need to address myself to a more methodical and structured approach to my work and to make me look at policy' (quoted from the evaluation of the pilot phase of the project and reported in Maisch and Winter, 1992, p. 25).

On the other hand, there are certain claims that we would not wish to make. First, the competence statements are not *final*. Tutors (and even external examiners) sometimes suggest amending one or other of the competence statements in the light of candidates' difficulties, usually attributable to the statement's vagueness or (conversely) its restrictiveness. And although the competence statements were phrased to be appropriate in a variety of contexts, it is clear that they are embedded in current professional culture and thus will need updating from time to time. In both respects, the limitations of our competence statements are no different from those accepted by NCVQ (see Training Agency, 1988/9, No. 2, p. 17). The current 'national standards' of the Training and Development Lead Body, for example, are quite different in both content and structure from those issued by the same lead body four years earlier.

Furthermore, we would not wish to claim that the language of our competence statements is 'unambiguous' (NCVQ, 1995a, p. 24, para. 3.4.5). Like all language-based rules, they always, on every occasion, need to be *interpreted* in the light of shared agreements among the users of that language (Wittgenstein, 1967, pp. 39–42) i.e., among the 'expert' professional community. Hence we accept that tutors and assessors need to *create* their shared understanding of 'acceptable', 'appropriate', and 'sufficient' evidence which 'demonstrates' a competence (see Chapter 6). This point also is strongly made by one of NCVQ's own consultants: assessment of competence, she says, is 'not an act of pure measurement'; on the contrary, it rests on 'a legalistic notion of . . . informed judgement . . . rather than a scientific one.' (Mitchell, 1990, pp. 24–5).[2] More importantly, this means that we recognize candidates' need to interpret the significance of the competence statements, in relation to their own work contexts, by working on a 'module action plan' (see Chapter 2).

We also recognize that even though our units of learning have been so painstakingly derived (as described in this chapter) they still cannot be taken as exhaustive or absolute. There is an important implication here, which we wish to make quite explicit, and which leads on to the fundamental argument of the next chapter. Our competence statements are not intended to define a standard of practice by means of a prescriptive *list*, as though they were indeed 'performance criteria'. That is why we do not use the term or the format, although what we call 'elements of competence' are in many ways as precise as NCVQ's performance criteria and could easily be rephrased to conform to the NCVQ performance criterion format (see Appendix F). We do not claim that our competence-based units are either exhaustive in their coverage of the total professional role or that our division into units constitutes the *only* coherent and rational subdivision of the structure of professional experience. In other words, the main purposes of our competence statements is to provide *guidance* to candidates and tutors concerning what portfolios of practice-derived evidence will need to demonstrate.

All this begins to take us some way from the format and procedures of the NCVQ 'standards' documentation, and inevitably so, since a key aspect of the

ASSET model rests on the argument that detailed competence statements only constitute a 'standard of practice' when they are used in conjunction with a set of *general* professional criteria. The significance of this aspect of the ASSET model is explained in the following chapter.

Notes

1   The Delphi technique was originally concerned with improving predictions, by amalgamating the views of experts, on such matters as the chances of nuclear war and the results of horse races (Lindeman, 1975, p. 435). Its aim is both to document the extent of a consensus and also to create it. However, although the oracle at Delphi did predict the future, it always did so with such ambiguity that the significance of its pronouncements usually only became apparent *after* the event! Hence, as Goodman says: any apparent consensus the technique seems to record should be 'viewed with caution' (Goodman, 1987, p. 733).
2   NCVQ are, however, increasingly recognizing that supposedly 'unambiguous' performance criteria are an insufficient basis for reliable and valid assessment. For example, the basic documentation for some NVQs now also includes 'Guidance to assessors', 'Knowledge evidence', 'Range statements', and 'Performance evidence required' (see Training and Development Lead Body, 1995).

4 The 'Other Dimension' of Assessment: A General Model of Professional Learning

In contrast to the format proposed by the National Council for Vocational Qualifications, the assessment process of the ASSET model has two basic 'dimensions' (see Chapter 2): the *specific competences* discussed in the previous chapter and the *general role requirements* embodied in 'Core Assessment Criteria' or 'Core Professional Criteria'. This chapter explains why this second dimension is so important, how these general 'Core' criteria were derived, how they are used in the programme as a necessary part of the assessment process, and how they differ from other apparently similar work.

A Limitation of Functional Analysis: The 'Holism' of Occupational and Educational Role Requirements

We have already noted, in the previous chapter, that the competence-based approach to the design of educational programmes is often criticized as being 'atomistic', in the sense that it seems to suggests that the essential quality of performance within a role can be expressed in a list of detailed specifications which can simply be 'added together' to indicate the required overall accomplishment (Ashworth and Saxton, 1990, p. 12; Elliott, 1991, p. 119). And, as Wolf (1995) observes:

> [The] goal of precision has proved elusive. In pursuit of it, English competence-based awards have become . . . ever more weighted down with detail.
> . . . The attempt to map out free standing content and standards leads, again and again, to a never-ending spiral of specification. (Wolf, 1995, p. 55)

We also noted that the NCVQ method of defining competences attempts to avoid this line of criticism by starting from a definition of the 'key purpose' of the role, from which the detailed competences are then derived ('disaggregated') in the form of a logical hierarchy. In this way, so the argument runs, details are situated within an 'overarching' conceptual framework (Mansfield, 1989, p. 5) which embodies 'the whole work role' (Fennell, 1989, p. 3).

But it is clear that a logical hierarchy (classifying details under general headings) represents a very incomplete way of describing the structure of human activities. The details of how I carry out a particular task can rarely be explained in terms of a simple chain of instrumental decisions ('I do this [particular act] *in order to* achieve that [general purpose]'). Rather, the details of my particular actions are shaped by a complex combination of various (and often contradictory) motives, feelings, understandings, bodies of knowledge, responsibilities, and values. It is this complex texture, rather than a simple classification of means and ends, which provides the unity (the 'holism') underlying the experience of occupational life and the experience of learning. We can call this complex underlying holism the 'structural unity' of role performances, and, following Bruner (1966) we would argue that an adequate grasp of a unified structure underlying separate requirements is essential to curriculum design. Thus, in the case of a practice-based vocational curriculum, it is the complex structure of the individual's occupational and educational experience which is central, and this is not adequately represented merely by assembling detailed requirements ('outcomes') under the heading of a general statement of purpose.

In order to appreciate the significance of this issue, we need to look more closely at certain aspects of the NCVQ model. Consider the following set of performance criteria taken from the document which presents the 'National Standards' for professional practitioners working in the area of Training and Development (Training and Development Lead Body (TDLB), 1995, p. 54).

Element D 112 Conduct Formative Assessments with Learners

a) The purpose of formative assessment and the use which will be made of information obtained is clearly explained to learners.
b) Learners are provided with clear and accurate information about the learning objectives and assessment criteria which they are being assessed against.
c) Suitable materials and facilities are provided to help learners to identify their achievements.
d) Assessments of current competence are valid, reliable and conform to any specified instructions.
e) Learners are encouraged to reflect on the ways in which they have been learning.
f) Learners are encouraged to feel comfortable to ask questions and express their views.
g) Learners are given feedback on their formative assessment in a positive and encouraging manner.
h) The process of formative assessment promotes equality of opportunity and learners' ability to learn.
i) Assessment records are completed correctly, passed to the relevant people and stored appropriately.

The term 'performance criterion' in the NCVQ documentation simply means that a statement includes explicitly *evaluative* terms or phrases (NCVQ, 1995a, p. 24). For example, from the above list: 'clear', 'accurate', 'suitable', 'promotes equality of opportunity'. Now, although NCVQ claims that performance criteria such as these should 'allow unambiguous interpretation by different users' (Jessup, 1991, p. 17; NCVQ, 1995a, p. 24, para. 3.4.5), it is clear that this cannot be the case in any strict sense: evaluative terms can only be applied to actual situations by means of further judgments as to how they will be interpreted: what will count as 'clear' information or 'suitable' materials must depend on the characteristics of different groups of learners (see, yet again, Wittgenstein, 1967, pp. 39–49). In other words, performance criteria such as those above do not prescribe *exactly* what candidates must do on a particular occasion; they merely indicate the *sort* of judgment which will have to be made. They thus assume that there will be consensus within a wide community of assessors as to how ('exactly') to interpret 'clear information', 'suitable materials' and what is entailed in 'promoting equality of opportunity'. This consensus needs to be applicable to an enormous variety of individual cases, and thus it needs to be guided by considerations which apply to *any* case, i.e., by the holistic awareness of the overall role requirements, for which we are arguing and which (we shall argue) the NCVQ performance criteria do not provide (but see Chapter 3, Note 2).

There are two theoretical points which can be made to support this argument. The first is from the long tradition of 'hermeneutics' (the theory of interpretation) which has already been mentioned; the meaning of particular details depends on the place of the detail within the whole of which it is a part, so that interpretation always involves moving in a 'circle' between part and whole. The second is a mathematical principle: to identify a point in one dimension you need a second dimension, or, more generally, to identify a point in N dimensions, you need to use N + 1 dimensions. For example, in geometry, you can find the mid point of a line by constructing a perpendicular to that line which intersects at the mid point. Thus, it is the 'vertical' dimension which identifies the required point on the 'horizontal' dimension. Applying both these theories to the context of assessing competences, our argument is that in order to identify the requisite form of competence in a specific case we need to see how it 'intersects' with the general role requirements. Of course, *if* we had a ruler, we wouldn't need to go to all this trouble, but although you *can* measure the length of a line with a fair degree of 'unambiguous' objectivity, no comparable measuring device exists where we are making judgments about learning. In the words of one of NCVQ's consultants, already quoted: 'The assessment of occupational competence [is] not an act of pure measurement . . . [it rests upon] a legalistic notion of judgment rather than a scientific one' (Mitchell, 1990, pp. 24–5).

Let us now look back at some of the criteria in the TDLB unit quoted above and see what problems are created by this lack of a 'second dimension' of guidance. For example, in criterion (b) ('Learners are provided with clear and accurate information about the learning objectives and assessment criteria which they are being assessed against') it may be that the organization has already produced this documentation, so that the member of staff, i.e., the candidate for the NVQ, merely has to take it from a filing cabinet, make enough copies, and distribute it, a wholly routine task; it could indeed be part of the responsibilities of an administrative assistant to ensure that this document is included along with others in students' introductory information. Alternatively, if this document has not yet been written, then the candidate has here the very complex task of making a succinct analysis of the essence of a particular educational process. Similarly, let us consider criterion (i) ('Assessment records are . . . passed to the relevant people . . .'). We cannot interpret this without knowing what degree of responsibility the candidate is expected to take for making what is an extremely sensitive decision about who does and who should have a right to see records. Is this an occupational role in which the candidate is given a list of actual names and told to stick to it, or is this a role where the candidate could be expected to challenge her/his organization's policy on access in the light of a knowledge of general legislation, equal opportunities awareness, and/ or a professional value base? Is this, therefore, a competence in which the candidate will show they have learned a particular form of obedience (*remembering* to consult a list)? Or a competence where the candidate will show a particular form of moral autonomy (challenging organizational policy)? Finally, consider the first part of criterion (h) ('The process of formative assessment promotes equality of opportunity'). The problem here is that, lacking a *specific* reference, we don't know whether candidates need to ensure that the assessment tasks they set are not ethnically or gender biased (requiring a complex knowledge base and a sophisticated cultural understanding) or merely that they should attempt to minimize personal favouritism by ensuring that assignments bear only the student's number and not her/his name (requiring only the implementation of a simple rule, which, again, the candidate may or may not have initiated as a policy.) In all cases, the end result is the same; when the criteria lack either the general dimension or the specific dimension, the basis for assessment is not only 'ambiguous', it is seriously inadequate. Our argument is that in order to provide adequate guidance in forming consensus among assessors, specific *and* general criteria need to be used *together* (as described later in the chapter).

In some ways, the most important problem is that these performance criteria are indeterminate as to the vocational role they seem to imply. Some of them necessarily require sophisticated professional skills (for example, (e), (f), (g)). At least one of them, in contrast (criterion (i)), seems less likely to specify the direct responsibilities of professional educators than those of their clerical administrators. And in some cases, as we have seen, candidates' practice might conform to the competence statements (i.e., the performance criteria) in a way which may be *either* entirely routine *or* in a way which requires a large degree of discretion in the application of specialized bodies of knowledge and even complex ethical judgments (for example (b), (c), and (h)). In other words, the competence statements do not indicate the level of understanding, initiative, or responsibility at issue, even though they are described as 'standards'.[1]

Why, then, we may ask, all these apparently obvious inconsistencies? The reason is not hard to find. NCVQ performance criteria are not intended in themselves to constitute a curriculum, i.e., an *educational* process which thus entails a particular 'standard' of achievement (understanding, knowledge, skills, awareness, etc). Rather, they define required 'standards' in terms of what will be needed *from* the individual *by* the employing organization, as indicated in the following quotation from one of the Training Agency 'Guidance Notes' on functional analysis:

> Each individual contributes to the organisation performing effectively . . . by carrying out those functions which lead to the organisation satisfying its mission or purpose. Functional analysis is the process of identifying those functions and breaking them down until they are described in sufficient detail to be used as standards. Functional analysis offers the opportunity to base the standards on the outcomes required, for example, by an organisation to satisfy its mission. (Training Agency, 1988/9, No. 2, p. 8)

Although they are intended to *inform* educational processes, therefore, the NVQ performance criteria also resemble 'quality control' documents, constructing the form of 'expert knowledge' which the *organization* requires:

> Knowledge that extracts from performance (whether of man or machine) objective measures that enable management to define standards of and targets for performance. (Hoskin and Macve, 1993, p. 28)

From this point of view inconsistencies in terms of the required educational and occupational *level* do not really matter. Indeed, NCVQ argue that competence statements in themselves have no necessary link with an 'educational level':

> One feature of the NVQ model is that units [of competence] are not assigned a fixed level within the levels framework. It is the qualification as a whole which carries level. (Oates, 1994, p. 23)

Admittedly, the NCVQ 'educational levels' framework (NCVQ, 1991, pp. 17–18) is in many ways an unsatisfactory document (see Winter, 1993a) but its sequence does represent an attempt to outline an educational progression. It is surely, therefore, a strange feature of the NCVQ format that its competence statements remain outside its levels framework, and that some of the criteria we have just considered could be equally well applied to assessing candidates' work within a vocational course equivalent to an A level (pre-undergraduate) qualification or the equivalent of a Higher Degree.[2]

To sum up, it is in order to avoid such inconsistencies as those outlined above that the ASSET model includes a general statement of role requirements evoking both an educational level and a set of vocational responsibilities. This is our statement of the underlying 'structure' of the individual's occupational and educational experience previously referred to. It is summarized in the Core Assessment Criteria, which will be presented below. The Core Assessment Criteria are used in conjunction with the detailed competence statements in order to clarify an appropriate level for candidates' work. This is described in detail later in the chapter. We also made use of an early draft of the Core Assessment Criteria during our analysis of the ideas contributed by practitioners. This was important because we intentionally used a very 'open-ended' sequence of questions, and so suggestions were sometimes made which, although perfectly relevant, reflected a level of requirement which was taken for granted and thus did not constitute an important part of the *challenge* of practice at the level with which we were concerned (the responsibilities of experienced 'professionally' qualified staff). (Examples here would be: keeping records up to date, punctuality.) In other words, our formulation of detailed competence statements started out from (and was conducted in the light of) a prior formulation of the general role requirements, which was used in selecting, phrasing, editing, and elaborating practitioners' contributions.

The ASSET version of this general dimension is presented here only as an *example* of the sort of analysis required. We would argue that *all* assessment of specific competences *also* needs a statement of associated general requirements if assessment decisions are to be soundly based. We provide here a general model of *professional* work at *honours degree* level. A different, (but not entirely dissimilar) analysis would be needed to identify the general parameters of other levels of responsibility in employment and/or other stages of education (see Chapter 9). For the ASSET Programme, the general statement needed to encompass the general educational demands of work at *undergraduate* level and the demands of the *professional* role. Together these comprise a set of requirements which involve specific intellectual, practical, and communicative ability, affective awareness, knowledge, and value commitments, as described below.

Towards a General Theory of Professional Work

This section presents the first of three investigations which led to the formulation of the Core Assessment Criteria. It is concerned with the professional role in general, but it is important to remember that the analysis was undertaken to inform the formulation and assessment of competences in social work. It was therefore conceived in relation to what might be called the 'person-oriented' professions, including, say, management, nursing, teaching, and law; how far it would need to be modified to take into account a profession which is more 'object-oriented' (engineering) is discussed later in the chapter. The analysis in this section is presented in five parts. The first considers professional work in relation to its inherent values, the second considers its inherent emotional dimension, the third considers the nature of professional knowledge, and the fourth considers the relationship between professional experience and learning. Finally the main ideas and implications from the analysis are drawn together in the form of ten linked propositions.

Professions and Values

Many would argue that professional work is defined by its involvement with ethical issues, just as much as by its specialized knowledge. (One of the two key dictionary meanings of 'profession' is indeed a 'vow' of religious faith.) The point is clearly made, in respect of the teaching profession, by Wilfred Carr (1989, pp. 3–4). He argues that teaching has its own *intrinsic* criteria, as opposed to *extrinsic* criteria such as cost-effectiveness, number of pupils achieving certain test grades, etc. The general argument is derived from Aristotle's emphasis on the importance of the category of 'Practical Wisdom', which is at the same time a virtue, a practical interpersonal skill, and a form of understanding — the ability to deliberate on 'what is conducive to the good life generally' (Aristotle, *Ethics*, p. 209). Hence, the argument might run, each profession is *intrinsically* concerned with a particular practical aspect of 'the Good Life' — teachers with the realization of the capacity for understanding, lawyers with the realization of justice, medicine with physical health, engineers with material comfort and public safety, nursing with the overall health of the sick, and social workers with promoting the well-being of the vulnerable.

Now, it is essential to moral principles that their application to particular cases involves the exercise of complex judgments and usually the management of dilemmas, since actual situations bring different moral principles into conflict with each other, e.g., through the competing rights to well-being, care, and autonomy of different individuals. The ability to make these judgments in an equitable and effective way is a dimension of the practice of experienced professional workers: 'lay' persons, in contrast, may be thought of as concerned to pursue their *own* legitimate interests, not to adjudicate between the moral rights of others. This also means that professional workers will at times feel called upon to challenge the ethical acceptability of procedures and policies within the organization which employs them.

Professional workers have an inherent responsibility to try to ensure that their services are available to *all* members of society, as entailed in a principle of equity, often enshrined in official 'codes of ethics' (Parsons, 1954; Freidson, 1994, p. 174). (This, in principle, is one of the key differences between a profession and a commercial 'business' (Parsons, pp. 37–8) and thus a cause of much current controversy.) Consequently, professional practice involves an obligation to avoid 'oppressive' judgments, i.e., judgments which make non-justifiable discriminations on the basis of age, gender, race, etc. The ability to implement this principle of equity is a particularly important aspect of a specifically professional understanding because of the widespread institutional and interpersonal processes tending to reinforce social patterns of privilege and disadvantage (see, for example, Goffman's well-known work on 'stigma' (Goffman, 1968)).

The Emotional Dimension of Professional Work

The role of the professional worker institutionalizes the process whereby the needs of one person (or group) are submitted to the authoritative involvement of another person (or group) (Parsons, 1954; Illich, 1975). The basis for this authoritative involvement is the professional's specialized knowledge, and one of its consequences is acceptance of the ethical and quasi-political responsibilities noted in the previous paragraphs.

There are a number of reasons why such relationships have an inherently emotional dimension. Firstly, the basis for professional work is that the client has a *need* and therefore a range of associated anxieties. (A 'need' may be defined as being a relatively complex state of affairs, in contrast to a straightforward intention, e.g., to make a purchase.) Effective attempts to meet the client's need thus also require some success in allaying the associated anxiety. Secondly, in order to understand the client's need, the professional must both empathize with the client's situation and its attendant anxieties and yet preserve an emotional distance, which thereby creates a characteristic emotional tension in the worker. Thirdly, there is a *power* dimension, created by the presupposition of the professional's authoritative expertise in relation to the client. This tends to activate some form of 'transference' effect: as an immediately present authority figure, the professional is someone onto whom clients can 'transfer' their anxiety and thereby (in part, and temporarily) relieve it through a form of 'blaming' process. Hence the potential for hostility in many professional/client interactions. This emotional pattern is magnified where the professional also has direct institutional power over the client.

The emotions associated with interactions involving need, anxiety, and power are not only inherent in professional/client relationships. They can be equally central in relationships with colleagues (with different, sometimes competing expertise) which are such an important aspect of professional work — the 'teamwork' process.

Professional work thus has an emotional dimension in the same way as it has cognitive and ethical dimensions: for professional workers, emotions (their own as well as their clients') are both a topic and a resource (see Salzberger-Wittenberg, *et al.*, 1983). Experienced professional workers will be aware of this. They will recognize the emotions underlying clients' statements, and will respond in ways which address the emotions as well as the words; they will also recognize that their own emotions are likely to be 'hooked' by those of the client (see Harris, 1973). They will therefore have accepted that complex and apparently 'irrational' emotions are not an avoidable and regrettable indication of professional failure but an inherent aspect of the professional situation, which (like its other aspects) needs to be understood and 'managed'. To put into practice this understanding is thus an integral part of the professional worker's 'interpersonal' and 'problem-solving' skill.

Professional Knowledge

According to the dictionary. A profession is 'a vocation in which . . . knowledge of some department of learning is used . . .', and Talcott Parsons' seminal essay (1954) interprets professionalism generally as the application of science and rationality to human affairs. Hence, a theory of professional work must entail an analysis of the relationship between knowledge and practice. This is the theme of this subsection and also of the next.

The simplest type of theory here is that represented by the 'Expert Systems' approach. This characterizes professional practice as a series of decision-making events, and professional expertise as a body of knowledge in the form of a system of general factual propositions which are applied in making professional decisions (see, for example Takenouchi and Iwashita, 1987.) If knowledge has this form it can be codified and computerized. There is no doubt that computerized programmes can, in certain contexts, be a useful support. For example, University College Swansea has constructed a computerized system to assist hospital staff with decisions involved in planning the discharge of geriatric patients (DISPLAN) (Crystal, 1989). Some, however, would go further than suggesting that such programmes may 'assist' staff and go on to claim: 'Expert Systems . . . *simulate* the behaviour and incorporate the knowledge of rational human experts' (Oxman and Gero, 1987, p. 4 [my emphasis]). This claim rests on the proposition that professional practice may simply be understood as a set of 'rule-generated operations' (p. 5). But this proposition relies on a metaphor from the manipulation of *closed* systems (logic, grammar, mathematics), and it is in principle inappropriate for the *open* parameters of empirical experience. In the real world, rules can only *guide* decisions, not govern, let alone 'generate' them: an inevitable act of interpretation always intervenes (Bennett, 1971). Decision-making in human practice (in contrast to that of computers) is never the following through of a systematic algorithm but 'appropriate deliberation', seeking 'good' but not 'optimal' solutions (Simon, 1982, pp. 88–90) since there can be no consensus as to what the optimal solution is, except (perhaps) some time after the event! Expert systems, therefore, can assist but never 'simulate' the knowledge processing activities of experts: they do not formulate a model of professional expertise. (The continually increasing sophistication of computer technology means that this long-standing debate remains highly topical — see, for example, Salt, 1995.)

The critique of expert systems is the starting point for the influential work of the Dreyfus brothers. One of the Dreyfus brothers wrote a book called *What Computers Can't Do* (Dreyfus, H, 1979). What his brother said they can't do is to model the relatively 'unstructured situations' which typify the world of professional work (Dreyfus, S, 1981, p. 3). Thus, according to Dreyfus (S.), experienced professionals do not possess and apply their professional knowledge in the form of systematic analysis based on universal rules and clear-cut factual propositions. On the contrary, he says, this is how novices, still dominated by recent book-learning, set about taking their first faltering steps into the practical world *before* they have built up the normal, experience-based forms of proficiency and expertise. In contrast, the fully proficient professional worker's knowledge is no longer in the form of rules and facts, but consists of rough guidelines, elliptical maxims, long-range goals which determine priorities, and a repertoire of typical examples which are available to be invoked as precedents. Dreyfus charts the stages of this process, and ends with a description of the 'expert' professional whose knowledge has become largely 'intuitive', locked into the context-bound 'situational understanding' where it originated (Dreyfus, 1981, p. 22). Hence; 'At the highest level of skill . . . understanding is created unconsciously from concrete experience, and cannot be verbalized' (op. cit., p. 38).

But this highlights an important problem with the Dreyfus model. If the highest level of skill is 'intuitive' and cannot be verbalized, then Dreyfus is closing off the possibilities for facilitating the development of that skill, and this strangely neglects the well-known argument that verbalization is part of the creative development of understanding (see, for example, Vygotsky, 1962). The Dreyfus model of professional knowledge shows the valuable learning resource which is present in practitioners' accumulated experience, and makes a strong case that professional work spontaneously *generates* knowledge: professional workers do not need to be *presented with* 'reconstructed theories' of their work. But what Dreyfus' theory lacks is an account of the process whereby practitioners' knowledge is deepened and refined by being continuously made *explicit*, through interaction, consideration of alternatives, and communicative verbalization. Hence, it is to professional work as a *learning* experience that we now turn.

Professional Work as a Learning Process

We have established that the analysis of the competences of professional workers will need to take into account the fact that professional knowledge develops through the accumulation of concrete experience. Hence, if we wish to describe such competences in such a way that they can form a framework of opportunities for professional development we need a detailed model of how professional workers *learn* from their practice experience.

Donald Schon's well-known work on 'The Reflective Practitioner' (Schon, 1983) is concerned precisely with this question. Like Dreyfus, Schon contrasts the 'artistry' of the experienced practitioner (op. cit., p. 140) with the merely 'technical problem solving' involved in routine situations (p. 133). Thus, the professional worker does not acquire a set of validated rules or categories but a 'repertoire' of past examples as a set of possible 'precedents' or 'metaphors' (p. 138). In this way, problems are 'reframed' so that solutions can be envisaged (p. 134), and subsequently the unintended consequences of the reframing are 'appreciated' (p. 135). One basic criterion for this process is coherence, but another, equally important, is 'keeping the inquiry moving' (p. 136). In other words, 'solutions' are not seen as permanent, because the practitioner's relation to the situation has the form of a 'conversation', in which the search for an adequate interpretation 'shapes the situation but . . . [the practitioner's] own models and appreciations are shaped by it' (p. 151). This involves a systematic recognition of the *client's* meanings in a *collaborative* dialogue where the professional's authority is always open to question (pp. 295–6).

Another approach to the question of how professionals learn from experience may be found in some of the literature on 'action-research' (see, for example, Elliott, 1991, Chapter 4). Like the well-known 'experiential learning cycle' (see Kolb, 1984), action research also entails a cyclical movement in which practice and reflection both develop by mutually informing one another. Recent work in this area has begun to analyse the nature of the reflective process in this cycle. It has been suggested, for example, that practice-based learning entails:

    a)   a collaborative stance towards clients and colleagues, recognising the validity of others people's interpretations;

b) a systematic commitment to learning from professional situations;

c) ways of understanding practice situations which facilitate 'critical' analysis, e.g., relating a situation to its contexts, noting its contradictions, and understanding it within a process of change (Winter, 1989, Chapter 4).

It is clear that the above principles devised for action-research (i.e., for sustained inquiry which is relevant to, but separate from, professional practice itself) are in fact closely related to Schon's description of the forms of reflection which occur *within* professional practice, as the process by which practice generates learning (see Evans, 1990). As Evans points out, many of them echo key points from Schon's argument, and the basic processes of 'experiential learning' are common to both.

Ten Propositions on the Nature of Professional Work

The following propositions are an attempt to distil the key implications from the foregoing arguments. They are numbered for ease of reference, but they are intended to form the interdependent elements of a unified process which links professional practice, knowledge, understanding, skills, commitments, and self-knowledge. (Their inter-relationship is presented in diagrammatic form in Appendix E.)

1 The nature of professional work is that situations are unique and knowledge of those situations is therefore never complete. Good practice, therefore, for professional workers, is practice whereby knowledge is developed through the forms of reflection which practice itself requires.

2 It follows that, for professional workers, a given state of reflective understanding will be transformed by further experience of practice, and that (by the same token) future practice will be transformed by the reflection which arises from practice.

3 Professional work involves commitment to a specific set of moral purposes, and professional workers will recognize the inevitably complex and serious responsibilities which arise when attempting to apply ethical principles to particular situations.

4 The responsibility for equitable practice which characterizes the professional role commits professional workers to the comprehensive, consistent, conscious, and effective implementation of 'anti-oppressive' non-discriminatory principles and practices.

5 Authoritative involvement in the problem areas of clients' lives inevitably creates a complex emotional dimension to professional work, and professional workers therefore recognize that the role involves understanding and managing the emotional dimension of professional relationships.

6 Consequently, professional workers recognize that the understanding of others on which their interpersonal effectiveness depends is inseparable

from self-knowledge, and consequently entails a sustained process of self-evaluation.

7 The incompleteness of professional knowledge (see 1 and 2 above) implies that the authoritative basis of judgments will always remain open to question. Hence, for professional workers, relationships with others will necessarily be collaborative rather than simply hierarchical.

8 Professional workers will be aware of available codified knowledge — e.g., concerning legal provisions, organizational procedures, resources, and research findings, but they will recognize that the relevance of this knowledge for particular situations always depends on their own selection and interpretation.

9 Professional workers will have at their command a grasp of the relationships (similarities and contrasts) between a wide range of situations (different clients, different legal frameworks, and different practice settings).

10 The process of analytical understanding which professional workers will bring to their practice involves:
   • creative translation of meanings between contexts (see 9, above);
   • synthesis of varied elements into a unified overall pattern;
   • relating a situation to its context (institutional, legal, and political);
   • understanding a situation in terms of its tensions and contradictions; and
   • understanding a situation in terms of its inherent processes of change.

(An important point to be made about this overall formulation, in the context of the general argument of this chapter, is its close links with current notions about the nature of higher education as a whole. Barnett in particular (1992, chapter 11) is willing to take Schon's model of 'the reflective practitioner' with its emphasis on values, critique, and 'contextual knowledge' as a model for higher education students in general (*ibid.*, p. 194).)

Clearly, the general model of professional work we have presented here is largely a theoretical construction. Before translating it into a set of general assessment criteria for our social work degree, we decided to test it by means of two empirical studies. First, we collected the 'personal constructs' of social work practitioners, and second, we tried to obtain a fuller account of the appropriate intellectual and academic requirements by conducting a survey of the categories used by academic examiners. This work is summarized below; complete accounts of both studies are included in Winter and Maisch, 1992.

Practitioners' Personal Constructs

The Repertory Grid method for eliciting Personal Constructs is a well-known and widely used social science research procedure, originally developed by George Kelly (Kelly, 1955). Like Functional Analysis, the Repertory Grid method aims at eliciting the views of those being consulted in such a way as to minimize the imposition of predetermined concepts by the investigator, by using a process of 'triadic comparison' (see below) based on elements of the respondents' own experience — in this case practitioners' perceptions of the professionally significant qualities of their colleagues.

Twelve of the social workers who had taken part in the Functional Analysis sessions took part in this study. First, they were asked to list the names of ten colleagues engaged in roughly similar work to themselves. They were assured that these names would not be disclosed to anyone else at any stage. Then they were asked to consider any three names and to write down a quality possessed by two of these people but not the third. This quality could be either positive or negative. Then they were asked to consider another group of three names and do the same, and to continue until they had considered all possible combinations of names and/ or had made a list of ten qualities. Against each quality they had noted, they were then asked to write down the quality which they took to be 'the opposite', so that they then had ten pairs of contrasted qualities. Finally they were asked to rank these pairs of qualities in order of their importance in good social work practice. The list of names was then detached from the sheet and we were given the ranked list of paired qualities.

The following list includes the pairs of qualities ranked first by each respondent (unless only one pair was ranked first, in which case the qualities ranked second are also included). For ease of presentation only, the list is divided into four broad (and admittedly questionable) headings: Practical Qualities, Emotional Qualities, Intellectual Qualities, and 'General' Qualities, which could have either an emotional or an intellectual reference, or both.

Practical Qualities

1 practical   (as opposed to) impractical
2 administratively well organized   (as opposed to) disorganized
3 hard-working   (as opposed to) lazy

Emotional Qualities

4 warm   (as opposed to) unemotional
5 cheerful   (as opposed to) miserable
6 compassionate   (as opposed to) aloof
7 empathetic   (as opposed to) unsympathetic
8 positive/supportive   (as opposed to) negative/undermining
9 approachable   (as opposed to) isolated
10 assertive   (as opposed to) quiet/withdrawn

Intellectual Qualities

11 understanding   (as opposed to) misses the point
12 clear thinking   (as opposed to) narrow minded/ muddled
13 perceptive   (as opposed to) dismissive

14	well-informed	(as opposed to) ill-informed
15	good at identifying relevant issues	(as opposed to) not good at identifying relevant issues

General Qualities

16	professional	(as opposed to) unprofessional
17	objective	(as opposed to) subjective/unprofessional
18	open	(as opposed to) dogmatic
19	informed and careful	(as opposed to) holding extreme views
20	gives careful consideration	(as opposed to) adamant
21	flexible	(as opposed to) rigid
22	enthusiastic	(as opposed to) entrenched
23	resourceful*	(as opposed to) bureaucratic*
24	holds back from precipitate action	(as opposed to) acts on ill-assimilated policy or new fashion
25	positive	(as opposed to) vague
26	gains confidence by seeking information, researching, learning	(as opposed to) overconfident
27	good listener	(as opposed to) poor listener
28	communicative	(as opposed to) non-communicative
29	sensitive**	(as opposed to) lacking sensitivity**

Note: * Ranked second after two first rankings, but included because of its suggestiveness (see discussion below).
 ** By far the most frequently mentioned quality.

Commentary

The following analysis of the practitioners' personal constructs is an attempt to draw out themes which would be relevant as part of our general theory of the professional role, in order to check, refine, and add to the ten propositions presented at the end of the previous section. (Numbers in brackets refer to the numbers against the qualities listed above.)

A The preponderance of 'general' qualities (i.e., those which straddle the emotional/intellectual distinction) points to an important dimension of the complexity of the role, and to an important aspect of its fundamental nature, which might perhaps be thought of as an 'intelligence of the emotions'.

B The widespread invocation of the term 'sensitive' is significant, since it has links with very many of the other qualities listed, which also refer to the need to be 'open' to the unique and unpredictable complexities of each situation. Altogether the list of qualities makes a powerful statement about the impossibility of utilizing predetermined ('bureaucratic') responses to pre-categorized situations, and hence about the need always to draw upon a *wide* range of cognitive, practical, and emotional 'resources' (see 23, above). In this context, 'aloofness' (6), 'subjectivity' (17), and 'extremism' (19) can all be seen as identifying a similar form of 'professional' inadequacy (16, 17).

C   The emphasis upon responsiveness to the particular situation links with the notion of having professional confidence *because* one is conscious of continually learning from one's practice (see 26), as opposed to the 'over-confidence' which — therefore — is implicitly associated with *not* realizing that professional work is a form of 'researching' and 'learning'.

D   But the emphasis on sensitivity to contextual factors is balanced by a contrasting emphasis on the confidence required in order to make crucial *judgments* about people, events, and situations (see 10, 25) and on the practical decisiveness involved in carrying out positive action, once the time for deliberation is over (see 1, 2, 24, 25).

E   Hence the need for comprehensive factual knowledge (see 14) and clarity of understanding (see 11, 12, 15).

Finally, one might sum up the key contrast between B) and D) by suggesting that the essence of practice is presented as the need to make 'careful' (difficult, delicate, risky) judgments in response to the vast range of possibilities — emotional, cognitive, practical — presented by the uniqueness of individual cases, and the need to live with the inevitable risks of having to act upon such judgments.

Academic 'Level'

The original purpose of this study was to establish a set of categories which could be used to indicate the *general* meaning of 'honours degree level' work, to support the references to mastery of a body of knowledge in the two studies previously presented. It involved collecting data on the terms in which academic staff operationalize their judgments concerning appropriate standards when they write reports on candidates' work for honours degree courses. At this stage we were concerned with general intellectual skills (which could be evidenced in professional practice just as well as in academic study) rather than knowledge of specific facts and theories, but during the Ford (engineering) phase of the work the latter also emerged as an issue, and this is discussed in the next chapter.

Altogether a total of 150 examiners' reports were scrutinized, on work submitted by students in the final year of various honours degree courses, i.e., in English literature, biology, law, nursing, environmental planning, and education. The work was in a variety of forms: projects, essays, examination scripts, coursework, and Accreditation of Prior Learning portfolios. The examiners' reports varied in length from three lines to a densely packed side of A4. The common assessment vocabulary gleaned from this study is fully reported in Winter and Maisch, 1992.

Unfortunately, however, a follow-up study (reported in Winter, 1994a) showed that most of the intellectual qualities noted as desirable by honours degree examiners were *also* implicit in the requirements for pre-undergraduate, A level work and also at *post*graduate level!

Fortunately, however, we had not attempted to include much of the detail of the honours degree assessment vocabulary in our final statement on the general role requirements, since many of the categories and phrases seemed already to be implicit in the requirements of professional practice (e.g., 'open-mindedness', 'conclusions clearly derived from evidence', 'thoughtfulness combined with emotional sensitivity'). What this means, however, is that those categories and phrases from the honours degree assessment vocabulary which we did include (e.g., 'careful, sensitive observation', 'analysis of issues', 'details related to general principles' — see Core Assessment Criteria, below) must be taken as indicating successful academic work in a very general way, rather than any specific and exclusive link with honours degree work in particular. Clearly, a lot more work needs to be done before we can speak with authority and certainty about the defining characteristics of educational levels (see Chapter 6 and Winter, 1993b; 1994a).

Nevertheless, from the point of view of the argument of this chapter, it is worth noting the qualities which, in our research, did seem to distinguish at least between the criteria and expectations of 'higher education' in general and those of 'pre-higher' education. These are summarized below (taken from Winter, 1994a, pp. 98–9).

Knowledge
• awareness of a wide range of relevant literature.

Intellectual Processes
• using personal experience as a starting point for the development of general ideas and as evidence to illustrate theory;
• analysing assumptions;
• raising questions;
• developing a personal philosophy; and
• taking responsibility for decisions.

Investigative Work/Practical Activity
• linking observations in practical work to knowledge derived from reading; and
• clarifying a personal stance in relation to the work.

General Qualities
• self-analytical.

Although this list is in itself unremarkable, it does at least have an encouragingly close connection with the characteristics of professional work which emerged from the two previous studies. First, there is the emphasis on knowledge, analysis, intellectual flexibility, and the ability to adopt a critical stance towards one's current understanding. Even more significant, perhaps, are the references to *personal* engagement and a sense of responsibility, since these have, in a sense, an even closer conceptual link with professional practice itself.

This in turn provides further confirmation of the general assumption behind the ASSET project, that professional practice can indeed be a highly appropriate arena in which to demonstrate and develop higher education qualities and abilities. Indeed in Barnett's powerful plea for the *rescue* of the essential characteristics of higher education *from* the limitations and distortions of competence-based education (Barnett, 1994) he particularly emphasizes the need for 'wisdom' and 'values', as opposed to merely technical knowledge (op. cit., pp. 144–53). But the foregoing analysis has surely indicated that our model of the general role requirements for practice-based learning in professional development (our 'second dimension' of assessment criteria) embodies the centrality of values, along with understanding and critique — two of Barnett's other defining characteristics of higher education (op. cit., Chapters 7 and 8). We therefore put forward our Core Assessment Criteria document in the following section with some confidence that it begins at least to encapsulate the essence of what higher education would wish to stand for, as well as the basic stance of professional social workers towards their tasks.

The Core Assessment Criteria and Their Use

The Core Assessment Criteria presented in Document 4 are an attempt to present the main ideas from the three studies outlined above in the form of a practical assessment guideline, accessible both to candidates and to assessors within the ASSET Social Work Programme. The use of the Core Assessment Criteria in conjunction with specific competence statements is described subsequently.

The Core Assessment Criteria document is used in the following way. In their work for the programme candidates compile portfolios of work-based evidence and a supporting commentary to demonstrate that they have fulfilled *simultaneously* both the competence requirements (derived through the functional analysis process described in Chapter 3) *and* the general criteria. They begin by drawing up an action plan for the module they are about to undertake (see Chapter 2), in which they consider how their actual (or potential) practice can link each of the listed competence statements with *one or other* of the core criteria in turn. In other words, candidates use the Core Assessment Criteria for *detailed* guidance in selecting their evidence for the competence statements, and this also allows them a considerable measure of autonomy in adapting the programme documentation to the details of their own practice situation or work profile.

Consider, for example, the module presented in Chapter 3 (Document 2). The first competence statement is:

[Candidates must] inform clients of the full range of relevant resources and services and the criteria for their provision.

The ASSET model Core Assessment Criteria (Social Work Programme)

Criterion No. 1: Commitment to Professional Values
Demonstrates understanding of, and commitment to, professional values in practice, through the implementation of anti-discriminatory, anti-oppressive, anti-racist principles.
  This involves demonstrating:

1 awareness of the need to counteract one's own tendency (both as a person and as a professional worker endowed with specific powers) to behave oppressively; and
2 respect for dignity, diversity, privacy, autonomy.

Criterion No. 2: Continuous Professional Learning
Demonstrates commitment to, and capacity for, reflection on practice, leading to progressive deepening of professional understanding.
  This involves demonstrating:

1 willingness and capacity to learn from others, including clients, supervisees, colleagues;
2 recognition that professional judgments are always open to question; and
3 ability to engage in self-evaluation, recognizing and analysing one's strengths and limitations.

Criterion No. 3: Affective Awareness
Demonstrates sensitivity to, and understanding of, the emotional complexity of particular situations.
  This involves combining sensitivity with effective management of emotional responses in the course of professional relationships.

Criterion No. 4: Effective Communication
Demonstrates ability to communicate effectively in complex professional contexts.
  This involves communicating in a form and manner which is clear, sensitive, and appropriately varied in style and medium according to particular audiences and purposes.

Criterion No. 5: Executive Effectiveness
Demonstrates ability to pursue the stages of a chosen approach in relation to a clearly established purpose.
  This involves demonstrating decisiveness combined with sensitivity in making difficult judgments in response to complex situations.

Criterion No. 6: Effective Grasp of a Wide Range of Professional Knowledge
Demonstrates an understanding of the relationship between various types of professional knowledge, and an ability to apply this understanding effectively through practice.
  This involves demonstrating:

1 comprehensive knowledge and critical evaluation of professional methods, policy, procedures, general theory, research findings, legislation; and
2 ability to relate specific details to other contexts and to general principles.

Criterion No. 7: Intellectual Flexibility
Demonstrates an open-minded awareness of alternatives.
  This involves demonstrating the ability to analyse issues in terms of dilemmas and/or to analyse situations in terms of continuous change.

Candidates might approach the task of demonstrating this competence in a number of ways:

- The obvious focus would be on core criterion 6, ensuring that the range of resources is very varied, detailed and comprehensive, and that the criteria for provision are explained in such detail that the principles underlying them are analysed.

- Alternatively, if the client has 'unusual' needs (e.g., if he or she is suffering from a rare disease) or if the candidate is inexperienced in working with a particular client group, then demonstrating this competence may involve investigative work, which would then enable the candidate to focus their evidence on core criterion 2 ('Professional Learning').
- Or again, if the client is one with whom communication is exceptionally difficult, then demonstrating this competence might create evidence for core criterion 4 ('Effective Communication').
- Or supposing that there is a painful discrepancy between the particular client's perception of his or her needs and the availability of resources, then the demonstration of this competence could create evidence for criterion 3 ('Affective Awareness').

What would *not* be acceptable as evidence for this competence would be to simply pass on to the client a pre-prepared list. This would apparently fulfil the competence statement as expressed, but would *not* demonstrate any of the core criteria. It is clear that although the social worker might do this personally, it *could* be carried out by the team clerk, which returns us to the argument presented above, concerning the need for general criteria to indicate the overall occupational and educational role. Simply in terms of organizational 'quality control' standards, it might well be quite acceptable practice, in many cases, simply to deliver a pre-prepared list of available services and resources, but this would *not* earn credit within the ASSET Programme, unless, of course, the list had been researched and prepared by the candidate.

It is not necessary to analyse all the possible permutations of the competence statements in Document 2 and the general criteria presented above. Readers can do so for themselves simply by reading each of the competence statements against each of the Core Assessment Criteria in turn. Not all permutations make sense, of course, but there are always two or three realistic possibilities. Each combination of specific competence and general criterion provides an intellectual and professional challenge and makes the demonstration of the competences a taxing educational process while retaining the basic format of practice-based assessment evidence.

In this way, the combination of specific and general criteria enables ASSET Programme assessment procedures to ensure the level of the work required for each element of competence, both in terms of its professional quality (the value base of the work, affective awareness, and executive effectiveness) and also its intellectual qualities (flexibility, the knowledge required, and the ability to learn through practice).

'Core Skills', 'General Principles'

The ASSET Programme is not alone in recognizing that adequate role performance cannot simply be presented in terms of lists of specific behaviours, but must include more general considerations. Eraut (1993), for example, draws a general distinction between 'performance' and '*capability*' in formulating professional competence, and elsewhere he discusses various ways of embodying 'ethics' in occupational standards

(Eraut, 1994a). The significance in this respect of the work of the ASSET project is emphasized by Mitchell (1993, pp. 14–16). But at this point it is worth drawing attention to the differences between the general dimension of the ASSET model and other apparently similar work.

For example, although the official 'Guide' to NVQs emphasizes that 'Core Skills' 'underpin most aspects of performance' (NCVQ, 1995a, p. 20) they are embodied in separate core skills units, even though it is recognized that the evidence for the core skills ('problem solving, communication, personal skills', etc.) 'emerges through inspecting how an individual performs the occupational functions detailed in NVQ statements of competence' (*ibid.*, p. 21). In view of our argument that one of the purposes of the Core Assessment Criteria is to determine the *level* of assessment, it is interesting that NCVQ present the core skills units at specific levels (see Oates, 1992, Annexe 1). But it is precisely by presenting the core skills in discrete units separate from the occupationally specific units that NCVQ ensures that the level of its 'occupational units' remains indeterminate (see our discussion of the TDLB unit above).

The one aspect of the work of NCVQ which begins to approach our combination of two assessment dimensions is the use of 'grading themes' in the assessment of *General* Vocational Qualifications (GNVQs). Beyond the awarding of a 'pass' (in relation to specific competence requirements) higher and lower grades are awarded for aspects of the candidates' general mastery of the learning process, i.e., planning, information seeking and handling, and evaluation (see BTEC, 1992, p. 14). These 'grading themes' thus constitute a further 'general' dimension, but they do not refer to the *occupational* role and they are not fully integrated into the assessment of specific competences since they are only used retrospectively to *review* the whole of a candidate's work when it is presented for a qualification (BTEC, 1993, p. 5). A recent study of GNVQ assessment procedures (Wolf, 1994) reports duplication of effort, overload, and confusion.

The various projects on 'transferable skills' (Blagg *et al.*, 1993) 'personal skills' (Allen, 1991) and 'enterprise' skills' (Boyne *et al.*, 1992) all wrestle in various ways with the problem of establishing effective links (in terms of learning and assessment processes) between general qualities and specific discipline-based knowledge and/or the detailed requirements of employers. BTEC finds a partial solution by assessing 'Common Skills' at the end of a complete programme of study (BTEC, 1991, p. 5) in the form of a project or an 'integrative assignment. The work on the 'professional competence project' based in the construction industry (see Ennis *et al.*, 1993) and on 'the personal competence model' in the context of competence-based management 'standards' (the Management Charter Initiative, reported in Fowler, 1994) both focus on general aspects of the occupational role, but, like the NVQ work on core skills, both studies lead to the presentation of separate units, in the same 'single dimension' format as the TDLB standards discussed earlier. However, Fowler's evaluation of the MCI personal competence model recommends that MCI should explicitly establish links between the 'personal competences' and the occupationally specific elements of the management 'standards' (Fowler, 1994, 'Recommendations', 8.2). In their different ways, most of this work seems to echo or anticipate Boyne *et al.* (1992) in seeing 'a potential tension' between 'generic' skills and narrowly conceived occupational competences (op. cit., p. 29) and calling for a 'synergy' between the two while remaining unclear as to the assessment procedure for achieving this integrative aim.

In view of the origin of the ASSET model in social work education (with its very explicit emphasis on its underlying 'holism' and its value base, it is perhaps not surprising that its closest parallels are with the work of the 'Care Sector Consortium'. In particular, the standards for 'Residential and Domiciliary Day Care' (RDDC) specify not only performance criteria for each element of competence but also 'Core Performance Criteria' which express the key values and interpersonal skills of the 'caring professions' (Care Sector Consortium, 1990). But these 'Core' criteria, unlike those of the ASSET Programme, are *not* intended to indicate the 'level' of the candidate's work (Care Sector Consortium, 1990; 1991a, p. 10), and they have an uncertain relationship to the 'specific' performance criteria of the individual elements of competence (as noted by Armstrong, *et al.*, 1992, p. 42). This means that they risk being relegated to the status of worthy background concerns which are not systematically used in the assessment process. Indeed, in later work of the Care Sector Consortium, the concepts underlying the RDDC Core Performance criteria are re-presented as 'Principles of Good Practice', which form the basis of a separate, compulsory 'Value Base Unit' (Care Sector Consortium, 1991a, pp. 9–13). As with the ASSET Core Assessment Criteria, the Care Sector 'Principles of Good Practice' are 'applicable' to each of the specific elements (Care Sector Consortium 1991b, Appendix B, p. 41), but, again (and in contrast to the ASSET model), the actual process by which they are to be 'applied' is not clear, except insofar as they may be invoked by assessors as grounds for a judgment that a candidate's work is not adequate.

The ASSET Core Assessment Criteria can also function in this way, but the ASSET procedure goes further and is more precise, in that it also states that the evidence for each element in each unit must be explicitly related to, and assessed in relation to, one of the Core Criteria, as illustrated in the previous section. The ASSET Core Assessment Criteria are also more broadly based, in that they reflect the generic qualities, skills, responsibilities and activities involved in both the occupational role *and* in the educational process. Indeed they may be thought of as *combining* the various notions of 'core skills', 'personal competence', 'effective learning themes', *and* 'principles of good practice' treated separately in the work discussed above.

General Criteria? Core Assessment Criteria in the Context of Engineering

Finally we must consider the question: how 'general' is this 'general dimension' supposed to be? To begin with, although we began with a theory grounded in the work of the 'person-oriented professions', our Core Assessment Criteria are specifically intended for use in a social work degree. The ASSET material has been used to inform developmental work in, for example, law (see Webb and Maughan, 1996), teacher education (see Moon and Mays, 1995, p. 236; McIntyre and Hustler, 1996), medicine, and accountancy. But it is clear that all professions do *not* share a single characteristic stance towards a set of underlying values and a body of expertise, and that the emotional dimension of practice varies considerably, depending on whether one's work focuses on the personal needs of human beings or on the problems posed by inanimate materials and objects.

It was precisely to examine the generalizability of the ASSET model that the Ford ASSET Programme in automotive engineering was initiated (see Chapter 2), and the leader of that project, Samantha Guise, undertook the following work in order to establish what amendments to the social work Core Assessment Criteria would be necessary to render them acceptable in a very different occupational and cognitive context. First, the personal construct method was used with thirty-one Ford engineers in order to ascertain how far the engineers' conceptions of their role were compatible with the themes of the seven core criteria of the Social Work Programme. Second, since the original study of examiners' categories had not included either a technological or a 'hard science' discipline, reference was made to assessment criteria concerning the requirements of degree level work in engineering published by Imperial College (London University) Mechanical Engineering Department and by the (national) Institute of Mechanical Engineers. Third, the qualities presented in the Ford Personnel Appraisal form were consulted.

As a result of this work, the following document was produced, and like the first version produced for the Social Work Programme, it immediately gained a higher degree of assent within the profession. The differences between the two documents are clear, both in terms of overall emphasis, and in terms of detail, but we were also interested, and pleased, by the extent of the similarity between the two versions, given our assumption that the divergence between the occupational cultures of automotive engineering and social work would be fairly extreme.

Conclusion

Clearly there are other points to be made concerning the degree of generality and authoritativeness that we would claim for either version of these Core Assessment Criteria. On the one hand it is important to note that the engineering criteria are partly derived from the assessment form used by the Institute of Mechanical Engineers, a nationally recognized professional association. Similarly, the social work Core Assessment Criteria embody a number of the key professional criteria laid down by the Central Council for Education and Training in Social Work (CCETSW, 1992, pp. 14–15) and that they have been adopted more or less unchanged by the Social Services Department of Glasgow, i.e., in a social and cultural context which contrasts quite sharply with the context of their origin (see Glasgow Caledonian University, 1994; Brodie and Whittaker, 1995). On the other hand the differences between the social work and the engineering versions illustrate how differing sets of criteria can be derived even from a single fundamental theory and method, when

Document 5

The ASSET Core Assessment Criteria (Ford Engineering Programme)

Criterion No. 1: Effective Grasp of Professional Knowledge
This involves demonstrating:

1 comprehensive knowledge and critical evaluation of theories/technologies/methods/ policy/procedures/research findings/legislation;
2 ability to relate specific details to other contexts and to general principles; and
3 ability to recognize when and where to search for additional information.

Criterion No. 2: Intellectual Rigour and Flexibility
This involves demonstrating:

precise, open-minded, challenging analysis of problems and the generation of a range of different solutions

Criterion No. 3: Continuous Professional Learning
This involves demonstrating:

1 willingness and capacity to learn from other people and from a variety of sources;
2 recognition that the changing environment demands constant updating of one's under- standing; and
3 ability to evaluate one's work, recognizing and analysing its strengths and limitations.

Criterion No. 4: Task Effectiveness
This involves demonstrating:

1 initiative, responsiveness, decisiveness and tenacity; and
2 ability to focus on a given objective and manage resources accordingly.

Criterion No. 5: Effective Communication
This involves demonstrating:

ability to communicate in a form and manner which is clear/accurate/concise/sensitive, and appropriately varied according to different audiences and purposes

Criterion No. 6: Interpersonal Awareness
This involves demonstrating:

1 awareness of the effect of one's own and others' feelings on work situations; and
2 ability to work collaboratively within a team.

Criterion No. 7: Commitment to Professional Values
This involves demonstrating:

1 acceptance of responsibility for the quality of one's own work and of the work for which one is accountable;
2 personal integrity, honesty and respect for others; and
3 incorporation into one's judgments of an understanding of the ethical/economic/environ- mental impact of one's work.

interpreted in the context of different types of occupation. Hence, there is clearly nothing sacrosanct about either document: they are *interpretations* of a body of theory and evidence.

Furthermore it could be argued that documents such as the ASSET Core Assessment Criteria will need to be continuously amended to reflect historical changes in the structure of professional roles. For example, it has been suggested that both the social work and the engineering versions of the criteria are ultimately derived from a 'public service' model of professionalism and thus do not sufficiently include the more recent *managerial* dimensions of the role (see Young and Guile, 1994, p. 14). However, there is a danger of overemphasizing the significance of such arguments. We would argue that, in principle, the more widespread introduction of managerial responsibilities would require the development of further units of competence (and perhaps the amendment of existing units), rather than a rework-ing of the Core Assessment Criteria. This is to emphasize, once more, the crucial distinction between specific competences (which will indeed need to reflect changes in occupational tasks and responsibilities) and the general, 'underlying' values, qualities, and processes which will continue to guide and shape conceptualizations of, and responses to, such changes. Thus, we would argue, the managerial task, like any other aspect of the professional role, involves value commitments, a grasp of bodies of knowledge, affective awareness, effective communication, and so on, as indicated in the Core Assessment Criteria. We recognize that of course there can be no *absolute* distinction between 'general' and 'specific': there is a sense in which all words (other than proper nouns) are general labels for the specific variety of individual experience. However, we have attempted in this chapter to indicate that there is a clear and important qualitative difference (in origin and function) between the ASSET Core Assessment Criteria and the sets of competence statements pre-sented in Chapter 3.

We also recognize that there is an implicit tension within our claim that the Core Assessment Criteria (a) embody the underlying/overarching *holism* of pro-fessional and educational processes, and (b) are used to provide guidance in the work for, and assessment of, *particular* episodes of practice and learning. This tension is expressed in the argument (already referred to) that a 'circular' relationship is involved in interpreting the significance of the whole in terms of its constituent parts, and vice versa. It is this argument which underlies our claim that the second dimension of the ASSET model provides a systematic yet flexible procedure for integrating the fundamental holism of professional and educational processes with the detailed specifications of a competence-based curriculum. The use of this sec-ond dimension is intended to enable the ASSET model to combine the practical, the moral, the affective, and the intellectual aspects of both professional work and the development of understanding. That, surely, is what a university competence-based vocational curriculum should aim to do. It is a bold claim, but ultimately a neces-sary one.

Notes

1   At this point in the argument, some may wish to object: what about 'Range Statements'? Are they not supposed to provide guidance as to the level required? First, it is not clear that they are supposed to do so, since there is doubt as to whether they indicate a *required* specification or a set of options (see Jessup, 1990a, p. 41). Also, it is often hard to see why range statements are given for some aspects of an element of competence but

not for others, see Winter, 1992, p. 106). Certainly, the range statements concerning the list of performance criteria quoted in this chapter do not even begin to address any of the issues raised, although it is highly significant for our argument that the matter of who has access to records *is* addressed in the range statement and in the 'Knowledge evidence required' for *another* element (i.e., in a different section of the document — see Training and Development Lead Body, 1995, p. 52, p. 53). This illustrates how useful a 'two-dimensional' set of assessment documents might have been. Alison Wolf comments:

> [Range statements] have become something of a rag-bag, containing any sort of information for which there is no other obvious home in the standards, and which the latter's authors think might make things clearer. (Wolf, 1995, p. 26)

For the element of competence with which we are concerned here, the statement on 'Knowledge Evidence Required' does not mention principles of confidentiality, although it does refer in very general terms to 'issues of equality of opportunity' and 'principles, processes and methods of assessment'. This suggests that crucial issues concerning assessment are addressed under the heading of 'knowledge', rather than in the performance criteria, which raises the issues discussed in Chapter 5.

2   The ambiguities as to 'level' are exacerbated by the fact that NVQ competence statements are presented in a 'depersonalized' format (see Appendix F). They therefore do not explicitly refer to what an *individual* must do and *could* be referring to group or organizational arrangements (see Ashworth and Saxton, 1990, for further criticism along these lines).

5 Practice *and* Knowledge or Practice *as* Knowledge?

Introduction

Of all the general aspects of role performance encompassed within the ASSET Programme Core Assessment Criteria, only 'knowledge' is consistently picked out by the NCVQ model as a necessary aspect of all assessment decisions.[1] This predominant emphasis on the cognitive dimension (at the expense of the affective and the ethical, for example) is not, however, surprising, since it echoes a widespread characteristic of educational curricula in general. In a famous comedy sketch from the 1960s Peter Cook tells us wistfully, 'I wanted to be a judge; only I didn't have the latin.' What make us laugh here is that Cook reveals the contradiction within a familiar phenomenon. That a judge should be required to 'know latin' seems, from one point of view, intuitively justifiable (the traditional idea that classical languages are a general training in practical logic, perhaps); but from another point of view the requirement seems an absurdity, since the knowledge requirement is so esoterically remote from any conceivable practical application that it seems like a *mere* convention, a 'senseless' rule creating a purely discriminatory barrier. This ambiguity in the assumed relationship between 'formal' knowledge and practical ability has long historical roots which run deep in our culture. On the one hand it continually threatens to place a question-mark against the 'relevance' of conventional educational qualifications (see Chapter 1), and on the other hand it suggests the need to specify 'underpinning knowledge and understanding' if competence-based curricula are to be educationally acceptable. It creates the complex theoretical and practical issues which are the topic of this chapter.

There have been two memorable occasions (so far) in the experience of the ASSET Programme team which suddenly revealed to us the full scope of these issues. The first was when we presented our first set of candidates' portfolios of work-based evidence to our external examiners, whose experience is mainly with academically based courses, and found ourselves faced with their question: 'Where is the "theory"?' The second occasion occurred when, at the end of a functional analysis session, looking round at all the flip-chart sheets listing all the things they needed to do in the performance of their professional role, a group of Ford design engineers complained, 'But what about all our knowledge?' For us this comment was totally unexpected: our previous functional analysis sessions, with professional *social work* staff, had always ended with the participants expressing pleasure at the extent to which the flip-charts seemed to encapsulate and to emphasize the complexity and value of their work. Why such different reactions? From this dramatic moment onwards, the engineering ASSET Programme began to develop a model which diverged significantly from the original social work model, and this chapter ends with a discussion of the basis for this divergence. But first, in order to appreciate the conceptual background to these two events, we need to examine, albeit briefly, some of the basic issues concerning the relationship between practical performances and their 'underpinning' knowledge.

Occupational Competence and 'Underpinning Knowledge'

Peter Cook's character bemoans the requirement of latin, but his stance is self-pitying rather than critical: he accepts that latin is, unfortunately for him, part of the legitimate 'rigour' of judicial training and assessment. In contrast, Gilbert Jessup, on behalf of NCVQ, would have liked to offer an immediate solution, by abolishing separate academic prerequisites:

> The early arguments [concerning 'the problem of knowledge'] within the competence movement went something like this. If a person performs competently we need not be concerned with what he or she knows. Any knowledge the individual requires can be inferred from their performance. (Jessup, 1991, p. 121)

This simple abolition of the problem draws philosophical authority from Gilbert Ryle:

> The boxer, the surgeon, the poet and the salesman ... are appraised as clever, skilful, inspired or shrewd not for the ways in which they consider, if they consider at all, prescriptions for conducting their special performances, but for the ways in which they conduct those performances themselves. (Ryle, 1963, p. 48)[2]

Jessup goes on to admit that matters are not quite so simple:

> The above argument ... would be sustainable if it was practicable to assess performance over the range [of situations] to which an element of competence applies. In practice this is seldom possible, especially at higher levels ... where the potential range of applications is considerable. (Jessup, 1991, p. 121)

Jessup's argument here converts the philosophical issue (the nature of the link between action and knowledge) into a practical problem of assessment procedures. The argument is as follows. It is not possible to make what lawyers would call a 'safe inference' (Mansfield, 1990, p. 17), on the basis of one observed competent performance, that a range of similar performances would be equally successful; the candidate's competence *may* be highly context-bound (Wolf, 1990, p. 33) or the one performance may even have been a lucky and unrepeatable 'accident' (Ryle, 1963, p. 44). Evidence of 'knowledge' is therefore required in order to make an inference of transferability, i.e., that a small sample of directly observed performances are representative of a *general* 'capability' (Eraut, 1994b, p. 200). At the practical level this becomes a debate about the appropriate balance between different types of evidence (see Chapter 6).

At the philosophical level, however, Jessup seems to retreat only slightly from the position of the 'early arguments' in saying that the current NCVQ model 'links knowledge assessments *directly* to competent performance' (Jessup, 1991, p. 123). The argument for this 'direct' link begins from the broad sense in which the term 'competence' itself is to be understood within the NCVQ model:

> [Competence] is a wide concept which embodies the ability to transfer skills and knowledge to new situations within the occupational area. It encompasses organisation and planning of work, innovation and coping with non-routine activities (all of which depend on an adequate knowledge and understanding). (Debling, 1990, p. 22)

(See also, NCVQ, 1995a, p. 17.) In other words, using a parallel argument:

> Knowledge is . . . simply a component of competent performance which should be associated with elements of competence expressed as performance requirements. (Jessup, 1990b, p. 23)

Hence, knowledge is seen as a *necessary* 'underpinning' which therefore can be 'unwrapped' or 'unpacked' from competence statements themselves (Wolf, 1990).

But we are still left with questions as to how we may understand these various metaphors and shorthand phrases, such as 'underpinning', 'unwrapping', 'components', etc. In particular we need to note that all these terms imply only that practice is *informed by* knowledge and diverts our attention from the process whereby practice also leads to the *development of* knowledge (see Chapter 4). In the next three subsections, therefore, we shall examine the issues in rather more detail (without trying to write a treatise on epistemology or repeating the arguments presented in the previous chapter) by considering in turn:

1 the different forms of knowledge which may be thought to 'underpin' action;
2 how far such knowledge can or should be prescribed; and
3 whether the knowledge dimension of competence can or should be embedded in competence statements or identified separately.

Together these three questions encapsulate a major aspect of the tension between conventional 'academic' higher education and the emphasis of competence-based vocational education. It is these three questions which receive contrasting answers within the two ASSET Programmmes, as described later in the chapter.

Propositional or Process Knowledge

Propositional knowledge is knowledge in the form of systems of descriptive statements or prescriptions ('propositions'). These propositions may be abstract (e.g., bodies of academic theory) or concrete (bodies of legislation, codes of practice). To the extent that the knowledge underpinning practice is seen as propositional knowledge, competent practice will be understood as the *application* of knowledge *to* practice situations; practice is thus seen as dependent on, determined by, its 'knowledge-base'.

However, as we argued in the previous chapter, this is an incomplete and even misleading formulation. Competent practice requires more than the 'application' of a specifiable knowledge-base; rather, it involves a *process* of selecting from alternatives, of interpreting situations as relevant to this particular theory, rather than another, as relevant to this particular piece of legislation or technical formula rather than others. It also involves *managing* the relationship between various types of technical knowledge in conjunction with the 'tacit' knowledge derived from personal and cultural experience (Polyani, 1962). It also entails understanding the nature and limits of one's knowledge so that one is able to adapt it to changing circumstances (Fleming, 1991) as part of a dynamically changing 'knowledge frame-work' (Moonie, 1992). It is this further form of knowledge which we would wish to emphasize under the heading 'process knowledge'. Process knowledge refers to the complex *process* by means of which propositional knowledge is actually *used* (Eraut, 1994b, p. 107).

Another way of approaching these issues is to distinguish between two conceptions of 'theory'. 'Theory' may be conceived either as a set of *generalizations* (to be applied where appropriate through a process of *selection*) or, alternatively, as a set of *possibilities* which are interpreted as potentially relevant through a process of speculative *play*. The significance of this latter conception is emphasized by Handy, writing about the 'learning stance' towards professional experience required by effective managers. (Handy, 1991, pp. 47–8) (see also our critique of the 'expert systems' approach to professional knowledge in Chapter 4)

Many would agree that it is this 'process knowledge', this ability to envisage possible interpretations, rather than the possession of propositional knowledge in itself, which is of particular significance in 'underpinning' occupational competence:

> Take electronics for example. How much circuit design — or calculus, or control theory, or programming — needs to be in a modern undergradu-ate course, when computer-based tools are relieving engineers more and more of such tasks? What is really needed in a first degree are courses which develop the ability to use such tools with understanding, which pre-pare graduates to learn more specialist techniques as necessary throughout a

career, and which enable them to participate intelligently in the work of
a project team. (Bissell, 1992, p. 17)

Similarly, at the beginning of a discussion reviewing the structure of engineering
degrees issued by the Engineering Professors Conference, the following main aims
are listed: 'To produce broad-based flexible graduates who can think integratively,
solve problems, and be life-long learners.' (Hogg *et al.*, 1993, p. 5). It is in the
context of comments like these that we must interpret the anxieties of Smithers and
his colleagues concerning the absence of 'theoretical knowledge' in competence-
based curricula, e.g., the lack of formal teaching of trigonometry in the education
of plumbers (Smithers, 1993, p. 24, p. 28).

Personalized or Prescribed Knowledge

'Propositional knowledge' is publicly available in the form of academic syllabuses
specifying bodies of theory, in published research findings, in legislative schedules,
policy documents, etc. Thus, insofar as the knowledge underpinning competent performance has a propositional form, knowledge requirements *could* be prescribed in
quite minute detail. This raises the question: what level of detail is appropriate?
Mitchell and Bartram (1994) quote from documents for a unit of learning on
'making sound recordings' where the knowledge specifications range from the very
general ('What standards apply to the recording?') to technical details ('signal-to-
noise ratio', 'logarithmic units') (p. 19). Clearly, any attempt to provide an exhaustive
and systematic account of the *detail* of *all* the propositional knowledge relevant to
even a limited activity threatens to become vast and unwieldly (see Mitchell, 1993,
p. 27). Mitchell and Bartram propose a practical solution to this problem by saying
that the knowledge specifications must be 'derived from and firmly related to . . . the
actions and decisions' which constitute the occupational activity, as presented in
the competence statements (p. 28) but their suggestions as to how this is to be
achieved indicate that it will be, at the very least, a highly complex research process
(pp. 22–8), comparable in scope to that involved in establishing the competence
statements themselves.
When we turn to 'process knowledge', the issues surrounding prescribability
are very different. To begin with, it is clear that there is as yet very little consensus
about its structure or its detail. For example, Soden (1993) enthusiastically proposes
an 'algorithmic' format (a 'problem-solving' decision sequence ultimately derived
from an analogy with computer simulations of human mental processes) which
Wolf specifically rejects (Wolf, 1990, p. 37). As Eraut says: 'The process of interpreting and personalising theory and integrating it with conceptual frameworks that
are themselves partly inconsistent and partly tacit is as yet only minimally understood'
(Eraut, 1994b, p. 157).
Part of the reason for this lack of consensus in formulating process knowledge
is, of course, that by its very nature the details of the process knowledge underpinning a given performance are very much bound up with particular contexts and with

individual experience and styles of thinking and learning. As such, these would be impossible to prescribe, except in very general terms. Eraut, as part of a general argument emphasizing the role in professional work of 'deliberation' (critical reflection upon one's knowledge and one's practice) quotes with approval the construction industry's learning unit entitled 'Identify, Re-frame and Generate Solutions to Complex, Indeterminate Problems'. This includes performance criteria such as:

- The probable factors out of which problematic conditions arose are plausibly identified . . . ;
- Aids and techniques are applied which inform and increase the reliability of decisions and judgements;
- Optional solutions and procedures, in which the probability of resolution is balanced against disruption and risk, are identified and justified on the basis of declared criteria and reasoned argument. (quoted in Eraut, 1994b, p. 154)

If this is the 'state of the art' of specifying agreed and public criteria for process knowledge, then it is clear how little prescription of detail is possible; and how much its assessment, therefore, will necessarily be concerned with the individual's *selection* of detail from their own particular context, from the particular practice situation, and from their own interpretive conceptual framework.

Embedded or Separately Identified Knowledge

At the beginning of this chapter we noted that for NCVQ the 'philosophical' problem of the relation between knowledge and action is essentially a practical question of assessment validity: how far can one extrapolate from one successful instance to a *range* of instances. It is not surprising, therefore, that some of the early statements on the NCVQ model suggest that the knowledge required to demonstrate competence may be adequately dealt with by being 'embedded' in a 'range statement':

> The addition of information on the range of application or variation in practice that might be expected . . . can be seen as an extension or clarification of the element of competence. This will often give clear indications as to what evidence of knowledge and understanding it will be necessary to collect for assessment. (Jessup, 1990b, p. 23)

But one of the purposes of the ASSET Core Assessment Criteria, as discussed in the previous chapter, is to face the philosophical issue directly, without recourse to arguments about 'lucky accidents' as opposed to 'safe inferences'. Our argument is that by linking demonstrations of specific competence to general aspects of the role (including grasp of knowledge along with commitment to values, etc.) candidates are required to show a full 'understanding' of their practice, so that a 'safe inference' can then be made of 'capability' and the problem of having observed a lucky accident does not arise. For this reason, range statements are not part of the ASSET model. Indeed, more recently, NCVQ itself has recognized that the issue of 'underpinning knowledge' is more complex than making inferences from observations and needs to be specifically addressed (Employment Department, 1993).

Another line of argument is that if knowledge specifications must be closely tied to the activities they underpin, they can be embedded in the competence statements themselves. Mitchell and Bartram give the following example:

> During the development of the standards for Certified Accountants, there were insistent demands from practitioners and accountancy lecturers alike that auditors needed to know about the history of audits and what audits could, and could not, achieve. After much discussion surrounding this issue, and persistent questioning as to how this would be apparent in, or would affect, practice, it became clear that many clients have unrealistic aims and hopes regarding audits — they think that they will achieve all kinds of things which are impossible from the history and use of audits . . .

> An additional performance criterion was developed . . . This was: The purposes of an audit are explained in a manner and at a level and pace appropriate to the client and their level of understanding. (Mitchell and Bartram, 1994, p. 13)

It is not immediately clear that a knowledge of 'the history of audits' is actually 'embedded' in this performance criterion. However, if we do accept the argument then it is difficult to see why, in another of Mitchell and Bartram's examples, the following items, presented under the heading 'Description of Knowledge and Understanding' in a unit of learning for registered auditors, could not, with very slight re-phrasing, be presented as performance criteria or elements of competence:

- Establishing the type and degree of accuracy of the information required;
- Collecting and calculating relevant financial and related material;
- Identifying and documenting areas of concern in relation to the completeness, accuracy and validity of the financial and related information. (Mitchell and Bartram, 1994, p. 23)

Clearly, although we can easily distinguish between knowing *about* an activity and knowing *how* to carry it out, it is not easy to distinguish between an activity and the knowledge which is actually embodied in the fact that it is being carried out. This is the basic theme of Ryle's original argument (Ryle, 1963) and the foregoing evidence suggests that the notion of competent practice with 'underpinning knowledge' retains considerable ambiguity. As Mitchell herself argued in an earlier paper, 'Adding knowledge into the standards [competence statements]as the missing ingredient is not the solution . . . Writing knowledge elements or knowledge criteria is, at best, *ad hoc*.' (Mitchell, 1990, p. 24)

In the light of this discussion, let us now turn to our experience of working with these issues in formulating and developing the two ASSET Programmes.

'Underpinning' Knowledge?: The Social Work ASSET Programme

To begin with, the documentation of the social work ASSET Programme suggests a primary emphasis on personalized knowledge rather than prescribed knowledge. For example, each set of competence statements is accompanied by a reading list. In general, reading lists, although they may reflect some degree of professional consensus, can never be exhaustive and are always subject to change, so that they are, by their nature, *indicative* (of a level of discussion) rather than *prescriptive* (of a body of knowledge). Above all they inevitably leave the actual choice of material to the *personal* discretion of the candidate, and thus provoke the question: how will the knowledge referred to in the reading lists actually be evidenced? The Programme Handbook contains a general list of 'Types of Evidence' (ASSET, 1995, p. 22 — see Document 7 in Chapter 6). This list emphasizes that 'commentaries' and 'explanations' should accompany both practice-generated documents (memos, minutes, plans, etc) and direct recordings or observations of practice. This evidence format (recording, observation, or practice document *plus* commentary/explanation) provides an opportunity within the portfolio for candidates to refer to their reading when evidencing their practice (see examples in Chapter 7).

Secondly, it is important to remember that within the ASSET Programme commentaries and explanations always have the purpose of showing how the evidence from practice demonstrates one of the competence statements and, at the same time, one of the Core Assessment Criteria. In other words (in the terms of the discussion at the beginning of this chapter) the original intention of the social work ASSET model was that the competence statements and the Core Assessment Criteria should enable candidates to 'embed' the evidence of their professional knowledge in evidence of their competent practice. From this point of view, then, let us reconsider these two key aspects of the ASSET model.

The first point to make is that many of the competence statements in themselves explicitly require evidence of knowledge. Consider, for example, the module presented in Chapter 3 (Document 3). The following competence statements quite explicitly require the presentation of *propositional* knowledge as part of the practice requirement:

1 Communicate to clients the full range of relevant resources and services and the criteria for their provision;
2 Advise clients concerning the policies and statutory responsibilities of local authorities and the legal framework within which they operate;

From the same unit, the following competence statements clearly require the presentation of *process* knowledge:

3 Help clients to recognize their own strengths and needs, and work with the client in assessing and accepting their individual starting points and capabilities;
4 Demonstrate an awareness of the differences between clients' perceptions

and their own, concerning achievable goals, and construct a plan which accepts the outcomes of negotiated processes;

8 Manage a professional relationship with clients balancing the exercise of appropriate authority against an understanding of the necessity for client empowerment.

In each case, here, the candidate will need to present evidence not simply of a single action but of a sustained *process* of decision-making in which each step will need to be informed by a developing 'knowledge framework' (Moonie, 1992). Element 7 (Demonstrate a practical understanding of the theoretical basis for the social worker's roles and responsibilities in work with clients) will clearly require reference to *both* process *and* propositional knowledge. Two further examples of social work modules are presented in Appendices C and D. They both illustrate that, in the same way as the example discussed above, almost all the competence statements clearly require evidence of knowledge and also that there is, on the whole, rather more emphasis on process than on propositional knowledge.

It is not surprising that knowledge, recognized as a key aspect of complex activity, in general and of educational processes in particular, is clearly embodied in most of the ASSET competence statements. As we explained in the previous chapter, the ASSET competence statements were consciously formulated in the light of a complex model of professional work, precisely in order to express and require that degree of complexity, and thus to indicate an *educational* level.

But there certainly are a number of competence statements where this requirement is *implicit* rather than, as in the examples presented so far, quite explicit, e.g., statements 5, 6, 9, and 10 in the unit 'Promoting Clients' Potential for Independence' (Chapter 3, Document 3). This is where the role of the Core Assessment Criteria becomes of particular significance, because, of course, candidates would need to provide evidence for these competences in association with one or other of the Core Assessment Criteria. A glance at the list of Core Assessment Criteria (see previous chapter, Document 4) immediately shows that some of these also explicitly refer to either propositional knowledge (criterion 6) or process knowledge (criteria 2 and 7). So, for example, evidence concerning the competence statement 'Make effective representations on behalf of clients' (Document 3, competence statement 5) *could* be linked with Core Assessment criterion No. 6, and would then include a theoretically grounded analysis of clients' needs and a comprehensive knowledge of the alternative facilities available, in order to show the decision-making process which led to an 'effective' claim.

Moreover, a further consideration of the details of the other criteria (commitment to values, affective awareness, effective communication, and executive effectiveness) suggests that in different ways they also refer to 'process knowledge': they require the analytical articulation of practice in terms of a complex sequence of decisions made in the light of a continuously developing understanding. Thus, 'Make effective representations on behalf of clients' might also be presented by describing (and explaining) a set of communication *challenges* and how they were overcome in order to achieve and sustain 'effectiveness'. In other words, the Core Assessment

Criteria embody a conception of the dimensions of professional awareness which is broader than the purely cognitve (i.e., including the affective, the ethical, and the communicative).[3] Thus, following from our argument in the previous chapter, we would argue that in this respect the Core Assessment Criteria *subsume* the notion of process knowledge within a more fully analysed model of professional work. From this perspective the ASSET Programme therefore goes *beyond* NCVQ's concern with 'underpinning knowledge', which, in comparison with the ASSET Core Assessment Criteria, we would say, is a rather narrowly conceived *political* response to the conflict between competence-based education and the existing cognitive overemphasis of higher education (see Barnett, 1994, pp. 151–2).

All this is, as it were, our claim: this is what the ASSET documentation and procedures *ought* to encourage and facilitate. And yet our external examiners (who are broadly sympathetic to the programme) responded to our first set of portfolios with some reservations concerning candidates' coverage of relevant theoretical knowledge. The following statement, quoted from the edited transcript of a discussion which took place in the summer of 1993, indicates the main themes.

External Examiner:
It was difficult to make a comparison with the work of an ordinary degree student because of the extent of these students' professional responsibilities. So one had to work out criteria for oneself; i.e., could these students defend their practice by using a range of theories in the social sciences (without necessarily identifying them)? I was looking for a kind of maturity of judgment, critical analysis, reflection — all those things that one would expect to find in a good first degree student (although, of course one often doesn't find it in a first degree student!). But all the time I felt I couldn't make this comparison, because these students' work is an emotional labour as much as an intellectual labour.

The portfolios I saw worked well. They illustrated the developmental stages of children, so the sociology and the psychology was also there. So there was no doubt that you could say, 'They may not be able to say what books they have read, because it was a long time since they read them, but they knew what they were tussling with.' And I was impressed by that, and excited, and I enjoyed reading them.

My area of concern was something that I suspect is difficult to do in the workplace, and that has to do with reflection, with the student saying, 'What ought I to be doing here? What do I know which helps me to do it?' There wasn't enough of questioning, of saying, 'What can I learn from this? What questions can I ask that might stop this kind of thing from happening again?' The sort of questions that can be taken back into the whole body of knowledge. We're asking a lot. I mean, I would see that as a student getting a first class degree. But let's aim for something high.

Such responses by our external examiners to the portfolios helped us (i.e., the ASSET Programme tutorial staff) to clarify certain aspects of our approach to the work submitted. In an important sense, what the examiners had said *confirmed* feelings that we were already on the brink of putting into words. Much of the discussion in tutors' meetings had been concerned with the issue of 'how much description' and 'how much analysis' was necessary. After listening to the examiners' comments we felt more confident in asking students to include more analytical commentary in their work, and this resulted in work which felt more like the 'level' of work we wanted the students to attain, and which also seemed to be much closer to the detail of the competence statements and the Core Assessment Criteria. We were also led to ask ourselves why we had not originally made this emphasis with sufficient clarity. We concluded that perhaps at first we had been very concerned about the volume of students' writing, and had emphasized that the evidence required *could* be simple and direct; initially, in response to our advice, this had led to the students producing largely descriptive accounts with somewhat skimpy references to the Core Assessment Criteria rather as a series of afterthoughts. We now realized that we needed to get students to focus from the outset on the Core Assessment criterion they had selected as well as the competence statement, thereby providing a clear emphasis on an *analytical starting point* for the work.

One of the main conclusions to be drawn from this series of discussions and reflections is as follows: even if in principle the knowledge dimension of professional expertise *is* 'embedded' in programme documentation (competence statements, etc.) the satisfactoriness or otherwise of submitted evidence is inevitably a matter of interpretation. Social work is indeed underpinned by theories which could in principle be specified, but the test of professional understanding lies in how the theories are *used* in the particular context. Perhaps, therefore, there is a crucial sense in which in the context of a practice-based curriculum the knowledge 'required' can never be fully prescribed.

This in turn serves as a reminder of two important general considerations. Firstly, an assessment process always requires an 'expert community' as a basis for decisions concerning adequacy (which is the general theme of Chapter 6). This will include, for example: a range of acceptable differences, typical forms of inadequacy, likely dimensions of exceptional impressiveness, etc. In other words, as we have mentioned before, assessment of occupational practice can never be so wholly codified that decisions can be determined, as it were *mechanically*, by means of documentation alone, no matter how detailed. (Assessment is never 'measurement' — Mitchell, 1990, pp. 24–5.)

Secondly, where the format of candidates' work is *unfamiliar* (to themselves and to tutors) as is certainly the case *at present* with competence-based portfolios, the creation of the necessary expert culture will take time and conscious effort (e.g., through frequent sessions in which assessors share material and alternative judgments concerning that material, and even through providing candidates with examples). Our experience has shown us that this process is even more complex than we had anticipated (see Chapter 6, pp. 1–7). As an example of this complexity, as it were 'in action', let us reconsider the final paragraph of the examiner's comments above. One interpretation of her words might suggest that for her, as a member of an expert assessment culture based on the 'assignments' of 'conventional' degree students, criteria for judging our portfolios remained problematic, in spite of the detail of the programme documentation and her sympathy with the programme aims. Thus, although we have emphasized that we found her final comments concerning the 'analytical' content of the portfolios to be extremely helpful in clarifying *our* thinking, it may be that in making the comments she actually had most clearly in mind a form of 'analysis' where the process begins and ends in a determined 'body of knowledge', which may be rather more central for a learning process located in an academic institution than for the more open and fundamentally interdisciplinary 'process knowledge' of *practice*-based learning. And the final comments in the quotation may be interpreted as a realization that what she is tempted to recommend is at the same time perhaps 'unrealistic'. It may not be a question of 'aiming high' but of being clear as to what would constitute a realistic yet worthwhile challenge. In 1993 we discovered, partly to our surprise, that we did not have this requisite clarity. We feel now, partly indeed thanks to discussions with our external examiners, that (after five years' experience) perhaps we do.

Underpinning Knowledge?: The Ford (Engineering) ASSET Programme

We have argued so far that, in a social work context, underpinning knowledge *can* in principle be 'embedded' in competence statements and Core Assessment Criteria. But, unlike the social workers, Ford engineers seemed to invoke a clear-cut distinction between their professional knowledge and their practical activity, in objecting that the knowledge dimension of their work had *not*, in their opinion, been adequately captured in their responses to the functional analysis questions as to the purpose of their work and what they needed to do in order to achieve it. Let us examine the nature of this distinction in an engineering context by considering the following document, which lists, in draft form, first a set of competence statements for the Ford ASSET unit 'Evaluate Test Results and Processes' and second the underpinning knowledge which these competences required but (it was thought) did not adequately specify.

Evaluate test results and processes
Competences:
- analyse, cross-reference, and extrapolate results;
- apply engineering and component knowledge to assess test data against acceptance criteria;
- document successful test completion;
- analyse test failures using probability and statistical techniques;
- report success/failure of component/system to management;
- project test data to assess risk;
- feed test data into computer aided engineering software, for realistic modelling;
- be aware of the correlation between vehicle, system, and component testing;

- analyse test results in relation to 'real world' circumstances;
- evaluate test data against competitor parts;
- keep abreast of changing customer requirements, and feed these into test specifications;
- use test information for future equipment procurement;
- use test data to consider redesign; and
- use test data to confirm or updata component/system performance predictions.

Underpinning knowledge (Relevant engineering knowledge and principles):
- properties of materials;
- production processes;
- structural analysis;
- engineering mechanics;
- fluid mechanics;
- thermodynamics;
- engineering mechanics;
- control theory;
- electricity/electronics; and
- operating principles of systems.

This was an early working document and serves merely to illustrate the nature of the perceived distinction between practice and knowledge. What emerges clearly from this document is that in an engineering context this separately described 'underpinning knowledge' is largely a matter of formal scientific and mathematical theory, i.e., in terms of our initial analysis, public, academically institutionalized (and hence potentially *prescribable*) *propositional* knowledge. (Hence the current concern about student engineers' lack of mathematics (see Sutherland and Pozzi, 1995) which is *not* paralleled by any particular current anxieties about social workers' lack of specific social science theory.) It was this distinction, then, which led the Engineering ASSET Programme to specify 'knowledge' separately in its units of learning.

In the light of the work of Mitchell and Bartram (1994) already referred to above it is not surprising that this is turning out to be an extremely complex task. One factor, however, which has made things so far slightly more manageable is that, as a result of a longstanding cooperative relationship between the Ford Motor Company and Anglia Polytechnic University, Ford managers fully accept the relevance of the Anglia Automotive Engineering Degree as a course of professional education for its staff. It has not been necessary, therefore, to consult the enormous range of very different engineering degree syllabuses in order to identify an appropriate academic base for the Ford ASSET Programme professional competences. Instead, the two members of the programme team with engineering expertise (Samantha Guise and Mike Holman) were able to take the documentation of the Anglia Automotive Engineering Degree and distribute each of its syllabus items into one or other of the competence statements previously identified through the functional analysis process. Further relevant items were obtained from various company training courses.

This elaborate 'cross-referencing' between competence statements and their underpinning academic knowledge also helped to clarify the wording of some of the competence statements, indicating more clearly both the purpose and the method of the practices referred to. Indeed, the Ford Programme Development Team agreed that there was a very close link between clarifying the 'purpose' of a competence statement and specifying the formal knowledge which underpinned it, in part because the 'same' competence had very different implications in a mechanical engineering context as opposed to electrical/electronic engineering. Both of these points are highly significant in the light of the argument presented in the final section of this chapter.

The following example of an element from one of the units of learning from the Ford ASSET Programme shows how the competence statement (in bold type) is matched against a variety of knowledge requirements.

Ford ASSET Programme Unit of Learning: 'Analyse Component/System Costs' (Element 1)

Estimate and analyse detailed product and process costs by assessing company, competitor, and supplier information

Knowledge required:
Management and economics:
- the business system with reference to marketing strategy;
- control of cash-flow in business; and
- cost methods.
Design for manufacture and assembly:
- basic cost analysis techniques; and
- elements involved in the total cost of a product.
Benchmarking:
- analysing internal process data;
- choosing benchmarking partners; and
- determining 'best-in-class' features.
Simplification engineering:
- constraints of the Ford costing system; and
- value-added and non-value-added concepts.

Even this document does not, of course, provide an exhaustive definition of the knowledge required. To begin with it presents only quite general headings and there are plans to analyse each of these headings in greater detail. In some units/elements this has already been accomplished. For example, for the element of competence 'Design experiments to optimize testing of component/system acceptance criteria using minimum resources' one of the headings for the underpinning knowledge is 'Probability and Statistics' and this is broken down into detail as follows: Probability axioms, set theory, laws of probability, Bayes' rule, random variables, probability functions for discrete random variables, and so on.

Secondly, where a number of different possible techniques might have been utilized (whether or not they are actually listed) candidates will be expected to include in their submitted evidence a commentary explaining their reasons for choosing one method rather than another, and, where practical formulae are used, the derivation of the formula must be explained (see example below).

As yet the final format of the Ford Programme's attempt to specify underpinning knowledge separately had not been established, and candidates are only just beginning to work with some of the early draft documents, so the Ford Programme's overall response to the issues presented at the beginning of the chapter is not available. However, an interesting insight into the competence/knowledge relationship in an engineering context is afforded by the following extract from one candidate's draft response to the above documentation format.

Document 6

Underpinning Knowledge: An Example from the Ford ASSET Programme

(The following is an extract from a candidate's draft portfolio, demonstrating competence No. 1 from the unit 'Analyse Component/System Costs' with particular reference to the knowledge heading 'Benchmarking'. The extract has been edited to protect Ford Motor Company information and procedures)

The benchmarking information of the various competitors was used to compare with the existing Car Model X system. From the comparisons, two major points were noted:

a) Very few of the competition were using heat protection for the batteries even with engine compartment mounted positions. Two possible reasons were identified for this. Either the environmental heat extremes exposed to the battery were lower than the Model X (possibly due to improved engine airflow characteristics) or that the detrimental effect of heat on the battery was not perceived as a problem by other manufacturers.

b) There appeared to be scope to improve the existing battery capacity requirements. It could be seen that the electric loads on the battery in the ignition key 'Off' position were far greater than those of the competition (14mA instead of 7mA). What this meant was that for a given period of time whilst left unattended, the battery was being discharged at a rate of approximately twice that of the competition. This was ultimately forcing the requirement for a larger capacity battery, and thus increasing both cost and weight for a given comparable vehicle.

The XYZ manual specified 31 days as the period of time for which the vehicle could be left unattended and still have sufficient battery capacity to start the engine. This is defined as approximately 50 per cent of the original capacity.

In order to make a direct comparison between the existing Model X system and the competition, I needed to calculate the estimated time supportable by the battery for a given battery drain — in this case XmA. The Model X batteries are in general specified by their 'Reserve Capacity' (C). This is the period of time in minutes that it can maintain a discharge current of 25 amps to a cut-off voltage of 10.5 volts (perceived as the minimum required to start a normal engine). The theoretical relationship between reserve capacity in minutes and nominal capacity (Cn) in Ampere hours is:

$$Cn = -144.7 + (123456 + 432.1 * \text{specified Constant}$$

(International Standards Manual IC 95–1, 5th edition)
[See Comment at the end of the document]

Therefore, for a given battery size (Car Model X) of 75 C:

$$Cn = -133.3 + (17778 + 208.3 * \text{specified Constant}) = 49.46$$

From previous investigations it was found that in general most vehicle batteries have only 75 per cent of their original capacity with everyday use. Therefore, to support a battery drain of 14mA (Car Model X) the following calculation was used to estimate the duration:

Cn (Ampere hours) * 24 (hours)	i.e., Ampere hour capacity in days
4 (for 25 per cent change) * XmA	i.e., 25 per cent loss of capacity
	(75 per cent to 50 per cent)

This equates to X days, which meets the XYZ Manual criteria.

By rearranging the formula it was possible to show that with a key off load drain of only YmA (similar to the competition) the battery would last for X + Y days or the battery capacity could be reduced to X Cn and still meet the same criterion. This proved that significant gains could be made if the key offloads could be reduced.

This underpinning knowledge, although not **specifically** identified as a requirement against this competence, is an example of the depth of investigation that is required to effectively demonstrate the competence.

(Andy Delicata, Ford ASSET Programme Candidate, June, 1994)

Comment

In her feedback to the candidate, one of the programme engineering tutors observed that this 'rule-of-thumb' formula needed to be explained; i.e., from which basic *principles* in mathematics or physics are these specific numerical values derived? A further interesting point is that although 'Benchmarking' is the starting point for the work on underpinning knowledge, Andy finds that he needs to introduce a further non-specified aspect in order to do justice to his particular practice context, and comments on the fact that he needs to do so. This may suggest that even when specific techniques have been listed in great detail the 'prescribability' issue discussed earlier could nevertheless still remain.

'Underpinning Knowledge': Context and Ideology

Having thus decribed the different ways in which the two ASSET Programmes have attempted to establish the linkage between competent action and its underpinning knowledge, let us return to the question as to why there should have been this marked difference in emphasis between the two programmes. To begin with, consider the following statements (based on edited transcripts of discussions between Maire Maisch, Richard Winter, Samantha Guise and Mike Holman) concerning the contrasting knowledge precesses in the two professions (social work and engineering).

Social Work and its 'Knowledge-Base'

In child care, for example, you go into situations in order to 'measure' the adequacy of relationships between parents and children, between children, and between parents; and you can't do that without knowing some of the psychodynamic theories about attachment, separation and loss. You can't make any statement without tracing it back in a direct line to what theorists would have said about those early relationships. Some of the original details of the theories have been discredited but there is a theme running through their work (Bowlby, Winnicott, Erikson) and it's the theme which you are aware of, rather than the individual theorists. Where it gets complicated is that it isn't straightforwardly applied; there are always so many other dynamics (line managers' ways of working, local authority policy emphases, and so on). You also have to decide how poor is a 'poor relationship', and how good is 'good enough'. That's where it becomes more complicated, and where the experienced worker will be making a judgement based on experience rather than straightforward knowledge.

Also, the knowledge base moves. For example, it used to be thought in Adoption work that a complete separation from the past situation was desirable, to make sure that the past did not get mixed up with the new situation. And then new research showed that *maintaining* contact led to children having better coping abilities later on: you need to work *with* your past, not cut it off. There isn't a *vast* amount of research on this; but you do know it, and it's no longer possible to work with the old theory (that a clean-cut separation is a good thing) because the legislation and the local authority policies don't allow you to. It's easy to have this knowledge (that you must work with the past) but then you find a situation where a child doesn't want to know about the past, or where the parent doesn't want to know about the child. So it's how you use the knowledge in a particular case which is the true test of how much of its intricacies and variations you have absorbed.

Engineering and its 'Basic Principles'

When I was designing a piece of equipment or a component, I had to make sure it had sufficient strength, so I had to undertake some form of stress analysis. This meant that I had to go back to my stress analysis principles, which were laid out in the textbooks. There are so many formulae, covering a range of different applications, for example: thin-walled tubes, thick walled tubes, plates, types of end-fixings, and so on. You had some basic principles (e.g., those for cantilever structures and for different end fixings) but there are so many options that the important thing was that you knew where to go for the information, and you had some idea of how that formula had been derived, so you could make an assessment as to whether that particular formula applied to your situation and its limitations. You often need to use formulas that you don't use frequently and therefore you haven't got them in your head, although it's there in general terms, (for example: calculations for vibration analysis). But when I need to do something very specific, then I may need to consult a text book ...

You have these formula books, but in real life your particular lump of metal is always different, and so you always have to assess which of the formulae will be the best fit; you are sort of 'working formulae together', to get them to match the reality which is in front of you.

Nowadays, of course the process operates in terms of computer modelling of possible situations. The computer simulates the conditions and the effect of variables, so this enables engineers to look at alternatives in a much more refined way. There is now so much software around that simulates engineering situations, and the engineer will select the one which best fits the particular situation, but in choosing it you still have to understand the basic concepts at work in the system you are working with.

It is clear from these statements that our original distinction between propositional and process knowledge is equally significant for both professions. But an equally important difference emerges. In working with people, knowledge must be applied *within* an interaction between professional and client. For example, *reluctance* to engage with past traumas must be gradually overcome through the social worker's skill in *handling* the situation in which the reluctance is being expressed; the worker does not (and cannot) leave the situation in which the problem is occurring, check up on relevant alternative theories, and return to the practice situation to pick up where he or she left off: the situation will have been drastically transformed by the worker's absence. The engineer, in contrast, can (and does) leave her/his 'lump of metal' and check on its theoretical possibilities with every confidence that when he or she returns the dynamics of the problem it presents will not have shifted. The difference here is both practical and fundamental. People, unlike lumps of metal, are always actively *responding* to the professional's work with their own theories as to what is 'going on'. Hence, in social work (unlike engineering) the problem-to-be-solved is always in a process of change.

This practical difference can be traced back to a difference in the nature of 'theory' in the two contexts. Engineers are not seeking to inform (through theory) their sensitivity to the particular characteristics of a given situation (the social worker's use of *their* theory) but to find a theory which will enable them to *convert* that situation into an abstract formula which will enable all situations of that type to be manipulated and controlled:

Take an example. At a roundabout, driving a car, when you modify your speed so that you don't have to stop, you are actually doing calculus: you are 'differentiating' in the way you appreciate the relationship between the fixed position of the roundabout and the changing speed of your car and the changing speed of other cars in relation to the time and space available. There's a very very sophisticated piece of maths going on, on the part of the ordinary car driver. But the important difference is between being able to drive your car safely and fluently and being able to turn that into an equation, to write the software for an engine management system that might enable *driverless* cars to negotiate the roundabout. *That's* engineering theory.

In others words, engineering knowledge seeks an absolute level of abstraction from the concrete situation (i.e., the mathematical). The tentative generalizations of social science knowledge, in contrast, always remain subject to the variety of factors which constitute the individual case.

Here, then, is an explanation why, compared with engineering, social work knowledge *must* be more directly embedded in practice; why more of it must be 'in one's head', and why, compared with social work, engineering knowledge can be (and frequently is) 'elsewhere', separate, a set of abstract technical possibilities to be 'consulted' before being consciously applied. The general argument is anticipated in Becher's analysis of the specific cultures underpinning different academic and professional disciplines (Becher, Chapter 1 and pp. 150–4). It also suggests that the issue as to whether underpinning knowledge can or should be separately described, and what proportion of one's expertise takes the form of a body of theory, is itself closely linked with the nature of the decision-making context in the two professions. It is not at all surprising, therefore, that with respect to these two questions the two ASSET Programmes were led in different directions and may ultimately need different forms of documentation.

These illustrations from social work and engineering permit some more general observations. Firstly, forms of knowledge are created by forms of action (see Messer-Davidov *et al.*, 1993) and one of the ways in which we can expect forms of knowledge to differ, therefore, is in the manner in which they are related to the action context where they originated. We know that a geographical map, a mathematical equation, and a psycho-dynamic theory can all be useful in informing certain types of activities, but no-one would think that they are to be used in the same way. Hence, it is clear that, in principle, when we say that different activities are all 'underpinned' by appropriate knowledge, we are referring to many different types of relationship between action and knowledge. The term 'underpinning', is, after all, merely a metaphor (from construction) and so we should not be worried if in different occupations it seems appropriate to incorporate knowledge requirements in different formats (e.g., embedded in competence statements or separately listed).

Secondly, claims concerning the forms of knowledge we possess are not 'innocent'. The social workers' claim that their knowledge is largely embedded in the subtle processes of interpersonal action is a claim to an informed personal sensitivity in response to experience, which transcends codification or prescription and constitutes the basis of their professional authority. In contrast, the engineer's claim to abstract theory is a claim to partake in the general cultural authority of science and technology, which subjects experience to 'objective' control, i.e., (precisely) to codification and prescription (see Habermas, 1978, pp. 308–11). (The gender-specific dimension of these two contrasting ideologies is not, of course, accidental — see Belenky, *et al.*, 1986; Harding, 1987). In other words, we need to treat with scepticism claims to, and descriptions of, required knowledge: they are inherently likely to contain elements of institutionalized self-legitimation. This again suggests the difficulties involved in attempting to establish an authentic and realistic account of the knowledge which is *actually* required within practice, i.e., beyond a refined and sophisticated account of practice itself.

Finally, we must not forget that different ideologies of underpinning knowledge are themselves situated within a wider managerial ideology. Since the days of Frederick Taylor management has tended to see its task as codifying practitioners' knowledge in order to centralize the prescription of practice as a management prerogative (see Braverman, 1974, p. 101), and Field (1991) criticizes the work of NCVQ as yet another example of precisely this process. This indeed may be another reason (alongside the cognitive emphasis of higher education mentioned at the beginning of the chapter) why the recent presentation of competence-based education has been associated, as we have seen, with the proposal that knowledge should be specified and prescribed.

Our own response to this proposal remains, on the whole, sceptical. On the one hand we have suggested that there are fundamentally different relationships between knowledge and practice in different professional contexts and that these may permit, or even require, quite different degrees of specificity and prescription in formulating the knowledge dimension of practice. In principle, therefore, we accept the possibility that in some professions and some scientific domains it may be appropriate to attempt a thorough-going codification. We also accept that in some professional/academic specialisms (e.g., engineering) the separate specification of 'knowledge requirements' may seem necessary to both tutors and candidates as a basic clarification of the 'meaning' of the competence statements and also as a clear signal of their interdisciplinary reference, which may otherwise be glossed over, leading to further confusion.

On the other hand, we doubt whether the task of creating detailed knowledge specifications will, in the end, turn out to be feasible, i.e., worth the enormous effort it will involve. In theory the task is infinite, even paradoxical.[4] Hence our other emphasis: while we do not doubt that evidence of competent practice must include (amongst other things) evidence of practitioners' knowledge, our general conclusion is that what this necessarily entails is not so much the prior codification of knowledge requirements but the encouragement of a personal, individualized formulation by learners of their own process knowledge as it emerges from and in their practice. We have already seen the emergence of this emphasis, somewhat unexpectedly, even in an engineering context (see Document 6), and we will see further examples in the extracts from candidates' portfolios in Chapter 7.

Notes

1   A possible exception here is the inclusion of 'Principles of Good Practice' in the standards for social care workers, but see Chapter 4.
2   But Ryle's jovial confidence in what he is quite prepared to call a 'behaviourist' solution to the philosophical problem (Ryle, 1963, p. 308) now seems very much a characteristic of his epoch. His book was originally published in 1949, the same year as Tyler's classic presentation of the objectives model of the curriculum. In the intervening decades, the

behaviourist solution has ceased to seem so self-evidently plausible: Michael Eraut, in choosing a 'philosophical guide' to this area, selects instead the *phenomenologist* Alfred Schutz (see Eraut, 1994b, p. 104).

3   Eraut explicitly includes the communicative aspect of professional work as one of the key aspects of its inherent 'process knowledge' (see Eraut, 1994b, p. 107, pp. 114–5).

4   'The Sisyphian project of complete enumeration is but a prolongation of the widespread misconception that knowledge is primarily a matter of registering and filing away facts, as though facts were given and did not need to be established. Textbook knowledge in vocational education runs the risk of concentrating on the product of academic work, not the process or the producer. . . . [Instead] engineers [should be given] an opportunity to know what it means to know in the manner of an historian or a physicist, that is to say to understand a particular mode of human inquiry and its terms of reference.' (from 'Building the Ideal Engineer', by Sincliar Goodlad, Director of the Humanities Programme, Imperial College of Science, Technology, and Medicine, London (Goodlad, 1995). Sisyphus's problem was, of course, that he was condemned for all eternity to engage in a task which undid itself as soon as he thought it had been accomplished.

6   Assessment: The Development of an Expert Community

The essence of a competence-based curriculum is that it is 'assessment-led'. The main thrust of the documentation is to make 'explicit' the learning outcomes (the 'standard' of work) which candidates need to achieve, so that they can exercise a degree of autonomy in selecting and preparing evidence of their learning, confident that they know what criteria they will need to meet. However, 'explicitness' is always a *relative* term, especially when we are concerned with the complex phenomena of occupational practices. Not for us, alas, the straightforward task of calibrating a measuring instrument analogous in some way to a yardstick or a thermometer. Instead, we have the complex problem (already referred to) of developing a community which shares an understanding of the meaning *in practical terms* of the documented form of learning outcomes and assessment criteria. This community must include not just assessors but candidates as well (if they are to exercise autonomy as learners), and its shared agreements (concerning required and feasible standards) must be plausible to outsiders if its award-making decisions are to be accepted as having widespread currency. Hence the title of this chapter.

In the context of the ASSET Programme 'assessors' differ in role, location, and function (see Chapter 2). An assessor can be either a 'supervisor' based in the candidate's workplace or a 'tutor' allocated by the programme administration. (Also, see Appendix G on the involvement of 'Peer Group' colleagues in the observation of practice.) With a given candidate the assessor's responsibility can be either mainly providing supportive advice ('formative' assessment) or making the final decision as to the adequacy and the standard of the work ('summative' assessment). Tutors can be either staff of the university faculty or staff of the employing organization training section. Since the Engineering Programme is still at an early stage in terms of assessing candidates' work, this chapter is largely based on the experience of the Social Work Programme, where the workplace supervisor has played a relatively minor role, for reasons explained in Chapter 8. Hence, the 'assessors' referred to are, unless otherwise indicated, programme tutors, most of whom are members of Essex Social Services Training Section staff.

The overall issues concerning assessment have been fully outlined elsewhere (see, for example, Heywood, 1989; Jessup, 1991; Atkins, *et al.*, 1993; Drew and Anderson, 1995) and a number of them have indeed already been discussed in the previous chapter. This chapter therefore does not offer a systematic analysis; instead, we present a series of commentaries upon the specific experiences which have contributed to the development of our thinking. The first two sections focus directly on our experience of developing shared understandings concerning an assignment format which is unfamiliar to the tutor. The third section tackles the vexed question of 'grading' versus 'pass/fail' assessment formats, and the final section concerns aspects of assessment 'validity' and the 'authenticity' of candidates' evidence.

Individualized Evidence: A Crisis for Tutorial Expertise?

Alison Wolf, reporting on a project investigating the assessment of occupational competences, writes:

> The project work confirmed earlier research of ours in showing that as a group, occupational experts tend to be very consistent in their ranking of responses — but not in where they place the competent/non-competent cut-off . . . The way people tackle higher-level tasks will vary enormously — appropriately so, since there is almost never a single 'right' answer. However, this means that it is not easy for assessors to 'line up' the individual assessments with the standards and be confident in their judgement of whether or not each criterion has been satisfied . . . One needs to develop marking criteria which relate to the specific assessment itself — to make them much more context-bound than the underlying standards. This is best done by discussion and consensus building among experts. (Wolf, 1994, pp. 4–5)

In other words, faced with portfolios of evidence of work-based learning, Wolf suggests, assessors find it easier to agree on how one candidate *compares* with another than on how each candidate compares with a descriptive criterion, even though all the published documentation relates to the latter, and gives no explicit mention of comparisons between candidates. At one of our early assessment boards, an external assessor experienced a similar worry:

> I'm still left with the question, though: what is 'good enough'? I can see that some portfolios are a 2:1 and some are a 2:2, but there's a 'good enough' level, and I'm not sure we've identified that.

Paradoxical though it may seem at first, this should not be a surprising discovery. The production of a rank order of candidates without explicit agreement about standards is typical of traditional educational practices, based on competition and grading. However, this is an approach to assessment which is increasingly criticized (partly, at least, due to the work of NCVQ) since its basis cannot be made open to public scrutiny and its decisions cannot be challenged; in the end it enables educational institutions to avoid accountability either to their students or (in the case of vocational education) to the clients with whom qualified students will be licensed to practice (see Winter, 1993a). Hence Wolf's suggestion that an effective assessment community requires the creation of even more explicitly detailed agreements concerning criteria for individual judgments.[1]

Academic traditionalists, of course, would entirely disagree, claiming that educational standards cannot in principle be explicitly formulated (Pring, 1992, pp. 21–2) and even that 'marking schemes are for dullards' (Newman, 1994) because an assessor's 'global response' is a more sensitive guide than any detailed analysis. Behind such arguments is the claim that the expert community required for assessment already shares such understandings as are necessary and only needs defending against uncouth intruders. We would argue that even in traditional higher education this is by no means the case (see Winter, 1994b), but we also agree with Wolf that the process of building a shared basis for reliable assessment does not end with the publication of competence statements and criteria.

However, we do not agree that the problem is simply that since general criteria statements are always open to various interpretations more detailed specifications are needed. Instead, in the rest of this section and in the next we discuss another fundamental source of assessors' uncertainty in responding to the documentation of work-based learning — its *unfamiliarity*. It is not simply that criteria lack detail, but that the format of the work submitted for assessment is unfamiliar to the tutor, so that the assessment of practice-derived evidence cannot draw directly on the tutor's prior experience of assessing formal 'assignments'. This leads to a significant shift of *control* away from the tutor/assessor to the student (even though, of course, the format of the work is at first equally unfamiliar to the student).

The issue concerning tutors' familiarity or otherwise with the format of candidates' work is of general significance for the process of educational assessment. On the whole, tutors have been used to a situation where, as assessors, they are responding to an assignment which they have thought about many times before and/or which they themselves have had to produce as part of their own education. This gives tutors a comfortable sense of their expertise relative to their students, and enables them to respond confidently to students' work with a list of suggestions as to what the student 'might also have included'.[2] These suggestions can be informative as guidance for students' future work, but they do not, of course, focus exclusively on *what is required in order to pass*, since this is not, in conventional educational processes, tutors' main concern (see section on 'Grading' below).

In a competence-based programme, however, where the emphasis *is* on an explicit statement of 'what is required', tutors suddenly find that they need to distinguish quite carefully between what they *could* say, based on their familiarity with the area of work, and what they *need* to say, based on their understanding of the requirements embodied in the pass criteria. They also need to shift their role. Instead of providing authoritative expertise derived from much greater familiarity than the candidate with the parameters of the assignment topic, they need to adopt a more facilitative role, based on their understanding of the process of gathering evidence and relating it to the programme requirements.

From this perspective, it is not surprising that tutors on the ASSET Programme initially experienced a specific set of problems. Tutors, for example, may not sufficiently recognize the importance of the distinctions made in the previous paragraph. Consequently, they may have to be dissuaded from always responding to a candidate's work with long lists of suggestions for improvement, without making clear that they are only suggestions and not requirements, and thereby creating undue dismay on the part of the candidate. Or they may be so concerned to contribute to candidates' progress that they do not spot that the sophistication of their response to the candidate's work strongly implies that all the 'basic' criteria have been met, when in fact they haven't. Some of the tutors for the Engineering Programme (all university staff) felt daunted at the outset by a sense that they no longer had confidence in their own expertise relative to the candidates, since they realized that the work-based learning portfolios would be highly *individualized*, in terms of their format and style and the candidates' practice context, knowledge framework, and knowledge-base. The tutors thus felt that they no longer had *control* within the assessment process, and explicitly expressed anxiety on this score (Guise, Holman, and Winter, [*Ford ASSET Programme Pilot Stage Evaluation Report*] 1994, p. 7).

Tutors based in the social services training section did not feel equally threatened in this way, perhaps because their professional function is generally and clearly facilitative rather than instructional. Hence the work-based learning portfolios did not face them with a sudden loss of a sense of expertise and authority concerning the candidates' work. However, this group of tutors, like those interviewed by Wolf, were very conscious that they lacked a sufficiently clear set of agreements as to how competence statements and assessment criteria should be interpreted to make assessment decisions in particular cases. In the absence of these agreements, tutors who have worked closely and sympathetically with a candidate preparing a highly individualized portfolio, and who fully accept the facilitative, non-authoritative version of the tutorial role, initially find it difficult to maintain a sense of the overall 'standard' expected, to inform their response to the candidate's work. Hence, tutors acting as 'second' assessors — making the final assessment decision after the first assessor has provided advice, critical feed-back, and support — find that if there is any disagreement concerning the grading of the candidates' work they always wish to revise the grade *downwards*.

Much of the above might be equally true in any situation where a curriculum is moving towards greater individualization of students' assignments, e.g., 'project work', or towards the introduction of criterion-referenced assessment. But there are also further issues which are particularly related to the difference between a theory-based assignment and a porfolio consisting largely of *practice-based* evidence from the candidate's workplace. This is the theme of the next section.

Assessing Practice-based Evidence

The question as to what counts as adequate evidence embodies key theoretical problems in competence-based vocational education, e.g., the relationship between practice and knowledge, as we noted in the previous chapter. Jessup (1990a, p. 40) presents a general distinction between 'performance evidence' ('natural observation', 'extracted examples within the workplace', 'simulations' of practice situations) and 'supplementary evidence' (including 'oral questioning', 'multiple choice tests', 'essays'), and NVQ units of learning often specify the various types of evidence appropriate for that unit. The ASSET model, in contrast, provides a *general* list of types of evidence, applicable to *all* units of learning, which helps candidates to select the combination of evidence best suited to their individual approach to any given unit.

Document 7

Types of Evidence
(From The ASSET Programme Handbook, 1996, p. 22)

A wide variety of types of evidence is potentially relevant to demonstrating any given element of competence. The following list provides a general framework, but is not intended to be exhaustive.

A) A report based upon observation of the candidate's practice by an assessor or 'Peer Group' colleague;
B) Practice generated documents, e.g., memo, assessment, letter, practice notes, case-history, care-plan, child protection plan, court report, agreement with client or group of clients (together with explanations of their relevance for a particular competence);
C) Audio-tape recording of practice, together with transcripted excerpts and an explanation of its relevance for a particular competence;
D) Video-tape recording of practice, together with an explanation of the relevance of particular sections for a particular competence;
E) An analytical and evaluative commentary upon practice;
F) An analysis of issues relating to the planning of practice, e.g., review of relevant policy, annotated list of relevant legislation, list of possible courses of action + commentary explaining prioritization;
G) A tape-recording of work with a client and/or members of the clients' network, together with a commentary;
H) A video-recording of an interview with a client, or group of clients, together with a commentary;
I) A tape-recording of discussion with colleagues, supervisor, or other professionals, together with a commentary, if necessary;
J) Data showing client response (e.g., evaluative questionnaire return, client's tape-recorded comment, client's written comment) together with candidate's commentary;
K) An analysis of a training experience or training materials, in relation to the candidate's practice.
L) An authenticity statement from colleagues/managers.

The evidence for each module must include:

1 evidence derived from workplace observation to demonstrate at least one element and not more than two elements; and
2 a recording of practice (as in C,D,G,H,I, above to demonstrate at least one further element).

It is significant, following the general argument of the previous chapter, that this list does not include separate 'tests' or 'essays' but 'commentaries' on practice-generated evidence. Clearly, the list makes available a wide range of possibilities, so that candidates' work can be highly varied in format, structure, texture, and balance — leading to the assessment problems outlined in the previous section. But there is one limit on this variety: despite the clear invitations to analysis and commentary, an ASSET portfolio is always predominantly a documentation of *practice*, based on practice-based evidence, and this leads to a characteristic set of assessment issues.

To a certain extent the problem is common to all situations of radical but *evolutionary* change, in which, for example, innovations are not claiming that they are to be judged by an 'entirely new' set of criteria but, in part, at least, by criteria which are already accepted. This aspect of most innovatory processes is both theoretically and historically inevitable, and not without its advantages: some measure of continuity prevents the innovatory emptying out of bathwater leading to the loss of valuable babies. More particularly, this means that, at present and for the foreseeable future, ASSET portfolios are inevitably going to be evaluated by staff whose own professional culture has largely been formed through the production and assessment of assignments related to theory-based taught courses. For example, one of our external examiners suggested a possible danger that ASSET candidates might be *disadvantaged*, in relation to their future colleagues, by the programme's lack of formal theoretical input or insistence that work be presented within a conceptual framework derived from an academic discipline.

In short, lacking any other well established norms and exemplars, when we assess work-based learning portfolios we cannot help being influenced by the norms of conventional assignment work and by our experience of responding to them. In some ways this has advantages — at least it provides us with an initial intuitive resource to supplement the inevitable inadequacies of purely verbal descriptions of matters we have not ourselves experienced at close quarters, i.e., the competence statements and criteria. (The assessors interviewed by Wolf (1994) could agree on a *ranking* of candidates' work, presumably on the basis of prior intuitive understandings, even though they could not agree on how to interpret the published criteria for adequacy.)

However, this reliance on our previous experience can also lead us to respond to work-based learning portfolios in inappropriate ways. As one of our external examiners recently observed:[3]

> You still keep on thinking that there are awkward questions that should have been asked and haven't been asked: why did you [the candidate] say that? why didn't you say that? even: why do you think that happened? And yet it's so hard for them to take breath for that in the context of a busy case-load. Take X's porfolio for example. We would be asking her to reflect and evaluate in the context of the most unbearable emotional *pain* in dealing with that case. In asking her to ask herself the question, 'How could that have been better?' you are demanding the most enormous *courage* as well as knowledge. And no student on a conventional course is faced with that.

It is as though the presentation of practice-based evidence gives an assessor many more opportunities to identify unasked 'awkward' questions, because the inevitably problematic nature of practice decision-making is there, visible, in the candidate's work. ('You can't hide behind an intellectual argument', as one tutor put it.) In a theory-based assignment, in contrast, students can control the flow of the argument and the illustrative examples to make sure that they raise the 'awkward questions' which they know they can answer and carefully avoid those they can't. It may be easier, in other words, for a conventional assignment to seem more *complete* within its limits, since those limits can be explained and justified in advance, whereas the open structure of a work-based portfolio means that the work can never feel 'complete' in the same way. Similarly, it is much easier to write an essay which continuously sustains a high level of coherent and progressive theory than to maintain an equivalent degree of theoretical coherence and rigour throughout a wide range of practice-based evidence drawn from a context structured by all the emotional, cultural, and political pressures of a client's life world, hard-pressed colleagues, and a resource-limited organization. The openness of a portfolio also means that in an important sense tutors can only *respond*, i.e., they cannot so easily provide guidance in advance, and thereby help students to avoid what tutors see as theoretical 'pitfalls'.

It may thus be quite difficult for an assessor used to conventional assignments not to be 'too critical' of practice-based evidence. The danger is almost that of committing a 'category error' — of judging practice *directly* by the standard of theory, a general methodological danger noted by social theorists from Weber's warnings about the use of 'ideal types' (which *never* correspond exactly to reality — Weber, 1971 [1904]) to Garfinkel's direct analysis of the problem (Garfinkel, 1984, Chapter 8). Perhaps, indeed, the proper assessment of work-based learning which is informed by theory (the work of the knowledgeable, critical, self-evaluative 'reflective practitioner') ideally requires a fuller understanding than we yet possess of the actual forms in which theoretically informed professional work can be realized in practice and subsequently presented. Meanwhile, our immediate assessment task is to ask *enough* of candidates (so that these new formats are gradually developed) but not *too much* (i.e., to avoid judging work-based learning as deficient in terms of inappropriate norms). As one of our external examiners observed: 'We are still at the stage of needing to explore what work like this *could* be like.'

From this general argument, it is clear that the development of an expert community for assessors of work-based higher education is not a simple matter. Hence, in designing a training experience for ASSET Programme tutors and supervisors we took very seriously the scope of the learning required, i.e., the difficulty of achieving a sympathetic yet just evaluation in a situation where the form of the candidate's work is unfamiliar to (and may even pose a challenge to) the assessor's own prior educational and practice experience. Consequently, we took the view that merely reading and discussing the programme documentation would not be enough. Instead, we require tutors and supervisors actually to undertake the same tasks as the candidates whose work they would be appraising: to gather evidence from their practice in relation to the competence statements of one or other of the ASSET Programme units and to relate each of them to one of the Core Assessment Criteria. (We also undertook this task ourselves, and a very enlightening experience it was!) At the same time, we ask new tutors and supervisors (as part of their training process) to work with a candidate or group of candidates: sessions of this work are observed and recorded, the tutors'/supervisors' self-evaluative analyses are submitted, and their written comments and assessment reports on candidates' work are checked. (The training process is organized into units of learning which earn credit within the university modular scheme.)

But to call this 'training' is perhaps to undervalue its significance. In essence, the process entails a shifting of professional culture, a change in conceptualizing the nature of knowledge and of evidence for knowledge. To this extent the process of establishing a trustworthy community of work-based learning assessors is not unlike the process whereby, in the seventeenth century, a newly emerging community of empirical scientists established criteria for accepting (as 'trustworthy') one another's experimental evidence, as described by Shapin (1994) under the fascinating title of 'A social history of truth'. In both cases the problem is how to *expand* criteria for adequate knowledge, beyond a previously taken-for-granted structure of authority, how to determine whose reports of their experience are to be believed, and the characteristics of believable reports. In both cases, it entails re-forging a shared basis for constructing, acknowledging and evaluating trustworthy judgments.

Grading and Passing: Who Owns the Learning Process?

One of the most highly contentious and difficult issues with which the ASSET project had to grapple concerned the relationship between a norm-referenced assessment format ('grading'), largely taken for granted by the university, and criterion-referenced assessment (pass–fail or pass–not-yet-pass), strongly urged by NCVQ.

With most current educational assessment procedures the main effort and concern is devoted not to deciding whether students' work is of 'pass standard' or not, but whether it is, for example, 'outstanding', or 'above average', or 'average' or (merely) 'satisfactory', in the rough pattern of a normal distribution curve. This is particularly true of the UK honours degree, which is officially and publicly classified in precisely the categories mentioned above (Council for National Academic Awards, 1989, Regulations 28 and 34). Although there is no explicit statement as to what is meant by these terms, the fact remains that they (or their equivalents) are felt by the public at large, and hence by many ASSET candidates, to be an important expression of the 'standard' of assessment outcomes. We could not, therefore, simply ignore them, in favour of the contrasting NCVQ assessment model, in which the decision is exclusively whether candidates have (or have *not yet*) produced sufficient evidence from which to draw a 'safe inference' that they are competent with respect to specified outcomes and criteria (Mitchell, 1989, pp. 60–1; NCVQ 1995a, 1991, p. 21; 1995, p. 30).

Conceptually the two assessment models are distinct and hardly compatible. Whereas NCVQ emphasizes that negative assessment decisions are provisional (*'not yet* sufficient evidence' rather than 'fail'), current higher education regulations emphasize the finality of the decision: after receiving a poor grade a candidate may not re-take the course in an attempt to gain a better grade (CNAA, 1991, p. 97) although one resubmission is usually possible after an outright failure. It is sometimes argued that detailed specifications could be published for each grade, thereby apparently synthesizing the two models, but this would also require that in principle almost all candidates *could* present sufficient evidence in relation to the performance criteria for an A grade (cf. Bloom, 1975, on 'mastery learning', p. 338) without causing a scandal about 'falling standards'. But those who propose this argument also agree that this could not be the case: any institution which produced such results would not be congratulated on the excellence of its teaching but accused certainly of lowering standards and probably of failing to understand the nature of the assessment process.

Our own educational philosophy led us to embrace the NCVQ (pass/not-yet-pass) side of this debate. Grading, we would argue, is unreliable (see Heywood, 1989, pp. 47–68) and hence invidious: the inevitably widespread use of the C grade ('average' rather than 'good') threatens unnecessarily to undermine the morale of ostensibly 'successful' candidates by 'damning them with faint praise'. Grading is also inappropriate in contexts where candidates are undertaking difficult professional decisions since it distracts attention away from the crucial question of 'good-enough' practice and thus from our accountability as assessors to the candidates' *clients*. On the other hand, we live in a competitive and grade-oriented culture (see Winter, 1993a). Many ASSET candidates consciously undertake the programme to retrieve a previously missed opportunity to gain an honours degree, and they would be disadvantaged unless the programme were clearly seen to be in every respect 'equal to' other honours degrees. In the light of all this it is not surprising that our formulation of assessment arrangements for a competence-based honours degree sometimes entailed difficult and not always entirely coherent compromises.[4]

First, we offer candidates a choice between two alternative awards: an honours degree and a 'graduate diploma of professional studies'. The degree will involve them in having their work graded, whereas the graduate diploma (equivalent to the degree in all but name) is awarded on a pass–fail basis only, which allows them to avoid grading (if they wish) at the cost of gaining a qualification the academic status of which is perhaps slightly ambiguous. We anticipated that the ASSET Programme would attract candidates who possessed a professional qualification in social work alongside an honours degree in another subject, and that these candidates would choose to work towards the graduate diploma; in fact most ASSET candidates so far have *not* possessed an honours degree, and so the graduate diploma option has hardly been used.

Our second 'compromise' is a response to the conflict between the university regulations, under which assessment outcomes, including failure, are relatively fixed and final, and the NCVQ emphasis that 'failure' must be conceived of as provisional and potentially temporary. There is an important educational issue at stake here. Given the difficulty of establishing a reliable basis for assessment decisions, there is always a risk that any particular assessment decision is unjust; but there is a big difference in the consequence of this within the two models we are considering. In one case a candidate is given a final negative label which is unjust in the sense that another assessor might well not agree with it, but against which there can nevertheless in principle be no appeal (see CNAA, 1991, p. 91). In the other case, within the NCVQ model, an unjust assessment would mean that a candidate may be *unnecessarily* asked to submit extra evidence or to engage in further learning, which is certainly regrettable but is not entirely without benefit to the candidate. Our 'solution' here is that assessors may continue to give formative feed-back to candidates, on a pass/insufficient-evidence-as-yet basis, until:

1 either the candidate and the assessor agree that the work is ready to be passed on to a second assessor for the final assessment, who may then still reject it as inadequate-as-yet and refer it back for further work; or
2 the maximum period of registration for the module elapses.
  The candidate is only allowed to register twice for the same module and when the maximum period elapses for the second time, the module is then deemed to have been 'finally' failed. However, this maximum period is set at several times the anticipated average period of time required for the work, so that in most cases the candidate will have chosen to withdraw before the official failure decision is imposed.

The ASSET model thus gives candidates an unusual amount of discretion as to the amount of time they may take to complete a unit of learning, compared with the greater rigidity concerning time permitted for other types of university units. It is arguable that this contributes to the high standard of work which ASSET candidates often achieve:

> The first group of students have just graduated from the programme. Their results are impressive, with three first class degrees and five with upper seconds (out of a total of thirteen). *Although one would not expect a conventional distribution of marks, as the students were able to pace themselves,* the standards achieved, whatever the time taken, showed a very satisfactory level of scholarship. (External Examiner's Report, 1995 (our emphasis))

This line of thought poses an interesting question, of course, to some conventional higher education notions of 'standards', and again it relates to Bloom's (1975) argument that students vary not in the level of work they are capable of achieving but in the time and degree of support they require. From the point of view of what might be entailed in genuinely broadening access to higher education, his argument is of the utmost significance.

Finally, we present below the ASSET Programme grading 'criteria' in Document 8.

It is clear that this document does not attempt to avoid the normative structure of conventional approaches to grading (e.g., references to 'outstanding', 'average'). However, it is important to note that the grade is not awarded in relation to each separate competence statement within a module but in response to the portfolio of evidence for the module *as a whole*.[5]

It could be argued that in adopting this holistic approach to grading we have reintroduced into the ASSET assessment procedures the uncontrolled use of assessors' 'intuition' which otherwise we have been at pains to minimize. This in turn means that the consensus-building processes described earlier are even more crucial, and that their effectiveness can only be judged on a long-term basis, since

ASSET Programme Grading Criteria
(ASSET Handbook, 1996, p. 24)

A = First class honours = 'outstanding':
All Core Assessment Criteria are met in every particular by exceptionally detailed evidence in relation to the statement of competence; each of the supporting commentaries explaining the relationship between the evidence and the criteria is exceptionally clear and insightful.

B = Second class honours, division one = 'very good'
All Core Assessment Criteria are met, some to the standard outlined for 'A' above and the others to a lesser standard; clear and detailed evidence is provided, together with fully argued explanations of the relationship between the evidence and the criteria.

C = Second class honours, division two = 'average'
All Core Assessment Criteria are met by means of clearly appropriate evidence and reasonably well argued explanations of the relationship between the evidence and the criteria.

D = Third class honours = 'below average'
All Core Assessment Criteria are met, and the evidence is quite acceptable; but some of the explanations of the relationship between the evidence and the criteria are not very clearly argued, even though the general line of the argument seems to be justified.

(The grade for the final award is calculated from the various module grades by equating them with numerical equivalents.)

tutors will necessarily require substantial experience with the portfolio format before they can feel comfortable in judging work as 'outstanding' or 'average'. Certainly, tutors currently find the grading process extremely difficult, although disagreements between the two tutors who are always involved in agreeing a grade for a portfolio always focus on 'adjacent' grades: A or B; B or C; C or D. In part this is symptomatic of the large degree of agreement concerning professional or academic values which tutors inevitably *import* into the process on the basis of their previous experience, even where the format of the work is unfamiliar. This is a reminder that even when one is engaged in the formation of a 'new' expert community we do not start 'from scratch' and that this prior experience is a necessary resource (in view of the initially unpredictable variety of the work) as well as a potential problem (as argued above).

On the other hand, it is also true that although tutors find grading difficult they nevertheless welcome the opportunity to go beyond the pass/not-yet-pass decisions concerning individual elements of competence and to consider a candidate's work holistically, as a substantial body of work which the candidate had intended to be 'complete'. As one external examiner commented at an early meeting:

With all the elements we lose a sense of the wholeness . . . I'm a little anxious that these students might be subjected to a different kind of rigour from students who go through a conventional course, because you have dared to break these things down into all the elements of competence in this way. It helps you to judge that the evidence for this element *is* enough if the rest of the elements allow you to say that *overall* this is good enough.

Or, in the words of one of the tutors:

> At first, the students' work is often rather fragmented. But then they become more skilful in presenting evidence in a way that gives a fuller feeling of the whole module. And I'm slowly getting more of a feel for what a module should look like.

There is a counter-argument here, however. A 'holistic', integrated impression *can* be an oversimplification; it can underestimate the complexity of a candidate's response to the contradictions and dilemmas of professional practice, which (one could argue) is appropriately expressed and appreciated through the variety and the fragmentary format of a portfolio of discrete elements (see Belsey, 1980, pp. 91–2, on the significance of 'plural texts'.)

Furthermore, although a holistic view can indeed *supplement* one's judgment of individual elements, it can also be a distraction, leading the whole edifice of precise specification to collapse. This is an important issue in general, and one which goes to the heart of the debate concerning the role of specification and intuition in educational assessment (see Pring, 1992 and Newman, 1994, cited above). But there is a particular urgency when one is considering the judgment as to whether or not a candidate's work is 'good enough' (see below), i.e., when one is considering the rigour of the pass/not-yet-pass demarcation. Two years or so into the operation of the programme the tutors were consulted on their experience of allocating grades to candidates' portfolios and we tape-recorded a discussion of what they had reported, from which the following significant extract is taken:

> **RW** So, do you think that tutors appreciate the opportunity that grading gives them to make an official differentiation when someone has done some really good work?
>
> **MM** No. What they are saying is: if we were using just a pass–fail system, I wouldn't be saying, 'This is a "C" or a "D" ' — I'd be sending it back for more work. They are saying that the grading gives too much flexibility to move off a 'fail' to a low [pass] grade.

There is an important point to be made about this, namely the general proposition that a grading system allows candidates with whose work a tutor is by no means satisfied to be awarded a weak pass, because it enables a tutor to protect his or her professional conscience while avoiding the interpersonal difficulties involved in an outright rejection of the work submitted. This suggests a profound disadvantage of grade-based assessment, especially where the educational qualification constitutes a 'license to practise' so that the well-being of a candidate's future clients is at stake. In other words, as long as there is a shared assessment culture the pass/not-yet-pass format creates a crucial dimension of *rigour* in assessment, whereas a shared *grading* culture cannot prevent a damaging ambiguity as to what is or is not 'acceptable' (see the quotation from Wolf at the beginning of this chapter).

As a result of this consultation with tutors we were alerted to the danger that our holistic and inevitably somewhat intuitive grading of the whole portfolio might undermine such precision as we had attained concerning the pass/not-yet-pass assessment of the individual elements of competence. We therefore clarified, for ourselves and tutors, that the major part of the assessment effort should be concerned with establishing the adequacy or otherwise of the separate elements without reference to the grading system; and that an overall 'D' grade nevertheless means that *all* the work conforms *fully* to the requirements of the competence statements and the Core Assessment Criteria.

It will have become clear from all this that one of our major fears about allowing grading into the model is that it might come to dominate a candidate's approach to the whole learning process, i.e., that it might serve as a distraction from candidates' wholehearted commitment to the professional and academic standards we had tried to embody in the programme documents. In the light of well-known studies by Howard Becker and his colleagues into 'student culture' (Becker *et al.*, 1958; 1968) we feared the 'calculative rationality' involved where students try to 'suss out' what is required to 'get an "A"' and the minimum needed to 'get by'. Becker *et al.* describe this as the student side of an implicit and speculative bargaining process which arises where staff dictate the form of students' learning without making explicit the exact criteria for different assessment outcomes — the inevitable consequence of a grade-based assessment format.

Becker and his colleagues were, of course, describing conventionally institutionalized taught courses (both academic and professional) for full-time students. In contrast, in the ASSET model we specifically hoped to create a learning situation appropriate for the autonomous responsibilities of the professional work role itself, i.e., a learning role in which candidates would be conscious of working for the sake of the development of their own practice and their own understanding, rather than to conform to standards imposed by tutors. (Hence, for example, our concern for professional realism in our development of the competence statements, as described in Chapter 3.) In an admittedly over-used phrase we wanted candidates to 'own' their learning, by *committing* themselves to it, not (as Becker *et al.* describe) by driving an advantageous bargain (calculating their effort in relation to an extrinsic reward).

Admittedly, this can seem to be a difficult ideal to achieve in practice. All candidates come to the programme burdened with many years' experience of conventionally teacher dominated 'schooling'; in particular, those who had recently completed their qualifying award responded to the exhaustive documentation in the programme handbook by bombarding their tutors with questions of the form: 'What do *you* want me to do? How much do *you* think I should write on this?' But this is only their initial stance, and in one way we succeeded beyond our anticipation. When at first we remonstrated with candidates at the unexpected bulk of their portfolios, they made it clear to us that this was not simply due to a failure on their part to identify what was truly relevant (as we initially suspected) but equally a matter of their pride in the value of their professional role. In other words, after candidates had grasped the programme procedures and their implications, it was indeed as though their work was no longer for *us* (tutors), it was work for *themselves; they* insisted on fully elaborated detail because their sense of the complexity of their work demanded it. When tutors say, 'Why don't you submit your work now?', candidates often respond, 'But first I just want to read X, Y, Z' or 'But first I just want to collect a bit more evidence on P, Q, R'. Unlike the students interviewed by Becker *et al.*, ASSET candidates did not wish to 'get by' with a minimum effort any more than one would if one were writing an autobiography. As one student put it, comparing her work for the ASSET competence-modules with work for a taught course:

> With the ASSET Programme you are more likely to produce work based on what *you* feel the competences mean, your own interpretation, knowing that others might interpret it differently but it doesn't matter, because different interpretations by different students are o.k. . . . You are the one who has to take all the initiatives, do all the planning, take all the decisions . . . This means that at the end of an ASSET module you feel in a sense that you have done more to achieve it, but on the other hand this makes it more of a strain. (Monica Peake, ASSET Programme graduate, 1995)

The unexpected intensity of candidates' efforts initially created a further problem. The ASSET competence-based modules were originally allocated a certain number of 'credits' within the University Credit Accumulation system. But ASSET candidates without exception produced much more work and devoted much more effort than students writing assignments for taught modules with a similar credit rating. After much thought, therefore, we successfully proposed to the university that the modules be *revalidated* at a higher credit rating, in order to achieve greater comparability with the workload of other students within the system.

This experience illuminated two issues for us. First, since it reduced the number of modules necessary to obtain the final award, it clarified that any notion that the ASSET Programme provided a 'complete' professional qualification did *not* stem from the 'coverage' of the activities of the professional role by the lists of specific competence statements in the different modules, but, rather, through the comprehensiveness of the Core Assessment Criteria. Second, it clarified that ASSET candidates are not basically engaged merely in documenting the adequacy of their current practice. The format of the work seems to generate an inescapable challenge to engage in a process of evaluation and change, which often entails the conscious development of their standards of practice and at the very least a considerable enhancement of their professional understanding. Which is why, as Monica Peake points out above, the ASSET model is *not* an 'easy' route to a qualification, and perhaps why, initially, a number of candidates enrolled but dropped out before completing their first module.

To sum up, then, although the current structure of the UK honours degree forces us to include grading within our assessment process, we attempt in various ways to ensure that the ASSET Programme does not *focus* on the allocation of grades but on the decision as to professional and academic adequacy. But there is nothing 'minimal' about the conception of adequacy embodied in the ASSET competence statements and Core Assessment Criteria, any more than there is, in principle, in the NCVQ conception of 'competence' (see NCVQ, 1991, p. 7; pp. 8–9 under the heading 'Breadth'). On the contrary, the concept underlying the ASSET Programme assessment process, the focus of our attempts to constitute ourselves as an expert community, is the complex ideal of 'good-enough' practice (i.e., precisely the concept which the assessors interviewed by Wolf felt they lacked (see Wolf, 1994, quoted above, p. 1). The term is intended to convey both the difficulty and the possibility of elucidating and evaluating subtle and complex activities, pursuing exacting theoretical ideals within the limitations of personal, organizational, political, and cultural constraints. The term in this sense is derived from Winnicott (1965) and is elaborated throughout Bettelheim (1987). It implies the reality of crucial judgments (concerning differences of quality) and yet the wide range of practices which can be 'adequate' — in different ways, in different contexts. It originates in the world of social interaction, but — in our terms — there can be 'good enough' carburettor designs as well as 'good enough' child protection. It expresses our sense that if the complexity of human activity is properly conceived, 'good enough' practice is not *'merely competent'*, it is the achievement of a very exacting standard.

Evidence: 'Validity' and 'Authenticity'

Finally, we address two further issues. Firstly we discuss the 'validity' of our assessment of the evidence presented in the ASSET portfolios, i.e., how far the portfolio format enables us genuinely to assess the quality of candidates' practice and their understanding of their practice. Secondly, we present examples of how candidates demonstrate that their evidence is 'authentic'. The two issues are, of course, closely connected.

The first issue, 'validity', arises from the complexity of the portfolios and hence the importance of the candidates' ability to present clearly a wide variety of material and to organize it coherently, so that it can be easily understood by an assessor who has had no prior contact with the candidate or their work context. This is no mean task, and it led one external examiner to comment that she thought that what differentiated candidates who had been awarded a high grade was their superior ability to organize a complex *text*, which does not seem, at first, to be central to the criteria of the programme. In other words there is a danger that the grades awarded may reflect candidates' ability to manage the selection and presentation of evidence and to articulate its relationship with the competence statements and the Core Assessment Criteria, rather than variations in the quality of their practice (and their understanding of practice).

Our first reaction was that if this is the case then it is an unfortunate displacement of attention away from the 'real' criteria of the programme, and thus indeed a source of 'invalidity' in the assessment process. On the other hand, it was agreed that this displacement of assessment emphasis from 'practice criteria' to 'assessment format criteria' is even greater when the assignment takes the form of conventional 'coursework' or 'an essay', as indicated in the following extract from a transcript of a discussion with an external examiner who had just assessed portfolios and assignments relating, respectively, to ASSET modules and to conventional taught modules with the same learning outcomes.

> **RW** If you compare ASSET candidates with students presenting work on a taught course, are you saying that the evidence presented for assessment in the taught course gave you a better sense of how much they understood and how effective as practitioners they were?
> **External Examiner** No. Less.
> **RW** So on the taught course you were only getting a sense of how well they had mastered the process of writing essays, and so on?
> **External Examiner** Except that those are extremes. But there was a tendency for the students on the portfolio [ASSET] route to present more evidence of how they performed as practice teachers.

So perhaps the problem is a residual one: no assessment format is entirely 'transparent': even when observers are physically present during candidates' practice they are partly assessing how well candidates can avoid being distracted by the physical presence of an observer.

Further reflection on this issue, however, suggested that the distinction between 'genuinely professional' criteria and 'assessment format criteria' may not be so clear-cut. Being observed in the workplace will be less distracting for a candidate whose practice is deeply client-oriented, for whom the observer's presence will even intensify their focus on the client by creating an awareness of the tensions created by the observer for the *client*. Similarly, the competence statements and Core Assessment Criteria were designed so that good practice would generate relevant evidence and commentary much more readily than poor practice. One could argue, therefore, that even though the assessment process does indeed focus partly on a candidate's skill in articulating the relationship between practice evidence, competence statements, and the Core Assessment Criteria, this emphasis nevertheless concerns key intellectual and personal competences underpinning the professional role. (This point of view is strengthened by our arguments about process knowledge in the previous chapter.)

Let us, then, finally, turn to the question of how candidates can convince assessors that their evidence is 'authentic'. This was an issue raised by one of the external examiners at an early assessment board meeting, and it is perhaps particularly significant for the ASSET model because, in comparison with the NCVQ model there is a relatively limited amount of actual observation of a candidates' practice (see Document 7). We would argue, however, that the rather limited use of observation evidence within the ASSET model does not undermine the overall authenticity of our assessment evidence, since in professional contexts the importance of the responsibilities involved means that practice is always extensively documented, to guard against possible future complaints and even legal proceedings. (Consider how much easier it would be to assess the practice of hairdressing if each appointment had to be documented by a pair of polaroid photographs of the client's coiffure —

'before' and 'after' — together with an agreed copy of the client's instructions duly signed!)

Nevertheless, one important question about the assessment of work-based evidence is how far candidates have been able to guarantee the authenticity of their claim to have demonstrated competent practice. Some illustrative examples are given below.

The most direct solution, from the candidate's point of view, as the 'List of Evidence' document implies, is the addition of appendices containing practice documents (e.g., official 'care plans', review forms, and memos) at the end of an account. This can begin to establish that an apparently impressive portfolio does indeed represent impressive *practice* (see examples in Chapter 7) but it is not without its problems. To begin with, tutors report that they have to work hard to convince candidates of the significance of direct evidence from their practice, although when they do finally realize that this is the case, the effect on candidates is very empowering, since it brings home to them the value (in terms of academic 'credit') of their day-to-day work. Secondly, early on in the project, one candidate found that she was blocked by a manager in her attempt to gain access to practice documentation relating to cases with which she was no longer directly concerned, and an official declaration had to be prepared, signed by the director of the social services department, indicating that the use of practice-generated material to authenticate work for the ASSET Programme is a legitimate professional purpose, and compatible with departmental rules on confidentiality (see ASSET Programme Handbook, 1996, Appendix A).

In general, candidates recognize that it is legitimate for tutors to ask them to document the authenticity of their work, and are quite prepared to find the appropriate materials and/or to ask colleagues, managers, and clients to sign declarations of accuracy, etc. The following example illustrates the involvement of a client in the process of authentication.

Document 9

Portfolio Extract: Involving a Client in the Evaluation of Practice
(by Valerie Dawes)

Module 3, Element 9
Involve clients in discussions and decisions which affect their situation (N.B. This example contains only extracts from the submitted portfolio)
Core Assessment criterion no. 7 Intellectual Flexibility

Background
Mr X sustained a neck fracture whilst driving on holiday abroad, causing a spinal cord injury. At the age of 20 years, the accident caused Mr X to be quadraplegically disabled. . . . He did nor want to believe that his paralysis would be permanent. He left decisions and arrangements to his family and professionals involved with his care. . . . Multi-disciplinary service efforts to assist Mr X on his return home were rejected by him, although welcomed by his family. He became a recluse, refusing to see anyone except his sister, whom he relied on for care. He tolerated his mother and occasionally a relief carer from the Spinal Injuries Association. All his friends stopped visiting because of his antagonism towards them. . . .

Practice

.... My initial meeting with Mr X was 18 months after his accident, when his family requested further social work involvement to assist with finance, form-filling, and help with Mr X who continued his self-imposed isolation. At this meeting Mr X made it clear that I was an unwelcome visitor. His attitude heightened my dilemma regarding his rights to privacy, autonomy and choice against his family's rights and need of assistance with him. Mr X's non-verbal body language of withdrawal and rejection, as he continued to remain in bed, facing the wall, felt very discouraging ... After a few visits, Mr X hesitantly participated more. He admitted to having made a couple of thwarted suicide attempts, berating himself as 'useless' ... Good communication is essential in casework. I endeavoured to develop this with Mr X, yet there were times when I couldn't comprehend what he meant. His sense of humour surfaced as I began asking him to explain his usage of many colloquial terms. At times he tried to shock me with revelations of his past 'Jack-the-Lad' escapades ...

[In the end] Mr X moved to his own flat, where he gets up and dresses every day. He is learning to cook, developing interest and flair. He has chosen his own furniture. ... He has visited his mother, brother, and grandmother, having joined in his first family meal since the accident ...

Appendix (Extract): *Letter No. 3*

Having been asked to write a confirmation of Val's university course work paper based on my case, here follows some comments that may be relevant. On the whole, I thought that it was accurate, with the exception of a few minor points.

It was noted that during our initial meeting I displayed extreme antisocial behaviour: not speaking, merely grunting in response to any attempt at conversation; and lying in bed, facing the wall with total disinterest. This ill-will was almost certainly due to my natural hatred for all social workers; being the meddling, busybody do-gooders that they usually are. From memory there is only one recurring thought that I can remember thinking during the time that Val was in my room, which was: 'Oh please God, make her piss off and leave me alone!' But needless to say, she was rather persistent. After a couple of visits Val came across as more likeable than I had expected; I begrudgingly decided to co-operate, much to my now quite obvious (although I'm loth to admit it) advantage. I found that, after several visits I was able to open up a little and tell Val about things that were getting me down. As time went on, I became more trusting in her, and was able to talk about feelings and problems that were uncomfortable to discuss with anyone else. It helped a great deal just to get things off my chest.

I will admit to deliberately throwing in a couple of sexist remarks into our conversations just to get Val's back up, but the suggestion that I was trying to shock was, I think, due to a clumsy attempt at being truthful about my past, rather than a deliberate intention, seeing Val as more of 'a friend to chat to' and not an interfering nuisance.

Whereas before meeting Val all I could see, as a future, was my inevitable suicide; now things to come do look a little more rosy and I must admit (again grudgingly) that I do actually enjoy certain aspects of my life. By making suggestions — in a not too overbearing manner — I was able to build up a self belief that had long been missing. It feels as if I am once again a whole and functioning person, thanks to Val's help in gaining a greater independence by moving out of the family home and realising a greater self-esteem in doing so.

MR. X

Commentary

This example indicates quite well the nature of the authenticity issue, and how 'evidence' can help to resolve it. Val presents an account of her practice which claims a degree of both sophistication and success. How do we know that it is not exaggerated? The letter from Mr X is presented as corroboration. How do we know that the letter from Mr X is genuine? Its internal details, the way it refers to the account, and Val's two carefully worded letters inviting Mr X's contribution (not included in the above extracts) are 'convincing' in the sense that they assure us that the work is 'genuine' because they reflect an idiosyncratic quality in the practice relationship. In this way, Mr X's letter not only 'authenticates' Val's practice (in a technical sense) but also helps to demonstrate its quality and itself contributes to that quality by involving the client and enabling him to sense the value of his contribution. There is no doubt that for a knowledgeable social worker assessing this work, Mr X's letter would constitute 'authentication', but in the end, we are still engaged in making judgments of *plausibility*: to consider that the above material is not genuine is implausible, and this judgment could be backed up by thorough discussion of its details.

A slightly different authenticity issue is raised by the presentation of observation reports, namely, how well qualified is the observer to make a judgment? We have attempted to address this issue by requiring that all reports by observers include an account of what they themselves have learned (concerning their own practice) from their observation. This approach is connected with the significant role within the ASSET Programme of *mutual* observation by members of 'peer-groups' of candidates (see Chapter 8), but it is also part of the general educational and social philosophy of the programme (see Chapter 2, on the educational values underlying the ASSET model), in that we are concerned to promote the professional self-esteem of candidates and thus to minimize the role of purely hierarchical relationships within the programme procedures (see Heckscher and Donnellon, 1994, p. 3, on 'Post-bureaucratic Organisations').

Document 10

Portfolio Extract: An Observation Report
(By Letitia Collins)

Module: Understanding mental disorder and its treatments
Element 9: Demonstrate an understanding of the need to take appropriate steps to ensure their own personal safety
Core Assessment criterion no. 3: Affective awareness (N.B. The original report covered *two* elements from this unit)

Observer's Own Learning
What I particularly learnt from observing this piece of work was twofold. Firstly, how it is possible to effectively present complex areas through handouts and flip chart diagrams using everyday language. I was impressed by Jan's ability to summarise and present key issues clearly. It will make me think again how I approach presenting material to groups. Secondly, Jan's ability not to 'professionalise' issues struck me. It is easy to use terminology which can exclude colleagues who are not professionally qualified, but Jan did not do this.

Nature of Practice Observed
The observation took place in a meeting room at the offices of the Community Rehabilitation Team at the XXX Centre. The Multi-Disciplinary Rehabilitation Team consists of 3 professionals (including the candidate) and 2 support workers employed by Social Services. This session

was organised by J. to include the 2 support workers. A student nurse on placement with the team also joined the session. Jan had planned a structured discussion session, timed for approximately 45–60 minutes, led by herself to cover the behavioural symptoms of people with mental disorder and ensuring personal safety. The session was recorded on audio tape.

Element 9

Jan had linked two aspects to this discussion to follow the above. Jan introduced consideration of personal safety issues when working with people with a mental disorder. Jan has carried out some research into studies that were available on staff safety and the incidents of violence within Social Services in field, residential and day care settings. Essex's own guidelines on staff care were not as yet available to the team. Jan asked participants to consider what they thought were the important factors for staff safety. This generated contributions from the group which Jan built on.

Following this general introduction and discussion Jan raised the management of incidents when staff had felt threatened. Both support workers had been in situations when they had felt 'unsafe' in their relationship with a client. Jan enabled them to discuss how much of the incident related to their own inexperience of the clients' own illness. Jan also raised two incidents that had been followed up professionally in the team. By doing this Jan was able to acknowledge the importance of not only dealing positively with staff concerns, but also of the need to continue to work constructively with clients and their own feelings.

On reflection I did wonder whether a concentration on a particular incident (together with everyone's agreement) might not have been a more effective way of exploring this issue within the discussion group. However, in so far as Element 9 is concerned I did think that Jan had demonstrated an understanding of the need to take appropriate steps to ensure her own personal safety. In addition by introducing consideration of gender and the sexual element in a female worker–male client relationship Jan did recognise her own limitations and vulnerabilities as a worker.

Core Assessment criterion 3 (affective awareness)

This was demonstrated by Jan in the respect of demonstrating sensitivity to, and understanding of, the emotional complexity of particular situations. I did wonder whether 'the effective management of emotional responses in the course of professional relationships' had been fully met, hence my reference above to the possibility of focusing down on Jan's management of a particular incident rather than a generalised discussion. However, on balance I think Jan did cover this by her sensitive management of the support staff during the session when they were talking about incidents in practice which had worried them. Jan was also able to acknowledge that not only did the support workers need to have professional support for themselves, but that the clients should also continue to receive a professional service for their own needs. I thought it was particularly effective that Jan used research material and altogether I was impressed by this well planned piece of work. The participants initially were not very talkative, in part I think because J. had made available such well planned material. I did wonder whether an evaluation of the sessions by the participants might not have been useful. I think Jan could afford to take on board more of their learning needs because she ably demonstrated the elements as far as the ASSET Programme is concerned.

(Observation report by Letitia Collins on Jan Jolly)

Commentary

In this example, the competence of the candidate's practice is authenticated not simply by the observer's judgment to this effect, but by the measured and balanced quality of the observer's account, and by the demonstration of her ability to note details in what she observed which can contribute to her own professional thinking. In this way, we can see how the observation report itself must provide a basis for its own plausibility, and hence for the authenticity of the practice on which it reports. In this way we address the question: how can we assess the adequacy of the observation?

In their different ways, then, both of these examples (of how the quality of practice can be authenticated by the presentation of 'evidence') lead us back to the theme of this chapter as a whole: that the development of sound assessment procedures in an innovatory programme, even where such procedures have ostensibly already been specified in exhaustive detail, involves building an expert community which genuinely shares a practical understanding of never-absolutely-explicit formulations of criteria.

Notes

1 In a later work Wolf also recognizes the limitations of this approach (Wolf, 1995, p. 56).
2 The importance of the tutor's own experience of producing work similar to that which they are currently demanding of students, as a basis for their expertise and the authority of their judgments, explains the otherwise puzzling phenomenon that newly appointed academic staff are rarely given explicit training concerning the standard of work appropriate for different assessment outcomes.
3 The significance of this observation became even more apparent some time later, when two candidates working in child protection explained their decision to discontinue their work for the programme by referring specifically to the emotional pain of the work, which made it seem intolerable to prolong an intense current involvement by further periods of documentation and analysis. (This throws light on the failure of child care workers to complete the programme, see Chapter 8) In contrast, the candidate referred to by the external examiner here was working *retrospectively* on a *past* case, which further illustrates how useful it is that the programme procedures can easily and routinely accommodate the documentation of 'prior learning' (see Chapter 2).
4 Of course, if we had been designing a certificate, diploma or higher degree qualification, then the issue would have been much less acute, since these awards do not have to be formally classified, and so candidates' work does not necessarily need to be graded.
5 In adopting this holistic and, in a sense, 'retrospective' approach to grading within a competence-based system we anticipated in some ways the approach adopted by NCVQ in their attempt to marry their basic criterion-referenced philosophy with the grading process required by the school system for their so-called *General* National Vocational Qualifications (GNVQs) (see BTEC, 1993, p. 5). But the difference between the ASSET procedure and the GNVQ approach is crucial — see Chapter 1 and Chapter 4.

7   Examples of Work from Candidates' Portfolios

In this chapter we illustrate the main aspects of the model which have been referred to in previous chapters, through extracts from candidates' portfolios. The choice of material has not been easy. To begin with, the work is so varied that it is difficult to take a few examples as 'representative'. Secondly, it is difficult to find a section from a portfolio which is short enough to be accessible to a general reader and yet intelligible without reference to other sections, dealing with other elements of competence. Thirdly, much of the material presented in many of the social work portfolios is highly confidential, and even to ask for its release might have caused distress to clients. Most of the work included in this chapter is drawn from the Social Work Programme, since the Ford Programme is still at a relatively early stage, and as yet rather few portfolios have been submitted, assessed, and verified by external examiners. The work presented below is among 'the best' submitted, since our purpose is to attempt to demonstrate that the ASSET model can generate student work of an impressive honours degree standard. Some portfolios, of course, fall short of this standard in a number of ways, while remaining 'good enough' (see Chapter 6). It might have been interesting for readers if we had included such work, but this would have been potentially misleading unless we had made explicit our reservations, and we did not consider it ethical to expose a candidate to public criticism in this way.

On reading through the students' work included here, we are struck by the fact that the bulk of it takes the form of analytical narrative and commentary, and that workplace documentation in itself (minutes, memos, letters, case-notes, etc.) plays a relatively minor role. In part this is due to our own editing and to the factors affecting our selection, as mentioned in the previous paragraph, but on the whole the balance is not untypical of ASSET candidate's portfolio material. This balance reflects in part the development of our explicit emphasis on analysis, which we discussed in Chapter 6, but it also reflects candidates' own insistence on *describing* their work, as part of a genuine professional pride. In a sense, therefore, the material in this chapter is beginning to formulate a new 'genre' of written work, midway between the workplace memo and the academic essay, as part of a necessary *exploration* of what 'the documentation of workplace *learning*' might need to look like. That the ASSET candidates have begun to develop *this* sort of writing has been part of our learning, as well as theirs.

Example 1: Christina Eldred

The first example shows in a straightforward way the use of a case interview report to demonstrate several elements of competence from a single module, together with appropriate Core Assessment Criteria. This example is used in the programme handbook where it is intended to be read by new candidates as an introductory guide to appropriate forms of evidence. It thus takes the form of a framework commentary (by Maire Maisch) with illustrative examples taken from a portfolio submitted by Christina Eldred, a candidate who completed the compulsory module: 'Implementing and Developing Anti-Oppressive Practices in the Workplace' (see Appendix D).

The work quoted in these extracts from her portfolio was used to demonstrate the following three elements:

- **Element 6**: Work with clients (or help others to work with clients) in understanding the impact of oppressive discrimination upon their life experiences.
- **Element 8**: Respond receptively to challenges concerning their authority, assumptions and beliefs.
- **Element 9**: Demonstrate an understanding of the need to ensure proper client access to information, records, and complaints procedures.
  The work for these three elements was associated with the following Core Assessment Criteria (see Document 4):
- **Criterion 1**: Professional values
- **Criterion 2**: Professional learning
- **Criterion 4**: Effective communication

In order to meet the above elements, the candidate submitted a report of an interview with the primary carers of a 32-year-old man with severe learning disabilities who attends the centre that she manages. The interview took place at the client's home.

The first part of the report demonstrates Element 6 in the following way: The candidate helped the clients to talk about their experiences as carers of a child with severe learning disabilities through to the child's adulthood. Mr and Mrs W talked about occasions when they had experienced discrimination, such as being refused access to public facilities and services because of DW's (their son's) disability. Mr and Mrs W were helped to recount many of their experiences which they understood as oppressively discriminatory. The following extract from the report is offered as part of the evidence for Element 6.

> Mrs W said that when DW was receiving phased care at T Village they closed the villa he was in. The hospital telephoned Mrs W to ask whether she would mind DW going into a ward with psychiatric patients who had challenging behaviour. She asked whether this meant 'aggressive behaviour', but they did not give a direct reply. The staff felt DW would be all right, so she agreed. During the night DW was badly beaten by another patient.

The interview ended with the candidate saying:

> I talked about the new assessments of need which are required under the
> Community Care Act and encouraged Mr and Mrs W to clearly state their
> needs. I also talked about the [Area] Information System, which is a regis-
> ter of people with learning disabilities and is used to project the need for
> future services.

The candidate commented in the report that she had helped Mr and Mrs W to see
that:

> DW had been rejected so many times by establishments and had been
> refused services, that they were fearful of criticising the services he cur-
> rently received in case they lost them.

The candidate decided that the relevant **Core Assessment criterion** here was
No. 1, 'Commitment to professional values': Demonstrates understanding of, and
commitment to, professional values in practice, through the implementation of anti-
discriminatory/anti-oppressive/anti-racist principles.

This involves demonstrating:

1 awareness of the need to counteract one's own tendency (both as a person
   and as a professional worker endowed with specific powers) to behave
   oppressively; and
2 respect for clients' dignity/diversity/privacy/autonomy.

She begins to describe how criterion 1 was met in the following passage:

> I became more aware from Mr and Mrs W's account of their experiences
> of caring for DW of how the caring services (Health and Social Services)
> had behaved oppressively towards them. They had been expected to cope,
> despite being refused essential services, they had suffered incorrect judg-
> ments and assumptions about DW's disability, information was not checked
> with them and they were not valued or recognised as people with knowledge
> and skills in caring for DW. I recognised I had contributed to this situation
> and I addressed this. See highlighted passages.

Here the candidate highlighted the parts of the report where she had encouraged
Mr and Mrs W to say what their needs were, where she had invited them to use
the complaints procedure and where she gave them information concerning a support group and where she had decided to ensure care was provided at Christmas
for DW.

The candidate then draws attention to the part of the report where Mr and Mrs
W (71 years and 65 years, respectively) talked about their ages, and discusses their
need for privacy and autonomy in their relationship with each other. The candidate

also highlights passages in this section of the report where she endeavoured to take account of Mr and Mrs W's views, feelings and rights as service users.

Finally, the candidate discussed the importance of maintaining a balance between supporting Mr and Mrs W (taking DW's needs into account) and not 'taking away' their responsibilities and expertise in knowing and caring for their son, i.e., of 'valuing' them as carers.

The rest of the report on the interview covered other aspects, which demonstrated Elements 8 and 9.

To provide evidence for Element 8, in the report the candidate describes how Mr and Mrs W challenged her on her decision to close the centre over Christmas. They said:

> We dread Christmas when the centre is closed for ten days. Christmas is an awful time, a nightmare, we get no rest. We dread it. Christmas is terrible for us like the elderly alone with no help.

The candidate comments:

> The centre closes for approximately ten days each Christmas. This is the only period of closure apart from Bank Holidays. We have closed because if all the staff take four days leave at the same time; that is 20 days when we will not be shortstaffed through the rest of the year. I used my authority to close the centre assuming that it will not adversely affect the families we work for, believing that it was the right thing to do. I now believe that I have made a wrong judgement and have put the needs of the establishment before the needs of this family. I intend to provide some day care for DW over this period through the use of our, or other, services.

This part of the report was also used to demonstrate **Core Assessment criterion No. 2**, Continuous professional learning: Demonstrates commitment to, and capacity for, reflection on practice, leading to progressive deepening of professional understanding.

This involves demonstrating:

1   willingness to learn from others;
2   recognition that professional judgments are always open to question; and
3   ability to engage in self-evaluation.

The candidate clarified her fulfilment of this criterion, as follows:

> The interview with Mr and Mrs W made me reconsider my level of awareness in relation to the difficulties some carers face in receiving essential services geared to their needs. We need to involve carers at a much earlier stage in the provision of services and although I believe I dealt with Mr

and Mrs W and DW empathetically and professionally I had not previously checked out with them or other carers, decisions made about the opening and closing of the centre over a holiday period. It made me review other decisions I had made as manager of the centre which affect the service users.

The candidate offered evidence for Element 9 by demonstrating an understanding of the need for proper client access to information, records and complaints procedures:

Mrs W had disclosed that her son had been deprived of respite care due to information supplied by DW's social worker to the care establishment. The report, it was felt, had over-emphasised aspects of DW's behaviour which led the care establishment to believe that they could not cope with him. I informed Mr and Mrs W that the department now has a Consumer Representation Policy which would enable them to complain and gain redress in situations of this type. I also informed them of their right of access to files held by the departments which would enable them to ensure that all information held on them was correct. I then offered to share DW's file with them and encouraged them to exercise these rights on behalf of their son. I told them that their representations would enable the department to assess service delivery and make changes when necessary.

Finally, the candidate demonstrates her fulfilment of **Core Assessment criterion No. 4**, Effective communication: Demonstrates ability to communicate effectively in complex professional contexts.

In order to do so, she highlighted parts of the interview report where she felt she had needed to communicate in a particularly sensitive manner:

Mr and Mrs W were distressed at their treatment at the hands of the different services. I listened carefully, summarising and reflecting back to make sure I understood and that Mr and Mrs W were aware that I was listening and responding. I had to be careful not to sound defensive and resisted the immediate temptation to offer practical solutions instead of allowing them to express their feelings. I tried not to use the 'Does he take sugar?' approach when referring to DW. Since DW cannot communicate his wishes and feelings in ordinary conversation this took particular effort.

Example 2: Geoff Wright

This example consists of work presented by Geoff Wright to demonstrate Elements 2 and 6 of General Module 1 'Implementing and Developing Anti-oppressive Practices in the Workplace' (see Appendix D). These Elements of competence state:

[Candidates must] recognise and challenge the power of discriminatory social and institutional pressures upon attitudes and practices (including their own) and work towards changing them.

[Candidates must] work with (or help others work with) clients in understanding the impact of oppressive discrimination upon their life experiences.

The candidate has chosen to present his work for these elements so as to fulfil **Core criterion No. 5**: Executive effectiveness: Demonstrates decisiveness in making difficult judgements in response to complex situations, (including) overall initiative, sensitivity and tenacity (and) the ability to relate the chosen approach to a clearly established purpose, and **Core criterion No. 7**: Intellectual flexibility: Demonstrates general perceptiveness and insight and an open minded awareness of alternatives, (including) capacity for careful, sensitive observation (and) ability to analyse situations and issues in terms of their dilemmas/change processes.

These elements of competence and Core Assessment Criteria are demonstrated by using evidence from a practice situation involving a family of mixed heritage whose 14-year-old son (O) had been excluded from school for 'behavioural problems'. This piece of work illustrates how easily a complex piece of work can demonstrate several elements. The first section of the portfolio is a descriptive account of the work and an explanation of its relationship to the competence statements and the Core Assessment Criteria. This is followed by a voluminous collection of practice documents (case notes, reports, letters, etc.) presented as reinforcing evidence and cross-referenced to the main account as a series of numbered appendices. There is not sufficient space within this chapter to allow us to include these appendices here, but one of our reasons for selecting this example is that the candidate's explanation and his references to his appendices are so clearly presented that the quality of his work can be ascertained even without reference to the supporting evidence. One highly significant letter ('Appendix 5') and a 'memo' to colleagues ('Appendix 8') are, however, reproduced at the end, as illustrations. The submission of so many appendices (even though they are indeed 'direct evidence') is not actually necessary to 'authenticate' the work, since one can usually infer from carefully *selected* appendices that other events, as described, have taken place.

> The family were referred to the Family Centre immediately prior to the school exclusion by a Child Guidance professional whose opinion was that the family had not responded to family therapy and that there was nothing more that they could achieve.
> Coinciding with this referral was another one from the school that O attended asking if he could have counselling as he had an attitude problem (Appendix 1, initial referral form) [not included].
> O's mother is black; his father is white, and O has a younger sister. O's mother's previous husband was black, and there are two children from this earlier marriage.
> Several visits were made to O at school and the family. At that time

I felt that racism may be an issue. Coinciding with this was O's exclusion from school accompanied by a report about events leading up to the exclusion (Appendix 2, recording from case file and exclusion report) [not included]. The report was four pages long and represented a number of incidents which O is alleged to have initiated. Nowhere (in this report) was racism, ethnicity or colour considered or addressed as a possible explanation as to what was going wrong for this young man and his family.

On 24th June I visited the family and talked to them about their rights. The family felt that they did not want to face an exclusion hearing, where they felt they would only hear more negative statements about their son. They felt that a new school would be more advantageous, giving O a fresh start, rather than delaying what they saw as inevitable. O was also voicing this. At the request of the family I drafted a letter to the school governors offering an explanation for O's behaviour in the incident which led to the exclusion and added their observations on what the school had not done to help. (Appendix 3) [not included]. The Governors upheld the exclusion and very little else was done because of the school holidays.

Immediately at the start of the school term I again assisted the parents in preparing a letter to the head of Parent Pupil Services for Essex County Council, this time pointing out that O was black and therefore likely to be disadvantaged further without access to proper education. Mr P arranged for an appointment at the school. (The school is Grant Maintained and is very conscious of league tables for attendance, performance and exclusions.)

With the parents and O's consent I talked to the school, indicating very clearly what support we would give this family, and directing the school's attention to teachers at his previous school whom I know would be taking account of O's positives and the fact that he has experienced racist taunts. Unfortunately he was not re-admitted to the school. (For correspondence and case notes on this phase, see Appendix 4) [not included].

O's family lives in a rural area which does not have the choice of schools that would be available in a town. It became clear at this stage that O was not going to get his educational needs met other than by home tuition. Discussion with the family and with colleagues confirmed that they felt the same. There seemed very few options open, so having talked to the family, it was agreed that all the correspondence would be filed and that I would help the family step by step through the legislation whilst at the same time increasing the pressure on the Education Department to meet their legal requirements (see Appendix 5).

In supervision on 18th October 1993 it was agreed with my line manager that O's emotional needs were being neglected because of the amount of work being done to try to find a school for him. A plan was agreed where I would work with the parents, that a recently arrived student social worker would work with O, and that I would act in a consultative role with her.

It was at the partnership meeting that I was able to identify with the family and the student the way in racism was being internalised and normalised in the family. The student drew up an agreement with the family in which strategies to combat the effects of racism past and present would be addressed. (Appendix 6 contains case notes on the partnership meeting, supervision, and on the agreement for working). The impact of racism was addressed in all subsequent meetings with the family, whilst continuing to record and increase the pressure on the Education Department to meet their legal duties.

In November 1993 another school refused O's admission, except on this occasion the refusal was not so direct. This school, either through accident or design, were able to find a way around outright refusal and said they may be able to reconsider a place for the following September. Further correspondence from the family assisted by myself and the student was sent to this school requesting that they reconsider their decision [not to consider admission before September] and advising them that the Family Centre were willing and able to support the school and O (Appendix 7) [not included].

The current situation with the family has become very complex, with many needs, and it has been necessary with the consent of the family to separate some of the work we are doing to help them. The student social worker and an experienced social worker are carrying out family therapy, addressing the identified difficulties in the family which includes their experiences of racism. My responsibility is to concentrate on the difficulties with the educationalists. This had not been possible before because of the operational boundaries of my particular role of counselling and not case working, and because of respecting the wishes and rights of the family at that time.

It would appear from the response from the schools that it is unlikely that we will find a place in a school within 15 mile radius of O's home. It is clear that the Education Department are not able to meet their statutory duties and that there may well be a case for the Local Government Ombudsman. In working with and supporting the family we have been able to follow the letter of the law and have explored all available resources. We have been able to keep accurate records of all correspondence which will be used for evidence of causing 'undue delay' in finding a school for O.

Element of competence No. 2: Recognise and challenge the power of discriminatory social and institutional pressures upon attitudes and practices (including their own) and work towards changing them.

I believe that in this piece of work I have 'recognised the power of discriminatory social and institutional pressures upon attitudes and practices.' The school exclusion of O and the failure to acknowledge his colour and the effect this had on him is an example of this.

The institutional pressures of having to produce league tables and publish results almost certainly influenced the attitudes of the schools when they looked at the school exclusion report of O.

The financial and operational pressures on the Education Department has limited their response. All of the schools approached have Grant Maintained Status which means that in future, pupils who need extra provision will have to be provided for from the school budget and not from the L.E.A. budget. This may well have been a consideration. I feel I have started to work towards challenging this by supporting and empowering this family in documenting and following the law in the fight to get O into a school. In changing the way in which we are working with this family and by seeking their permission to represent them in future meetings with the Education Department I have demonstrated a commitment to seeing this through (see Appendix 5).

I have also undertaken responsibility for setting up a number of workshops for teachers and home tutors addressing 'oppressive practice' and personal and professional values. These will be of an informal nature initially with a view to inviting more experienced people in to discuss issues of racism and discrimination (see Appendix 8).

One of the learning experiences from this piece of work has been the recognition of not how much I know, but what I did not know.

Element of competence No. 6: Work (or help others to work) with clients in understanding the impact of oppressive discrimination upon their lives.

The evidence is clear in demonstrating that I am working with the client to help them understand the impact of oppressive discrimination particularly in the way which one aspect of it is affecting their lives at the moment and in how it has been internalised by some members of the family. I believe that in joint working this case with a student I am also helping her to work with this client, gaining experience in understanding the impact of discrimination.

This has been quite difficult for me — I cannot close my eyes and pretend I am black and imagine what it is like because I know when I open my eyes I am still white, probably middle class in a relatively powerful position and part of the oppressive institution. On reflection I feel patronising trying to show an oppressed person how this has affected their lives when it has affected mine to a far lesser degree.

Core criterion No. 5: Demonstrates decisiveness in making difficult judgements in response to complex situations.

1 'Overall initiative, sensitivity and tenacity'
I believe that initiative has been demonstrated in the way in which a planned approach to dealing with the Education Department has been used. For example using the law exactly, following the procedures to a point where the family have a well prepared case should they wish to proceed with a grievance against the Local Education Authority.

Sensitivity is demonstrated in the way in which the clients' rights and wishes have been reinforced and respected from the outset. This is further demonstrated in the clients' ability to talk about their experiences of racism which is evident in my case notes and other documents.

Tenacity is demonstrated in the way in which we have continued to work with the family, separating off areas of work to others in order to follow the school exclusion process through to conclusion. It would have been far easier to have accepted home tuition as an alternative and concentrated on counselling O individually.

2   'Ability to relate the chosen approach to a clearly established purpose'
This is demonstrated in that I and the family have documented every action taken in a way which allowed them to make the decisions and prepare a strong argument for further discussion on how the Education Authority have, so far, failed them. (The clearly established purpose being to get proper education for their son.)

Core criterion No. 7: Intellectual Flexibility Demonstrates general perceptiveness and insight and an open minded awareness of alternatives.

1   Capacity for careful, sensitive observations
This is demonstrated in my recognition that O's emotional needs and the family's overall needs were not being met because of the work being generated in trying to find a school placement for O. It was clear that this was becoming the focus for a number of deep rooted, long standing difficulties, and from this observation it was possible to explore other issues with the family and to introduce another worker to carry out family therapy, ensuring that emotional needs were addressed as well as the schooling difficulties.

2   Ability to analyse situations and issues in terms of their dilemmas/ change processes
One way in which this is demonstrated is in being analytical with the family about the issues relating to Grant Maintained Status. The schools were very conscious of the truancy, exam and performance tables they were expected to produce. They were also aware of the extra pressure that special or additional teaching would make on the school budget, especially so now that they would also have to pay for home tuition if they took on O and then had to exclude him again. It is now clear to the parents that the schools do indeed have a dilemma. Understanding this has led to a firm resolve by the parents to see this through where they might have given up.

What I learned from this piece of work

Although I have attended a number of training sessions on anti-discriminatory/anti-oppressive practice, when it comes down to it I missed the signs of racism before O was excluded. I did not address this soon enough. I think that on reflection I should have persuaded the parents to attend the exclusion meeting and gone with them. It was my lack of experience and short-comings that prevented this as much as their powerlessness.

I am conscious of how patronising I feel trying to tell a client how oppressed they are when I go home to my comfortable home at night. I have reservations about doing this again, it would have been better if there had been a cultural advisor to help with this.

I think that in completing the other elements of this module and previous modules I had become complacent. This case has served to remind me of what I did not know, most of which was about myself and my own attitude to racism and oppression.

I realise now that oppression and discriminator practices do not have to be intentional to exist. I am now more aware and more willing to undertake training and be challenged myself rather than look for other peoples faults. My hope for the future is that I have helped this family, only time will tell.

Post-script

2 February 1994 — The family received a communication from one of the schools that had previously denied O a place (Copy of letter — Appendix 7) [not included]. They have reconsidered all of the evidence submitted and the fact that some issues were not considered in the original exclusion and they are able to offer O a place starting on 21st February 1994.

Extract from Supporting Evidence (1):
Letter drafted by G.W. in consultation with and on behalf of O and his parents
(see reference to 'Appendix 5')

[Home Address]

7th September, 1993

Mr C.F.
Parent Pupil Services
Essex County Council,
Chelmsford.

Dear Sir,

I am writing to you about my son O.Z., born 11/1/1980. He was excluded from school before the summer holiday and for a short time received home tuition.

Please can you tell me when he will be admitted to a school, so that your department can meet its obligations in educating my son. He is already disadvantaged by being black in a virtually all white community; not to have an education will further disadvantage him, and I urge you to do all that you can to get O. back into mainstream school as soon as possible.

If you are unable to meet his needs in a day school because of his difficulties, then I want him assessed as having special needs and if necessary a boarding place found for him.

Yours sincerely,

Mr & Mrs Z.

Extract from Supporting Evidence (2):
Copy of circular from G.W. to all home tutors attending the X
family centre
(see reference to 'Appendix 8')

To All Home Tutors

I am considering a series of mini workshops on professional and personal values, and I wondered if any of you would be interested. I am only inviting home tutors who attend the X Family Centre, so it should be a nice informal group.

I would particularly like you to suggest times etc and subjects for discussion.

I thought the first session could be around issues of confidentiality — oppressive behaviour, gender issues etc.

Please add your names below if you are interested.

Geoff Wright.

Commentary

The tutor's view of this work was that, quite apart from the clear presentation of evidence, the material presented demonstrates a high standard of professional practice. The commentary on 'Element 6' is particularly thoughtful and does not fall into the trap of seeming self-congratulatory or self-justificatory, which is quite difficult to avoid when one is arguing that one's work demonstrates given criteria. On the contrary, it is clear that Geoff is adopting a questioning stance towards the competence statement even while demonstrating it:

I feel patronising trying to show an oppressed person how this has affected their lives when it has affected mine to a far lesser degree.

The explanations concerning the Core Assessment Criteria are exemplary in their clarity and detail. However, the appendices should have been more carefully selected, and a supporting statement from the student involved in the work could have substantiated Geoff's claim that he helped her to understand the effects of oppressive discriminatory practices on O. Finally, the 'post-script' indicates the overall effectiveness of the work.

This extract also illustrates how the elements of competence and the Core Assessment Criteria challenge candidates to *analyse* the rationale for their practice, and how in doing so they articulate the 'process knowledge' (see Chapter 5) which informs their work. In this way, Geoff's 'underpinning knowledge' (as well as his 'underpinning values' and 'underpinning affective awareness', for example) are made apparent through the presentation of practice itself, without recourse to explicit reference to bodies of theory and without engaging in explicit 'research'. The memo proposing staff workshops on values is particularly significant, in that it shows how Geoff's work for this module stimulated an initiative on his part to undertake specific innovation and further learning, even though the immediate focus of the work is a 'description' of a practice episode.

Example 3: Andy Delicata

Andy Delicata is an engineer with the Ford Motor Company. This is an extract from the porfolio of work he submitted to demonstrate the element of competence 'Assess the cost of product complexity' within the module 'Analyse Component/ System Costs'. He chooses to demonstrate this element in relation to the Core Assessment criterion concerned with 'Intellectual Rigour and Flexibility' (see Document 5, Chapter 4). He explains in his introduction how the work was undertaken within a Ford training workshop called 'Value Engineering' and he structures his material by dividing it into two distinct 'activities' associated with different phases of the workshop process.

Introduction: The 'Value Engineering' Workshop
The final part of this module was completed during a three day 'Value Engineering' workshop. This process has now been adopted as a basic methodology by Ford Motor Company. I have been fortunate to pioneer this process for power supply technology within Ford and led a team of key personnel through the workshop. The workshop and the underpinning knowledge gained have given me tools which in combination now assist me in my everyday work.

Activity A: Assess current system 'Value' Ratio
(value = function/cost)
This phase of the workshop was aimed primarily at identifying opportunities for improvement. To do this it was necessary to produce a 'value ratio' figure for the current system to which any future suggestions could be compared. A set of ten key criteria were identified and a weighting assigned to each to show relative importance. This was necessary to avoid less important criteria from influencing the decision making process unless the number proved to be significant.

I led the team through a process of rating the current system against the criterion and assigning a number to each. This number represented the ability of the current system to meet this criterion. This was completed using a scale of one to ten, 'one' meaning the criteria was not met at all and 'ten' meaning 'fully met'. [An appendix was submitted — not included here — showing the full 'worksheet' generated by this process.]

One such criterion was 'complexity', to which a relative importance of five (5) was agreed. At this point the experience gained from previously designed systems was brought to bear. For example the total number of alternators used on previous [X model] vehicles was sixteen. This was dependent on the engine size, transmission variant and feature content of the vehicle. When combined with the possible combinations of battery size and cable size, the situation was poor: it would have undoubtedly led to expensive alternators since the volume produced would have been low for each variant. Storage would also be required and there would be additional problems associated with identifying each alternator and the potential to build vehicles with incorrect parts.

At the target setting stage of the activity, complexity was a key consideration, and thus a severe target was imposed. By commonising between different engine variants and by optimising the alternator output the complexity was envisaged as being reduced to three. This had prompted the team to assign an importance value of eight (8) against complexity for the current system design. For each of the criteria a number was assigned in the same way. Each number was multiplied by its relative importance (e.g., in the above case: complexity (8) × importance (5) = 40) and then the total numbers were added to give an overall 'weight rated' function number.

Having completed the cost versus function worksheet it was a simple process of dividing the function number by the cost for each of these functions, thus giving a value ratio, in this case 7.5.

This number was used later in the proposal selection phase as a basis for comparison.

Activity B: Define alternative design proposals to meet functions
Having now set out a definitive value ratio for the current system any new ideas could be evaluated and compared in the same way and analysed for their viability later. The process to be followed for the next part was to brainstorm the system for any new concepts, focusing primarily on areas with maximum opportunity.

The objective of the brainstorming being to generate as many ideas as possible with the emphasis on quantity and not quality, which can be evaluated at a later stage. To ensure this process could work to maximum effect it required a complete mindset change. The team was prepared for this by introducing us to the factors that limit or enhance this creative thought:

Limits	Enhancements
• fear	• curiosity
• criticism	• courage
• reluctance to change	• imagination
	• inspiration and relaxation

This was designed to show how, given the right environment, people can be very creative. This was proven when after only two five minute brainstorming sessions, split by a concentrated look at various competitor vehicles, the team produced a total of 213 ideas. The sessions were split to allow a chance to reflect on the ideas and to look at various competitor vehicles brought to the workshop for comparison.

After producing these ideas they were grouped together, categorised by physical part or by function, and ranked as follows:

A   easy to achieve with high payoff
B   hard to achieve with high payoff
C   easy to achieve with low payoff
D   hard to achieve with low payoff
X   'no hopers'!

To optimise the time available it would not be possible to look at each idea in detail. By general agreement, a set of ten ideas were chosen to be evaluated in the next phase.

Core Professional Criterion: Intellectual rigour and flexibility
In Activity B the brainstorming session was used for the purpose of generation of new ideas to improve the value of the power supply system. The emphasis for the process is on quantity and not quality. One of the main reasons for our success as a team in this part of the workshop (i.e., 213 ideas in 10 minutes) was that of a mindset change that was made; a ('Paradigm shift').

I was introduced to this term during the workshop and again when I attended the Ford Quality Engineering course (Sept 94). Paradigms and Paradigm shifts are referred to in Thomas Kuhn's controversial book *The Structure of Scientific Revolutions* (1962). 'Paradigms are models. They are not the truth. They are models which attempt to explain how a particular system functions and self-regulates through laws, principles, axioms etc. Much of our scientific research is concerned with developing models or paradigms which explain the nature of the universe around us ... The disorganised and diverse activity that precedes the formulation of a scientific principle eventually becomes structured when a single paradigm becomes accepted by a scientific or engineering community.'

I interpret this to mean, it is human nature to try and comprehend the way the universe functions. When a new, revolutionary or controversial theory is introduced even when this is backed up with supporting data, it is human nature to distrust this theory on the basis that it does not fit the normal pattern (paradigm). When it can be proven beyond reasonable doubt it is generally accepted and thus becomes the norm (paradigm shift).

Commentary

The Ford Programme tutors were impressed by the quality of this section of the portfolio, although one of them did note that he did not entirely understand all the details of Andy's explanation of Activity A. It is interesting to see that Andy uses a workplace training session both to provide evidence for the element of competence and at the same time to further his work task; and also that he finds his own way of organizing his material (i.e., as separate 'activities'). (This highly individual response is characteristic of candidates' portfolios, as the difference between these examples illustrates.) Again, there is something unpredictable about Andy's linking of Kuhn's 'paradigm shifts' with the creative displacement of 'mindsets' during a brainstorming session, and a philosophy specialist might remain unconvinced; but in the context of the portfolio it draws attention to Andy's explicit awareness that what was at stake during the work was indeed 'intellectual flexibility' and thus a genuine 'creativity' (in some sense) rather than more effectiveness. Thus, although his own commentary under the Core Professional Criteria heading is rather more *external* to his work than one might have expected or hoped, his argument is nevertheless relevant, since he shows that his participation in (and leadership of) the workshop sessions was informed by a theoretically based understanding of the concept of 'intellectual flexibility'. The whole passage is an illustration of our claim that work-based learning is a continuous opportunity for the 'interdisciplinary' understanding which Barnett sees as one of the key features of higher education (Barnett, 1994, Chapter 9).

Example 4: Janice Whitaker

This piece of work was submitted by Janice Whitaker to demonstrate **Element No. 2** of Social Core General Module 2: 'Sustaining Morale, Developing Practice'. This element states: '[Candidates must] manage issues of confidentiality arising from the mutual sharing of professional experience.'

The candidate has chosen to present her work so as to fulfil Core Assessment **Criterion No. 6**: 'Effective grasp of a wide range of professional knowledge'.

The work below consists of an analysis of the issues surrounding confidentiality in professional contexts where staff from Health and Social Services are based in one team to provide a service to clients. The candidate has interpreted the element of competence fairly broadly, to mean the tensions inherent in the exchange of information concerning clients records where two major agencies are involved, but working to different policies and procedures. She has numbered the paragraphs of her account so that she can cross-reference the account with her subsequent argument that the account fulfils the Core Assessment criterion. Paragraphs 1–9 present the background information affecting the issue, and paragraphs 10–13 describe the candidate's response to the issue within her practice, leading to an initiative on her part to try to bring about a procedural change within the Social Services Department. At the end of her account she adds, as evidence, part of a correspondence between herself and her Principal Officer. A tape-recording of a meeting (referred to after paragraph 13 of the account) was also submitted as part of the portfolio. The contents of the tape are outlined and then referred to within her argument that the work fulfils the Core Assessment criterion. The tape-recording itself authenticates the evidence, i.e., confirms that the meeting took place, and could be consulted if one had doubts about the analysis as presented.

1 Chelmsford's mental health social workers are integrated in the local health led community teams. The N.H.S. and Community Care Act 1990 encourages close working between health and social service departments. Currently there is no single method of referral or an integrated records policy. Both health and social services departments are subject to legislation concerning confidentiality and access to records.

2 The Data Protection Act received Royal Assent in 1984. The principles as determined in Schedule 1 set out a standard whereby a computer user my be judged. These conform to articles 5, 7 and 8 of the Council of Europe Convention.

3 The first principle states 'The information to be contained in personal data shall be obtained, and personal data shall be processed, fairly and lawfully.' This is interpreted in the notes to the schedule as meaning that information was obtained unfairly if, 'any person from whom it was obtained was deceived or misled as to the purpose or purposes for which it was to be held, used or disclosed' (R.A. Elbra 1985).

4 The Local Authority Circular (LAC)(88)16, paragraph 13, notes 'Where there are arrangements for joint working with the health services of other organisations and there are joint records, who is the "data user" for these records in responding to a request for access is a matter of fact, depending upon the details of the arrangements in each case.' The circular adds that the D.P.A.'s Registrar's guideline No. 2 and the authority's lawyers should be consulted where necessary. This is reflected in the 'Guidelines on Access to Records and the Disclosure of Information' produced by the Policy, Planning and Development branch in 1990. This document also states that all entries in joint records made by social work staff employed by Essex will be accessible, and recommends that entries made by Social Services employees are made separately.

5 LAC(88)16 clarifies the health order appertaining to Data Protection, that is, that the power to withhold information only extends to the data subject on the grounds of 'risk of serious harm to a person's physical

or mental health', whereas the social work order 'allows information to be withheld if there is a risk of serious harm to the physical or mental health or emotional condition of another person as well as of the data subject himself'.

6   Further guidance relating to the keeping of joint records is produced in LAC(88)17. Part 1 para. 12 acknowledges the need for co-operation between health and local social services authorities and directs health authorities and health professionals to share personal health information about those in their care.

7   The U.K.C.C. code of professional conduct for registered nurses, midwives and health visitors requires them to 'work in a collaborative and co-operative manner with health care professionals and others involved in providing care.' But to 'protect all confidential information concerning patients and clients' which could place them in a professional dilemma about what and how much to share.

8   Further legislation established a right of access to records by the individuals concerned and other persons (Access to Personal Files Act 1987 and access to Health Records Act 1990). These acts encouraged health and social services authorities to develop a practice of 'live' record sharing on an ongoing basis. Clients are involved in and encouraged to participate in their own plan of care and participate in any recording made about them. They are also asked what information can be shared with others involved in their care.

9   The Essex guidelines on access to records and disclosure of information conform to the requirements of LAC(88)16 and LAC(88)17 in the matters of how personal health information can only be passed to a third party with the health professional's consent (Part B para. 4) and concerning entries by social services employees in joint records (Part C para. 10). There are no other policies or procedures on integrated records.

10 To manage an integrated records system in Chelmsford, I have worked with my health colleagues to develop the following system, which is in operation in the Community Mental Health Team (CMHT), the Community Rehabilitation Team (CRT) and Community Drug Team. Social workers use health files which are numbered and subsequently filed in the main health filing system. When a social worker accepts a new case, an additional social services PRN number is allocated by the worker informing Chelmsford locality office of the client's name, address, date of birth etc. The case is then entered on the social services HUBBARD database. Social workers record their work on social services forms which are photocopied onto yellow paper. This enables accessibility and conforms to the guidelines and circulars mentioned above. All documents which cannot be printed on yellow paper, letters, reports to Mental Health Tribunals etc, are identified with yellow dots stuck at the top right hand corner.

11 Although this system conforms to the guidelines and instructions available, several question relating to the rights and dignity of clients arise.

1 If all records are stored together, health and social services workers have access to all recorded material. This could contravene the 'need to know' basis on which we presently share records in all other social work teams.

2 LAC(88)17 states 'Local Authorities will also need to make arrangements for informing users of their services, and organisations and individuals with whom they exchange information, of the procedures set up for the safeguarding of personal information.' There are no specific arrangements made to conform to this, for example, social workers use health authority headed stationary which does not indicate the multi-disciplinary nature of the team (although they would indicate their status following their signature). G.P.s have been concerned to find that patients they have referred to the C.M.H.T. have been entered onto a social services database.

3 Social workers should make it clear to their clients who they are and which authority they work for, but should this responsibility rest entirely with individual workers? For example, The District General hospital has a multi-disciplinary Community Care Reception Team which is responsible for co-ordinating discharge arrangements, including referrals for district nursing services only. A social worker has not been involved in the majority of these cases, but the patient's details are entered onto the HUBBARD system. The patient has a right to know where his/her details are recorded, but who has informed them if a social worker has not been involved? This Practice also creates anomalies in data collection from multi-disciplinary teams as only a small proportion of referrals to the mental health teams are entered on HUBBARD (see process outlined above). In an attempt to begin to manage these problems I have written to the Principle Officer responsible for mental health in Mid Essex, (see Appendix 1) but have not received a reply to date.

12 Essex Social Services department is currently undertaking a major review of information systems with the intent of purchasing a new system that will encompass departmental needs following the N.H.S. and Community Care Act 1990. The Departmental Information Systems Group agreed that 'the Community Care specification would benefit from additional input in the area of options for sharing data with other agencies as a way of enhancing joint working arrangements'. However, 'it was acknowledged that the final point presented difficulties particularly since the creation of the internal market had given client details the profile of market information and that the stand-alone nature of the fifteen National Health Service Trusts in

Essex was seen as largely incompatible with data sharing on a macro, or Countywide level'. (Departmental Information Systems Group minutes, 4th August 1993).

13   The Mid Essex mental health partnership will be joining the next wave of Trusts. The implications from the creation of an internal market, therefore, may have a major effect on the way joint records should be managed in the future, indeed, if such schemes can exist at all.

The discussion on Tape No. 2 is evidence of a meeting held between myself, the co-ordinator of the mental health teams, a social worker from one of the teams and a colleague who works in mental health in a different area of the group. We discuss our present system for managing joint records and the issues of confidentiality that arise from this system. We acknowledge that the system presently used was devised prior to April 1st 1993 and that the new forms, particularly the D.S.S. 695 does allow for the client to be asked to give consent for contact and sharing with other agencies. It was accepted that, in X (town) audits were joint agency, although the discussion did not explain that I, as the Social Services Representative, would only have access to files which have been worked on by a social worker. Towards the end of the tape, we discussed access to records by those other than members of the team. An example was given of a G.P. accessing files, apparently without the clients' agreements. I state that clients should have been contacted and the co-ordinator explained the process of application the to health ethical committee prior to any work being undertaken.

At the end of the discussion, we consider the implications of the mental health partnership receiving Trust status in conjunction with the Community Unit of Mid Essex Health Services and agree that the issue of joint records should be revisited in the light of these significant changes.

Core Assessment Criterion No. 6: Effective grasp of a wide range of professional knowledge

1   Comprehensive knowledge and critical evaluation of professional methods/policy/procedures/general theory/research findings/legislation

In the above account, paragraph 10, I note the method that has been developed for the recording of social work in mental health records.

Tape 2 also describes this and there is some discussion of the strengths and weaknesses of the system, particularly with reference to the volume of recording engendered by social work involvement, primarily by long term placement issues.

In paragraph 7 I note the policy of the U.K.C.C. in relation to the sharing of information and the rights of patients to confidentiality.

In paragraph 9 of the above account, I note the procedures as outlined in the Essex guidelines on access to records and disclosure of information. I point out that there are no further procedures devised for joint working in paragraph 9.

In paragraph 11, I pose questions which relate to the rights and dignity of clients. These questions recognise the underlying theories of common human needs, the need to feel valued as a human being.

Paragraph 12 indicates the extent of my research in this area appears to be in its infancy and much will be learnt as the implications of Community Care are evaluated.

Paragraphs 2 and 8 explicitly note the legislation under which health and social services are required to act in relation to confidentiality and access to records.

In tape 2 I refer to LAC(88)16 and mistakenly relate its contents to the Access to Records legislation rather than the Data Protection Act to which it belonged. In fact, the Access to Health Records Act (1990) allows for access to be withheld if the 'information is likely to cause serious harm to the physical or mental health of the patient or of any other individual'.

2   Ability to relate specific details to other contexts and general principles

In paragraph 11 of the above account, in discussing the client's right to know where his/her details are recorded, I give an example of entries being made on the social services department database, apparently without the knowledge or consent of the client. This is discussed again on tape 2 where I explain that referrals that are merely clerked through the system are entered on the database.

In paragraph 13, I note the difficulties stemming from the creation of the internal market and the status of the National Health Service Trusts.

It would seem that the principle of closer working underlying the N.H.S. and Community Care Act could be eroded by the new boundaries being created. The impact of G.P. fundholders is yet to be felt, as is the consequences of the purchasing arrangements in health and social services.

Bibliography

Elbra R.A. 'Implications of the Data Protection Act' NCC Publications 1985.

Department of Health LAC(88)16 'Data Protection Act 1984, social work etc orders: Individual's right of access to information' July 1988.

Department of Health LAC(88)17 'Personal social services: Confidentiality of personal information' September 1988.

Essex County Council Departmental Information Systems Minutes 4th August 1993.

Essex County Council Policy, Planning and Development Branch 'Guidelines on Access to Records and Disclosure of Information' 1990.

Mid Essex Mental Health Partnership 'Background and Principles Underlying the Access to Health Records Act 1990', July 1991.
UKCC Code of Professional Conduct.

Supporting Evidence:
Memo to principal officer, mid-Essex regional area

(from: Janice Whitaker, team leader, Chelmsford office,)

Recording of work from Community Mental Health Team (CMHT)
and Community Resource Team (CRT) on HUBBARD

I am conscious of the need to enter data in a uniform manner across the Group to obtain reliable statistics and of the need to comply with confidentiality rules and the Data Protection Act. Could you share your views on the following points?

The protocol for the multi-disciplinary reception team at Broomfield Hospital allows for the recording of all the team's work on HUBBARD, including referrals requesting, and undertaken by, the team's nursing staff.

Are there any Groupwide agreements for the recording of all mental health multi-disciplinary teams' work on HUBBARD? At present, we are only recording the cases undertaken by social workers. This promotes anomalies in statistical data obtained from HUBBARD. Cases which normally either would be undertaken by social workers if a separate social work team (or more social workers in the C.M.H.T.) existed, or which have a significant co-working/advisory input, do not appear.

A further anomaly exists with cases worked on by the M.I.S.G. assistant social workers in the C.R.T. The case co-ordinators are health professionals and, therefore, would not normally be recorded on HUBBARD.

This problem of data collection has been highlighted by the inclusion of the C.M.H.T. in the research project being undertaken by the Chief Executive's Dept. The true amount of mental health assessment work will not be reflected by studying the work of one social worker, whose caseload comprises largely of long term provision, case management and review work. I am concerned that Mid Group will miss out on an equitable allocation of posts if this is not recognised in adequate data input.

Are there any guidelines about informing clients, seen by health professionals, that their details are entered on a social services dept. data system? Do the mental health unit's confidentiality rules and the Data Protection Act allow for entry onto two systems? I understand there is some work being done by the Centre on a health/social services integrated data collection system, has there been any progress?

Janice
(June 1993)

Note

Shortly after this memo had been sent, the Social Services Department introduced a new computerized information system, and the problems raised in Janice's memo were addressed at senior management level through the process of implementing this new system. This included providing training events, in which Janice participated.

Commentary

This work was agreed to be of a high standard: if all the elements of competence were demonstrated in this way then the portfolio as a whole would warrant an 'A' grade (see Chapter 6). In her introductory paragraphs Janice demonstrates that she has researched relevant legislation, Local Authority guidelines and codes of conduct regarding the management of client information. In this way she shows the 'wide range of professional knowledge' required by Core Assessment criterion No. 6, and she explains how this criterion is fulfilled. In the latter part of the extract Janice describes a system she developed to manage integrated records, and this is authenticated in the memorandum to her Principal Officer. This part of the work involves a consideration of the effect on clients of the implementation of existing policies and procedures, which *implicitly* also fulfils Core Assessment criterion No. 1 ('Professional Values'), and thus also contributes to the professional quality of the work described. This last point illustrates how the Core Assessment Criteria are not simply demonstrated separately, but also operate together as an integrated guide to a model of professional practice.

In contrast to Example 2, Janice's work shows how the competence statements can be used as the basis for exploratory work which explicitly challenges current practices and which entails the consultation of bodies of relevant knowledge as a prelude to subsequent practice. It thus shows how Core Assessment criterion No. 6 ensures that candidates demonstrate a high level of relevant knowledge while avoiding the need to specify 'underpinning knowledge' for every element of competence.

In a sense this is the key chapter of our book. These examples illustrate what exactly ASSET 'students' *do*. Is it acceptable 'honours degree work'? Is it 'reflective'? Does it represent a response to 'intellectual challenge'? Does it *adequately* 'demonstrate' an acceptable 'quality' of professional practice and an acceptable grasp of professional knowledge and understanding? These are the essential questions underlying the ASSET project; our book is an explanation as to why we feel we can answer these questions positively, but readers will, of course, make their own judgments.

8 The Organizational/Employment Context: An 'Educative' Workplace?

If education can be 'work-based', it follows that work can be 'educational', and indeed it has been one of our basic underlying arguments that this is so; that work *can* be the basis for an educational process. We have argued that educational aims, conceptions of knowledge, and educational assessment processes can be closely associated with occupational practices (Chapters 3, 4 and 5) and we have described some of the consequent shifts in role and procedure which the ASSET Programme has required of the university and its staff (Chapter 6). But the essence of work-based education is that its main location is *outside* the educational institution, in the candidate's place of employment, so we now need to consider in detail what is needed *in the workplace* if the educative potential of work is to be realized in the practical experience of those who seek to be at the same time both professional practitioners *and* 'students'.

Arrangements within the workplace are largely under the jurisdiction of employers, of course, and programmatic statements concerning the employer's required contribution to the realization of the educative workplace are readily available. Jessup, writing on the 'implications for employers' of competence-based education, notes the need

> to create an infrastructure and a culture within companies and other employing organisations in which it becomes normal practice for employees at all levels to continue learning and enhancing their practice. (Jessup, 1991, p. 95)

He goes on to list the components of the 'infrastructure', which include:

- Training or the development of human resources will need to be written into the corporate plans of every company and time and money will need to be devoted to it.
- Managers and supervisors will need to have the development of their staff clearly written into their job descriptions and they will themselves require training to become trainers (or more specifically the planners and facilitators of learning).

- Managers and supervisors will also need to become assessors . . .
- Jobs will need to be analysed to see what learning opportunities they provide. The experience of employees will need to be extended through job rotation and job enlargement.
- In addition to learning directly through work, experience will normally need to be supplemented by inputs of training. (Jessup, 1991, p. 97)

Although Jessup's list seems very demanding, we might nevertheless expect it to be acceptable in a management climate where the published advice of Tom Peters has achieved an almost talismanic status:

Train everyone — lavishly;
Invest in human capital as much as in hardware;
Train everyone in problem-solving techniques to contribute to quality improvement;
Train managers every time they advance;
Consider doubling or tripling your training and retraining budget . . . (Peters, 1987, pp. 322–4)

Peters' advice on training is part of a hard-headed managerial strategy for 'beating the competition through skill enhancement' (p. 324). In similar vein, another well-known management consultant argues that in order to be able to adapt and develop without sudden and wasteful upheavals organizations need to become 'learning companies'. For this they require a 'learning climate':

In a Learning Company managers see their primary task as facilitating members' experimentation and learning from experience. It is normal to take time out to seek feedback, to obtain data to aid understanding. Senior managers give a lead in questioning their own ideas, attitudes, and actions. (Pedler, *et al.*, 1991, p. 23)

However, as Duckenfield and Stirner imply, in their review of recent work-based learning projects funded by the UK Employment Department, the fact that an employer has adopted a *policy* 'specifically aimed at fostering a "learning culture"' merely heralds the arrival of what turns out in practice to be a fundamental dilemma:

How can a balance be maintained between the short-term business and commercial needs of an organisation . . . and the long-term learning needs of its employees? (Duckenfield and Stirner, 1992, p. 26, p. 29)

In the context of a Social Services Department, the organizational needs are 'operational' rather than directly 'commercial', but the key issue is the same: current employing organizations are *not* in practice attuned to giving high priority to the development needs of their staff, in spite of the rhetoric of management theory itself (see above) and in spite of the committed partnerships between educational and employing institutions within which work-based learning projects (including the ASSET Programmes) have been established. In this chapter, therefore, we recount and try to interpret six long years' experience of grappling with the difficulties involved in trying to turn a familiar but innovative *concept* into a practical reality.

'Partnership': The Harmony of Educational Aims and Organizational Policies

Both of the ASSET Programmes were established as 'partnerships' between the university and an employer (see Chapter 2), and in both cases the employers had their own clearly perceived organizational motives for setting up the programme. Both Essex Social Services Department (SSD) and the Ford Motor Company wished to increase the opportunities for their staff to acquire academic qualifications: in the case of Ford, the UK staff were apparently 'less well qualified' than comparable staff in their German establishments, so there were important considerations of avoiding negative investment decisions on the part of the parent company in the USA and thus of securing continued employment; Essex SSD, for its part, had a wastefully high rate of staff turnover, and the management thought that by improving educational opportunities for their staff they would not only be conforming to government and professional policies concerning a 'continuum of training' but would also facilitate recruitment and improve staff retention rates, thereby making substantial financial savings. The competence-referenced, work-based format of the ASSET model seemed to offer a mode of training which would be *relevant* (as opposed to 'academic'), *flexible* (easily adapted to local needs and purposes) and *cost-effective*. Calculations easily demonstrated this last argument (see Maisch and Winter, 1992, Appendix D): although the costing of educational provision is notoriously inexact, it seemed obvious that, in principle, the ASSET model would require less absence from the work place by staff undertaking training and (once the initial documentation had been developed) less preparation and input on the part of tutors. Admittedly, the complexity and unfamiliarity of the procedures made these savings less than had been originally anticipated, but with growing familiarity in the part of all concerned, it could be predicted that the cost-benefit calculations, initially acceptable, would continue to improve. At this level, then the commitment of the employer to the programme seemed to be secure.

The organizational framework for the development of the work also attempted to ensure that the new programme would be fully 'owned' by the organizational management. In the case of Ford, operational managers were involved from the outset in regular monthly meetings to oversee and inform the sequence of decisions and documents. In the case of Essex SSD matters were complicated by the fact that the line management was regionally devolved while the training section had remained centralized, so that once the programme had been agreed in principle by the SSD management (as a county-wide initiative), the details were negotiated *not* with the (regionalized) line managers but with the (centralized) training section, whose own relationship with the regionalized line management was somewhat unclear.

The link between the social work ASSET Programme and the line management structure of Essex SSD was thus rather indirect. This may perhaps have contributed to the significant long-term issues described later as well as to early difficulties, e.g., over arranging for practitioners to be freed to attend Functional Analysis sessions, in marked contrast with the Ford project, where the direct involvement of line management enabled staff to be freed for this purpose relatively easily. Hence, in order to broaden the basis for our partnership with Essex SSD, and in an attempt to compensate for our lack of a direct link with the line management structure, we negotiated and documented a commonality of purpose and activity with the SSD Inspectorate; the SSD Policy, Planning, and Development section; and the Research section. Through a comparison between official policy statements representing these organizational dimensions and the emergent documentation of the ASSET Programme, common purposes were easily identified concerning the involvement of practitioners and clients in planning, developing, and evaluating the quality of the services provided (see the ASSET Programme handbook, Section 8).

In other words, the ASSET Programme seemed to offer a mode of professional development which was closely allied with the purposes of the employer since it was closely linked with the requirements of effective practice.[1] As one candidate observed:

> The competence based modules are excellent, very useful. It is helpful to look at your own practice. Theory is useless if it is not tied in with your practice. You can tell when you go on a taught course if a Tutor has not recently been in the workplace. These modules are about our practice — good practice — and the workplace is the best environment to examine your practice. You have to keep asking why you do such and such, and to know which theories are influencing your actions. The best place to do this is in the workplace with your clients.

This reference to tutors who have not recently been 'in the workplace' is significant. The tutors on the social work ASSET Programme are not university staff but members of Essex SSD Training Section. Without ignoring the complexities of our arguments concerning the relationship between practice and theoretical knowledge in Chapters 4, 5, and 6, it is important to note that this identification of programme *staff* with the employing organization rather than with the university has been helpful in avoiding conflicts between the practice-oriented criteria of the ASSET Programme and academically focused interpretations which could have been perceived both by candidates and their managers as somehow *extraneous* to the needs of the workplace.

Indeed it is precisely the practice focus of the ASSET Programme which appeals to candidates' line managers, as illustrated by the following quotations from managers' comments on recently completed evaluation forms:

> ASSET appears to be an effective method of continued learning which is valuable as it originates mainly in the workplace and can be the cause of instigating change.

In my view the ASSET model of training provides an effective method of ensuring that participants have not only assimilated knowledge by researching but have also confirmed it by practice application.

The positive aspect [of the programme] is the opportunity it has given the entire team (multi-disciplinary, qualified and unqualified) to join in and benefit from an ability to share ideas, value their own input, and learn.

Altogether, then, candidates' work for the programme promised to be completely aligned with practice itself. So much so, indeed, that we had to include in the handbook a detailed explanation as to how the programme staff would handle issues of academic confidentiality in relation to their wider professional responsibilities towards the department and its clients if candidates' work for the ASSET modules should inadvertently present evidence that was of legitimate concern to management — i.e., evidence of unacceptable individual practice or of inadequacies at the level of management, policy, or resources (see ASSET handbook, subsection 8.6, ASSET, 1996). Similarly, in order to avoid misunderstanding, the ASSET handbook also had to include a clarification that the programme was actually quite separate from the organizational 'Staff Development Review Scheme', all the more so, perhaps, because the official booklet explaining the scheme announced a set of purposes which seemed to echo exactly those of the ASSET Programme:

- the setting of agendas for professional development;
- the assessment of staff success in meeting agreed objectives;
- the establishment of a framework for constructive support of practitioners by management;
- the enhancement of staff morale; and
- the identification of training needs.

This harmony of purpose between the Social Services Department and the educational programme enabled the Training Section to allocate specific *funding* for staff undertaking ASSET modules, namely a sum equivalent to three hours per week 'remission' for each candidate for the notional duration of his or her work for the programme (in the light of our analysis of the average time required). This sum was allocated to the budget of the candidate's line manager for use as they see fit, in order to reduce the candidate's operational duties.

Tensions (1): Support and/or Assessment?

So far, so good. We had created a situation, it seemed, where the educational aims of the training programme coincided point-for-point with the aims of the employing organization, and where the employer was officially funding candidates to undertake the requisite work. Nevertheless, we were from the outset doubtful about the suggestion by NCVQ that the candidate's line manager should play the main role in both supporting and formally assessing the work undertaken (see NCVQ, 1989,

p. 73; Kelly, *et al.*, 1990). Our doubts were as follows. In general, any assessment procedure sets up a power relationship — of the assessor over the assessee. If the assessment outcome is to be seen as legitimate the roles of assessor and assessee must be institutionalized in such a way that this relationship of unequal power is non-problematic. Otherwise, the justifiability of the assessment is liable to be contested, which is why driving a car is more peacefully learned from a licensed driving instructor than from a spouse. In educational institutions the power of teaching staff (i.e., the assessors) is reinforced in two ways which help to make it relatively non-problematic, i.e., unlikely to be challenged: 1) with respect to the institution, staff are permanent, students are transient; 2) with respect to the area of knowledge, staff are experts, students are novices. But in the context of workplace assessment of professional practitioners by senior colleagues these features are not present: senior staff carrying out assessments will not necessarily have been longer in post, and their superior *status* as managers or team leaders will not *necessarily* be seen as conferring superior *expertise*, especially in relation to the practitioner's particular case load or responsibilities. In other words, the perceived legitimacy of assessments will be much more fragile when transferred from the relatively safe hierarchical order ('teachers' and 'taught') of an academic institution into the complex and ambiguous structure of professional working relationships.

We therefore decided that it would be safer to divide the role of the workplace supervisor into two components, support and assessment, and to place only the support function in the hands of the candidate's line manager, on the assumption that if this had any impact on their relationship it could be beneficial. The assessment function (which we saw as potentially more problematic) would be carried out by *another* senior colleague, i.e., not the candidate's line manager but perhaps the line manager of another candidate, so that any possible controversy surrounding the assessment would not carry over into an ongoing working relationship. This arrangement is more expensive, in that it may often entail travel, but we argued that this would not be a major difficulty since workplace observation formed only a relatively minor proportion of the evidence which candidates would provide (see Chapter 6). We also introduced this broad division of functions (support/summative assessment) into the tutorial role (see Chapter 6).

However, these issues (safeguarding the perceived legitimacy of assessment by managers and preventing the assessment process from having a disruptive effect on workplace relationships) were soon overtaken by another, even more important problem, namely that candidates' line managers often seemed unable or unwilling to become sufficiently involved in the programme to offer formal support for the candidates' work. In the light of what we said previously concerning the harmony between the aims of the programme, the purposes of practice and organizational policies, this seemed rather surprising, and this is the topic of the next section.

Tensions (2): Practice *or* Education?[2]

The basic problem is that the availability of *budgetary* support does not necessarily imply any other practical commitment to encouraging candidates' work for the programme on the part of their line managers. And line managers are under enormous operational pressures set by their own departmental heads: to meet deadlines, to achieve targets, to allocate cases to workers, to balance budgets. All of this takes place in a context where the number of available staff is progressively being reduced by the economic pressures being exerted by competitive market forces, either directly (as in the case of the Ford Motor Company) or indirectly, i.e., mediated through government policies of reducing 'public spending' (as in the case of social work). As two contributors to the *Personnel Journal* report:

> Getting budgets approved for training is hard today. Squeezed by unpar-
> alleled pressure for cost control and incessant demands for productivity
> gains, line managers are forced to make tough decisions between Human
> Resource-related programs, such as training, and alternative investments,
> such as automation. (Montebello and Haga, 1994, p. 83)

Managers thus often feel that they are not *able* to prioritize the effort of supporting the training of their staff.

This lack of support places candidates in a difficult position, as the urgent priorities and 'unexpected' emergencies of the practice setting continually swallow up time which participants had hoped to use for their ASSET Programme work. As one candidate put it: 'It's a bit like sitting officer-training exams whilst in the trenches under fire.' In other words, if they are physically present in the workplace the pressure to continue with operational duties is overpowering. One tutor reported the situation of her candidates as follows:

> Support from most of the managers really has been minimal. It depends
> mainly on the candidates. At one candidate's meeting a group told new-
> comers to the programme that they must just book the time in their diaries
> and just go away and do it. And that works, because managers won't stop
> them doing it; they just don't make it easy, because the operational demands
> are so acute. Some candidates have been able to build their work into their
> performance review, by saying that one of the performance objectives they
> wish to include is that they will complete an ASSET module. And then
> managers can't get away with it, once they allow it as a performance
> objective. So there are structures around that candidates can use. Some of
> them have managers that are better than others. The SSD has made the
> money available, it's just a question of finding out how to make sure you
> use it. The problem is that too much onus is still on the candidates to find
> out how to do it. The managers aren't being helpful or innovative.

This quotation brings out several important problems. We have already indic-
ated the pressures upon managers which mean that they will not be able to create space in which to be 'helpful' unless they succeed in being 'innovative' in responding to a work regime in which decision-making is circumscribed by formalized 'performance objectives'. Within such a regime, some candidates have clearly spotted

that staff training can be (and might need to be) protected by being itself expressed as a performance objective, both for themselves and (we may add) for managers. In other words, it may be quite possible (and very important) to establish that the 'performance' of managers is to be officially evaluated by (among other things) the training achievements of their staff. (This procedure is reported as already being implemented in a nationwide chain of retail stores — see Knasel and Meed, 1994, p. 52.)

Naturally, candidates report a variety of experience. Some candidates reported that their managers, who had undertaken conventional higher degrees, professed to have completed the work in their own time, and therefore expected the candidate to do likewise. Some managers may even experience a sense of threat when their staff undertake ASSET modules, not only because it may result in a situation where one of their supervisees may become more highly qualified than they are themselves, but also, in particular, because the production of a portfolio of evidence drawn from the workplace necessarily entails a description and examination of work practices for which the manager is accountable. From this point of view, some managers might even have their own motives for preferring conventional, theory-based training for their staff. On the other hand, some candidates used their participation on the programme to involve other team members, either by presenting material to them or leading a discussion, and involved their line manager in creating evidence for the programme by using 'supervision' sessions to record case discussions concerning clients the candidate was working with or had previously worked with. The most positive situation of all is where managers have themselves undertaken the ASSET Programme and are anxious for their team members to benefit from, and share, their experience. This state of affairs is becoming steadily, if slowly, more frequent: half of the thirteen candidates who graduated from the programme in January 1995 were first line managers, and in every case members of their staff have subsequently enrolled on the programme.

However, as yet this degree of support within the workplace is rare. More frequently, candidates describe the low morale and shortage of staff which make them feel guilty about putting extra pressures on their colleagues through their work for the programme. One candidate said her team saw it as 'having a day off'. Another candidate said she was asked to give up the ASSET Programme by a team member because the team were 'too pushed'. Maybe this partly explains why candidates are so insistent that they are 'doing this for themselves'. One candidate said:

> I have learnt to be particularly thick skinned in taking time for myself to work at home. On my last study day I was phoned at home at least five times and couldn't concentrate on anything. I told my Manager I was taking another study day instead and he was really put out.

Another candidate observed:

> It is a problem if you are making it too obvious that you are doing it [writing up material] at work, so I do it at home.

Clearly, these are very painful pressures, and some candidates respond not by blaming the short-comings of their colleagues or their managers but by blaming themselves for their own 'lack of self-discipline', and commenting that they 'need to organize their time more systematically'. This points to a further dimension of the problem: in a work situation which is so highly determined by external deadlines, it actually may be very stressful to be given, suddenly, so much responsibility for organizing one's own time and to decide upon one's own purposes. Hence there is a risk that one side-effect of the programme may be to reveal to candidates the extent to which they have been socialized into dependency upon the very external pressures which they resent. In this way, a programme aiming to enhance morale through providing an opportunity for staff to take control of their own professional development could result, ironically, in undermining candidates' self-confidence. From this point of view the very flexibility of the programme procedures is ambiguous: on the one hand it feels positive, because, as one candidate put it, 'it allows you to think widely and to tailor the study to your own needs'; on the other hand it feels negative, engendering insecurity and anxiety, due to the lack of a clear external directive as to 'what is required'.

This 'internalization' of the tensions of the workplace as a site of education was more common in the first two years of the programme, when we were all (candidates and tutors) relatively unprepared for the strains that the novel format of the work would generate. More recently, the tension between the programme and the workplace has created a rather different emphasis, namely a sense (for some social workers at least) that their workplace is not an environment in which the elements of competence described by the ASSET Programme can be demonstrated. The work of one candidate, for example, drew the response from the external examiner that it indicated a 'poverty of experience', that she seemed professionally 'isolated', that she needed to 'change her job', and, as the candidate's tutor confirmed, needed 'colleagues that she can talk to'. In some cases, indeed, candidates have found themselves facing a stark choice: seeking an alternative position within the organization or withdrawing from the programme. Sometimes, in such cases, tutorial support has been increased, and, if the candidate requests it, liaison with the line manager has also taken place. The majority of those workers who in the end decided to change jobs were already dissatisfied with particular practices and/or management styles, and enrolment on the programme was the catalyst for resolving their situation.

Considerations like those mentioned above have led us to become increasingly concerned over the disproportionate number of social workers in Child Care fieldwork teams who have been unable to complete the programme because of the crisis-ridden nature of their work and the demands of the workplace in terms of time and emotional energy. None of the first cohort of thirteen candidates who recently graduated is from a fieldwork Child Care team, although this area of specialism was the original focus for the ASSET initiative. At the request of these candidates, therefore, representation from the ASSET Programme Committee has been made to the manager responsible for Social Services training, which may result in greater support for Child Care workers undertaking the programme.

In this way, the attempt to use the workplace as a location for professional education has begun to pose a series of challenges to existing workplace arrangements. However, the tensions involved go beyond merely matters of support and encouragement. Many candidates found that, having examined the ASSET Programme competence statements and Core Assessment Criteria, they are in the position of having to address the *conflicts* between the demands of the competence-based training programme and the demands of an employing organization which seems to have a different approach to professional intervention and even a different value-base. Consequently, at a meeting of the Programme Committee in 1995 candidates' representatives voiced a desire to meet with the Director of the Social Services Department to express their concern that current levels of staffing and resourcing were leading to practices which did not conform to the standards embodied in the ASSET Programme competence statements and criteria, and that this was beginning to limit the ability of staff to present adequate workplace evidence to fulfil the programme requirements.

This state of affairs was not entirely unexpected. The ASSET Programme was intended as a vehicle for the *improvement* of practice standards, and thus, implicitly as a basis for challenges to current practices. Indeed, some competence statements assume that the organization will not always act wholly in the client's best interests, since it necessarily operates within a culture and a set of economic circumstances where the government as a stakeholder may shape and constrain the organization's activities according to policies which seem (in effect at least) to be inimical to the needs and interests of many social work client categories. One of the arguments of Chapter 4, in particular, is that the professional role is not simply to 'follow' existing organizational procedures, but also includes identifying occasions where the individual's responsibility is to submit current practice to critical evaluation and, if necessary, to challenge them. Hence the inclusion within the programme of such competence statements as:

> Apply appropriate pressure to local authorities where local policies do not fully comply with legal requirements. (Core Social Work Module 3)

> Work with colleagues to help them develop strategies to guard against unrealistic expectations (their own and others). (Core Social Work Module 2)

> Recognise and challenge the ways in which legislation, regulations and policies can be used to justify discriminatory judgements in particular cases. (Core Social Work Module 1)

Thus, one candidate, for example, as part of her work for the programme, photographed the outside of the Social Work Area Office to show how inaccessible it was to clients with a disability and called a meeting with senior members of staff to draw their attention to the problem; this resulted in structural changes to the building and the provision of extra parking spaces.

In other words, some of the competence statements appropriately spell out the potential *tension*, to be expected within any actual workplace, between professional values and material constraints. Indeed, it is from this tension above all that the motive and the pressure for developmental change arises, and management *theory* recognizes that an organisation *needs* a critical, evaluative stance on the part of its staff if it is to remain 'responsive' to its clients and its environment, and hence if it is to survive:

> Knowledge workers . . . must motivate themselves. No one can direct them. They have to direct themselves. Above all, no one can supervise them. They are the guardians of their own standards, performance and objectives. They can be productive only if they are responsible for their own job. (Drucker, 1991 [1974], p. 242)

> It is important to identify the process *owners* [i.e., 'front-line' staff, 'practitioners']. These are the people who influence and control the process on a minute-by-minute, daily basis and are therefore well qualified to advise and comment . . . Do your staff feel able to criticise each process? (Hakes, 1991, pp. 14–16)

> In Total Quality Control middle management will frequently be talked about and criticised. Be prepared. (Ishikawa, 1985, p. 89)

However, as we have already noted in the case of the commitment to training, there is always a gap between the policies that management as a whole espouses and the practices that specific managers enact. In particular, candidates notice the discrepancy between, on the one hand, managerial values of supportiveness and consultation and, on the other hand, the sometimes oppressive styles and practices they experience in their own work context. The question then must be: can the ASSET Programme be instrumental in shaping and changing organizational cultures, or do candidates have to 'play safe' and only make 'challenges' which are within the policies and practices of their organization and acceptable to their immediate superiors? We have learned over the past few years not to underestimate the power that individuals can exercise in an organization. Many candidates on the ASSET Programme are highly motivated, critical and self aware; they have joined the programme in order to develop their understanding and to reaffirm their practice value-base, which they feel is being eroded by organizational pressures. And in many cases this is indeed the focus of their work — see Chapter 7, example 4.

In the light of these various considerations, then, it is not surprising that the arrangements for providing support for candidates' work have not turned out to be simply an extension of the workplace relationship between the candidate and their line manager, as our interpretation of the current emphasis of so much management theory had led us to hope. These relationships may indeed be *potentially* supportive, but in practice the supportive dimension is so eroded by the external pressures upon both parties, that its supportiveness is, at best, vulnerable to continual interruption.

In any case, our problem turned out to be much simpler: once the pilot stage of the work had ended we found that managers did not enrol for the mentor/supervisor training modules which we had devised from the outset, thinking that they would be crucial in the delivery of the programme. Our original plan had been that candidates would enrol on the programme at the same time as their line manager (enrolling for the mentor 'supervisor module') but after the pilot phase we were faced in almost every case with candidates who wished to enrol, but whose line manager felt unable to do more in the way of support than to sign a form indicating that he or she was in general agreement that the candidate should undertake the work.

Our disappointment in this respect has been echoed in the experience of the staff implementing the ASSET model in Strathclyde Social Services Department (Glasgow, Scotland): they also are finding that line managers are experiencing enormous difficulty in ensuring that candidates are provided with time in the workplace to undertake the preparation of their portfolios, and that managers are *not* volunteering to undertake the supervisors' training modules.

It is important to stress that this is not simply a tension between operationally driven managers and educationally eager practitioners, but (also) a tension *within* management culture (see below). Neither is it uniquely a feature of social services departments. In the Ford ASSET project, for example, there was, as in the Social Work Project, no difficulty in recruiting a small number of supervisors to take part in the pilot phase of the work, and their enthusiastic support was noted by candidates in their response to an interim evaluation questionnaire (Guise *et al.*, 1994, p. 6). However, the Ford supervisors also drew attention to 'lack of proper and systematic resourcing' (op. cit., p. 8), explaining in a collective memo to the Programme Team:

> We haven't really adequately resourced the training effort; e.g., loss of people to [training] means we're understaffed . . . We need to get some consistent policy on candidates' time allowance at work for work not directly 'work' based, i.e., ASSET overhead . . . Ford need to re-align budgets to formally recognise training effort, e.g., an engineer on [a training Programme] = 80 per cent at best of a head. Recognising this will help supervisors with realistic budgets, so enabling proper training time to be allocated to engineers [engaged in study]. Ditto supervisors' time.

It therefore seems likely that in the Ford context also the familiar tension between organizational operations and staff development will begin to emerge, once the intense initial efforts made possible by external funding and the halo effects of a high profile innovation gradually give way to the routine procedures and expectations of an established training model.

The ASSET Programmes are not alone in noting this tension. On the one hand, in principle, managers fully appreciate the benefits to the employing organization of their involvement in work-based education:

> I don't know if this is peculiar to pharmacy, but the supervisors were absolutely delighted to be in on the act. They were saying to us we're finding

that we are learning from this, because we're having to be on our toes to keep up with what we're supposed to be telling the students. (quoted in Duckenfield and Stirner, 1992, p. 28)

Involvement in work-based learning has been a sort of indirect staff development for us. (Learning from Experience Trust, 1993, p. 17)

See also the appreciative comments from Essex Social Services managers quoted above. And in principle also, a 'learning environment' in the workplace *can* be created by the way in which work itself is organized and by grafting supportive functions onto colleague relationships (as with 'mentoring') (see Knasel and Meed, 1994, pp. 51–4). However, on the other hand, it is equally true that many managers find it difficult to sustain *in practice* a sense of the importance of the training and development of their staff. Gerald Dearden, reporting on work-based learning initiatives in computer manufacture, car production, construction, and in the civil service, observed:

There is no doubt that one of the reasons for some withdrawals from the project was lack of interest and support from line managers. (Dearden, 1989, p. 18)

Space for Learning: The 'Peer-Group' Process

In order to respond positively to this situation we decided that the programme needed to provide further support for candidates' work, in a form which would be less dependent on the candidate's line manager. This 'alternative' supportive relationship, which has become central to the organization of the ASSET model, although it was initially introduced rather as an afterthought, is the 'Peer Group Process', i.e., a series of meetings between candidates ('peers') engaged in preparing a module portfolio, where candidates share their planning and examples of evidence, etc., and where a tutor acts in the role of facilitator for the group process. The following brief description of the arrangements for peer groups is taken from the Social Work Programme handbook. (The full description of the arrangements is reproduced in Appendix E.)

The principle underlying the Peer-Group Process is that, given a properly structured sequence of meetings, a group of candidates can provide sufficient support and opportunity for their own mutual learning, so that:

a) The role of Supervisor becomes less crucial, and thus will *not* necessitate prior training;

b) Tutors will only need to provide individual support intermittently, except when it becomes clear that a candidate is having difficulty in meeting the requirements of the process;

c) Observation of practice (otherwise undertaken by a Supervisor) can be undertaken on a mutual basis by the group of candidates (i.e., in a group of five: A observes B, B observes C, C observes D, D observes E, E observes A), with the tutor monitoring the quality of the observation reports.

For each module there is a sequence of five meetings. These meetings will be in work time. The first meeting usually involves peer discussion of draft Module Action Plans and discussion of individual candidates' workplace support. The second and third meetings usually concentrate on peer discussion of examples of evidence in relation to competence statements and Core Assessment Criteria (together with commentaries and explanations) and peer discussion of observation reports. The fourth meeting may consist largely of individual tutorials and the fifth meeting involves peer discussion of draft module portfolios.

The significance of the Peer Group Process as the critical mode of learning support within the ASSET model is echoed by Engestrom's emphasis on 'learning as collaboration' in his report for the International Labour Organization on new methods for effective work-based 'training for change' (Engestrom, 1994, p. 37 ff.). Many of the detailed procedures for the work of the peer groups are derived from those of 'action learning', in which a group of staff agree to work collaboratively to support one another in practical problem-solving tasks, as a way of liberating the learning process from the dependency relationships characteristic both of employment contexts and of conventionally taught educational courses (McGill and Beaty, 1992, pp. 12–13). McGill and Beaty argue that although the outcomes of learning may be 'practical', the process requires the provision of 'a concentrated period of time . . . for reflection [as] the essential link between past action and more effective future action' and that this time for reflection does *not* spontaneously occur within the pressures of everyday experience (McGill and Beaty, p. 17).

This last point is of key significance. The ASSET tutors report that an ongoing theme of Peer Group meetings is mutual support for individual members in trying to cope with the absence of direct support from their line managers in resisting the pressures of the workplace. One candidate, for example, left a meeting saying, 'Right, now I'm going back there and I'm to keep saying to myself, "Just say, No!"'. The importance of this aspect of the work of the groups means that one of the first issues that peer groups need to discuss is that of *commitment* to the Peer Group process, i.e., to attending all meetings, bringing along evidence for discussion, and supporting and challenging one another (see McGill and Beaty, 1992, pp. 19–51).

Within the Peer Group the learning process is derived from the balance between the similarity of members' agendas and the difference of their individual resources, in terms of the variety of their knowledge and experience. So far we have interpreted this to mean that all members of a peer group must be undertaking the same module but in different work contexts. Clearly, this entails a significant loss of flexibility within the overall model (i.e., a limitation in candidates' potential choice of modules to those selected at the same time by a number of other candidates), and so it seemed important to experiment at least with peer groups whose members are simultaneously undertaking *different* modules. At present we are only trying this arrangement with groups of candidates who have already successfully completed at least one competence-based module, but the indications are that it is proving to be feasible (see Chapter 10). In this case the *similarity* of agenda is represented by the sequence of tasks involved in the process of analysing the competence statements and Core Assessment Criteria, identifying appropriate evidence in relation to these two dimensions of specification, and organizing the portfolio into an easily readable text.

The learning process, then, is one of *sharing* one's ideas, as *possibly* relevant, and *listening* to the ideas of others in order to re-frame their potential significance for oneself. The interchange focuses on the relationship between the competence statements/Core Assessment Criteria and the details of one's own practice experience, and moves between the exchange of anecdotes and the exchange of theoretical interpretations to become a process of raising awareness concerning issues in evaluating standards of practice. Differences in perspective and experience between Peer Group members are thus group resources for learning, but this of course requires an openness to alternatives which is only potentially liberating because it usually requires a conscious effort on the part of group members. Hence the importance of the tutor's facilitative role, if only in drawing the group's attention to their own previously agreed ground rules for the interactive process (e.g., no interruptions, politeness in framing disagreements, acceptance of criticism, etc.). Tutors do also contribute their own ideas, of course, and even learning materials, on the basis of their familiarity with the module content and the programme procedures and their own experience of preparing and presenting a portfolio (see Chapter 6).

In this way, the Peer Group aims at constructing a 'safe space' for the exploration of possibilities, and thus necessarily a space of *trust*, free from the hierarchies and competitiveness of *organizational* relationships, where an open disagreement or an innovatory proposal can often feel like the taking of a serious risk (see next section). ASSET candidates have commented on the reality of this contrast between the 'freedom' of the learning focused relationships of the Peer Group and the defensive, even fearful tone of the 'operational' relationships of the workplace. The nature and origins of this contrast are discussed below, but at this stage two important points need to be made. The first is that each learning group needs to *create* its own sense of trust and this requires significant interpersonal skills on the part of its members (McGill and Beaty, 1992, Chapters 9 and 10). Even though in theory these skills correspond exactly with the ideal 'teamwork' skills of the professional role (the ability to listen, to empathize, to give and receive feedback, for example) most of us tend to interact spontaneously in ways which fall far short of this ideal, and so there is always a substantial task (above all for the tutor) of dispelling anxieties and/or of managing emotional tensions, both those imported from the workplace (e.g., concerning differences in status and length of experience between group members) and those inherent in the learning process (e.g., concerning one's perception of one's own 'ability' and the 'difficulty' of the task). The second point to be made is the importance for effective learning of trust and self-confidence on the part of learners, and the negative impact on the ability to learn of anxiety and fear. This is one of the relatively few uncontested areas of educational theory, drawing support from traditions as disparate as behaviourist theories of the superiority of 'positive reinforcement' over 'negative reinforcement' and counselling-based theories of 'positive regard', and echoed by management theories of 'open-ness' (see Senge, 1990, Chapter 13) and the 'no-blame culture' (for example, Handy, 1991, p. 104).

To illustrate the nature of the 'supportiveness' of the Peer Group, and how its tensions are addressed and managed, we include here extracts from one tutor's notes, based on a tape-recording of a group meeting.

> **R** then asks about using evidence for more than one element, and I hold back and let **M** [a more experienced candidate] answer. I realise that two more recently qualified members haven't said anything for a while and offer them the opportunity to come in, recognising that we might be moving too fast . . . I ask if everyone is o.k. about this element, and as the group seems to be clear, I go on to discuss the Core Assessment Criteria. I am aware that **F** has not contributed as much as everybody else: is she struggling with what is required, or simply gaining from listening to the others? There is always the danger of those with more experience taking the lead and widening the distance between them and the less confident members.
>
> **B** says that she feels left behind because everyone else is more experienced. The group immediately spring into action and reassure her that she is not at a disadvantage because, being fresh from the [qualifying] Diploma, she is not stuck in one way of thinking and that she had done more recent work on the subject. **M** says that although **B** might think what a lot of experience the rest of us have had, it was quite a stuggle for them to pick out the relevant bits and put them into the right form. **S** agrees, saying that her qualifying course was so many years ago that she isn't trained to think in this way. **B** goes on to say that each situation is challenging, and is interrupted by **R** who says that is how it should be and is (he is sure) for each one of them. **D** talks about a general raising of awareness in relation to the issue and **R** says that because of people's experience there is a danger of working by rote and missing a lot of stuff, and therefore having to change their practice, whereas **B** is coming to it all fresh. . . .

Our general argument is that this mutually supportive interaction and encouraging facilitation is what is *required* for effective learning. We agree that, in principle workplace relationships between colleagues and between managers and their staff *could* provide support of this order and consistency. We also note that many writers on organizational management even argue that workplace relationships *need* to be supportive and educative, if the organization is to be effective in its own terms.

However, the current reality for many ASSET candidates is that their workplace does *not* easily foster relationships which provide this form and level of support for staff education. We therefore concluded that the educative process of the programme could not simply rely upon workplace relationships, and that a separate form of relationship needed to be established to provide this necessary 'space for learning'. Hence the significance of the Peer Group Process within the ASSET model.

However, we cannot leave this crucial issue, the feasibility of the notion of the educative workplace, without considering the *generalizability* of our experience and our solution. Is the ASSET Programme's reliance on peer learning groups perhaps the result of an *unfortunate* experience, a regrettable compromise, ignoring the possible transformation of the workplace *itself* into a directly educative environment (as some management theorists seem to envisage)? Or is the ASSET Peer-Group (or something like it) perhaps a *necessary* feature of effective long-term institutional partnerships between higher education and the world of work? Are there, in other words, such deep-seated differences between an educational process and a system of production or service delivery, that the two cannot simply be *merged* but require a specific 'bridging' element? In the final section of this chapter we attempt to construct a theoretical perspective with which to interpret the ASSET experience, in order to confront this issue in general terms.

The Educative Workplace: A Theoretical Evaluation

We have already noted that some ASSET candidates have experienced positive and substantial support in the workplace from their line managers but that others have not. How shall we set about understanding which of these two differing experiences is the more significant, and why? Let us begin by emphasizing that *both* experiences (the positive and the negative) seem to have echoes in the general literature on organizations.

On the one hand, there is a specifically 'educational' theme in much recent literature on organizational management, and this theme is not presented as mere theoretical speculation but as urgent practical advice:

> The most successful corporation of the 1990s will be something called a learning organisation. The ability to learn faster than your competitors ... may be the only sustainable competitive advantage.
> Learning Organisations [are] organisations where ... new and expansive patterns of thinking are nurtured, where collective aspiration is set free, and where people are continually learning how to learn together. (Senge, 1990, p. 4; p. 3)

Some educationalists may perhaps raise an eyebrow at Senge's emphasis on 'collective' aspiration and on learning *together*, wishing to argue that 'education' is typically an *individual* achievement, but others, with no particular commitment to work-based education, could equally point to the general literature on the value of 'collaborative learning' (Vygotsky, 1962; Barnes, 1976; Hopper, 1987) and to the ancient notion of the university as a 'community' of scholars who learn from each other at least as much as from a formal 'teacher' (Newman, 1982 [1852], p. 110) as well as to recent theoretical formulations of truth and self-understanding as located in the interchange of free and critical conversation (Habermas, 1978; Rorty, 1979). For the present argument it is also significant that for Habermas *work* and *power* are (along with language) the 'media' in which knowledge and understanding are expressed (Habermas, *ibid.*, p. 313). We have, then, a strongly articulated theory of a potentially close link between educational processes and the activities of organizations producing goods or delivering services.

But let us contrast this with an authoritative negative vision of *anti-educational* organizations presented by W.E. Deming, the originator of many of the ideas behind 'learning organizations' and one of the classic exponents of modern management theory in general. In 1986 he published a portrayal of a profound economic, cognitive, and ethical 'crisis' of organizational life. Organizations, he says, are dominated by lack of long-term planning, by short-term financial policies, by decision-making based on superficial performance indicators which measure only what is easy to measure, not what is important, by 'job-hopping' managers and staff committed only to their own careers rather than to the quality of their work, by resistance to 'new knowledge' because 'it may disclose . . . failings, and by an oppressive climate of fear generated by the invidious comparative 'appraisal' of individuals, leading to the inhibition of creative team-work and rivalry in the pursuit of reward and the avoidance of blame (Deming, 1986, Chapters 2 and 3).

What is the relationship between these two visions? We might, for example, follow Brown (1995) and see Senge's optimism and Deming's gloom in terms of the contrast between the 'espoused culture' of modern organizations and their 'culture-in-practice'. 'Espoused' culture refers to a 'desired state' of the organization and 'culture-in-practice' refers to the actual culture as experienced by employees (Brown, 1995, p. 26).

> The recognition of the existence of separately identifiable cultures-in-practice in organisations helps us to understand why so many organisational cultures appear confused and contradictory. Interestingly, large numbers of individuals seem to be able to tolerate high degrees of inconsistency between the espoused and actual cultures of the organisations in which they work. (*ibid.*)

Brown goes on to suggest that some individuals fail to distinguish between the two while others accept the differences as part of the psychological contract they have entered into on joining the organization.

How, then, shall we understand the coexistence within one organization of very different perceptions of its culture? McGregor's (1960) explanation is in terms of differences between individuals, i.e., that different individuals subscribe to one or other of two general belief systems concerning 'human nature'. Those who accept

McGregor's 'Theory X' believe that, on the whole people are self-centred, irresponsible, resistant to change, and in need of authoritative direction. In contrast, adherents of McGregor's 'Theory Y' believe that 'by nature' people are responsible, creative and innovative, and that effective management involves not 'direction' but creating the conditions in which staff can realize their potential for development and autonomy (Handy, 1985, p. 33).

This would seem to suggest that the problem of establishing an educative workplace is a problem of finding enough of the 'right sort' of individuals to lead the initiative and of gradually 'converting' the rest. But this leaves us with three further questions.

1) What factors affect individuals' commitment to one of these belief systems rather than the other?
2) In a given employment context (in which we may wish to institute an 'educative' approach to organizational life) what ratio of Theory X and Theory Y staff are we likely to encounter?
3) What are the chances that Theory Y-oriented managers will be able to persuade their Theory X colleagues and subordinates to a 'change their minds' and alter their behaviour?

As regards the latter question, at least, the influential work of Argyris (1982) emphasizes the difficulties involved. He notes that people can often easily spot contradictions in others' behaviour, but are bewildered by their inability to avoid similar behaviour themselves (op. cit., p. 38). Thus, Argyris reminds us that people may become *trapped* into counterproductive modes of thought and interaction by a contradiction between their purposes and forms of action sincerely intended to realize those purposes.

The work of Argyris therefore alerts us to another and more helpful way of conceptualizing the relationship between our two contrasting images of organizations, namely that they are generated by contradictions inherent in the structure of organizational life itself. This approach accepts the equal reality and significance of both images, the real possibilities for an educative workplace and the real difficulties, both of which we have seen illustrated in the experience of the ASSET Programme candidates and their managers, as described above. The argument, then, is by no means that the problems identified by, for example, Deming are insoluble; on the contrary, the existence of a contradiction means that something somewhere, somehow is going to have to change. But it does mean that the problems are deeply rooted and that change towards the ideal articulated by, for example, Senge will be a lengthy process. In the next subsection, therefore, we identify three illustrative examples of *inherently* problematic features of current organizational life (see Winter, 1995a, for further examples) each of which suggests that although there are indeed indications that the realization of the educative workplace may be theoretically possible, there are contradictory features which suggest that it will be difficult to achieve in practice.

Three Problems for the Learning Organization

Firstly, perhaps the most widely influential concept in modern management theory's projection of organizational life as site for learning is the Quality Control Circle (QCC). This is intended to create a commitment on the part of *all* staff to corporate objectives by enabling them to participate in determining and developing the quality of organizational work through team discussion and critique of current procedures (Hutchins, 1988; Hakes, 1991). Quality Control Circles, then, are intended as an organizational structure which will increase staff morale through the decentralization of innovative initiative. And yet Ishikawa, probably the most influential exponent of QCC theory and practice, introduces the concept as follows:

> When the management decides on company-wide quality control it must standardise all processes and procedures and then boldly delegate authority to subordinates. (Ishikawa, 1985, p. 112)

But if 'all processes and procedures' have already been 'standardized', what is left to delegate? Policies and objectives, perhaps? (This is certainly the intention behind Kitson's (1990) 'Dynamic Standard Setting System' for nursing staff in hospitals.) But Ishikawa is quite clear that policies and objectives are to be set by senior management (Ishikawa, 1985, p. 60). In other words, there is a contradiction within the QCC concept between a central managerial authority and the aim of universal initiative in organizational decision-making. This in turn suggests an ambiguity in the very notion of 'a collective' identity and hence of *corporate* 'commitment': Ishikawa apparently sees no problem in assuming that 'consensus' will routinely be achieved on matters where there will inevitably be, as he himself asserts, a variety of viewpoints (Ishikawa, 1985, p. 51). The first contradiction, then is between hierarchical structures of organizational authority and the need (if that authority is to be effective) for widespread and decentralized initiative on the part of staff.

Secondly, a further contradiction emerges when we consider the function of *measurement* in organizational life. The measurement of outputs is central to the running of formal organizations, if only because information concerning the achievement or otherwise of organizational goals has to be communicated from the point where the work is taking place to centres of decision-making (prioritization, allocation of resources) located elsewhere. This was, indeed the origin of 'quality control', i.e., Deming's *statistical* methods of analysing the acceptability of variations in the 'quality' of organizational outputs. However, the problem is that many of the key factors are, in principle or at least in practice, impossible to 'measure' (as we have noted in parts of our argument about the assessment of educational outcomes). This is another of the main themes of Deming's own book, in some ways a gloomy retrospective evaluation of the impact of his own ideas:

> Focus on outcome (management by numbers, MBO [management by objectives] work-standards, meet specifications, zero defects, appraisal of performance) must be abolished. (Deming, 1986, p. 54)

He argues that managers frequently place too much emphasis on 'the bottom line' rather than on 'the actual problems of production' (Deming, 1986, p. 123) (or, we may add, on the 'actual' quality of professional services), and that decisions are all too often based on 'visible figures, with little or no consideration of figures that are unknown or unknowable' (*ibid.*, p. 98).

Clearly, if significant organizational authority is devoted to measuring matters which staff do not perceive as central to their professional values, we have a disincentive for staff to engage in an 'educative' sense in the development of their professional practices. Hence, a whole body of literature is emerging on the theme of how to evaluate (and indeed to measure) apparently unmeasurable 'extra' or 'discretionary' staff qualities (such as altruism, commitment beyond requirements, tolerance, supportiveness) under the heading of 'Organisational Citizenship Behaviour' (see, for example, Deluga, 1994; Posdakoff and Mackenzie, 1994).[3] But there is a danger that the attempt to measure and differentially reward such qualities will itself inhibit them; and in estimating the chances that organizational accounting procedures will be able to accommodate support for *educational* processes, it is particularly significant that Plant and Ryan conclude that even though it is possible to 'validate an organization's investment in training', it is nevertheless 'impossible' to measure its 'benefit' in the sense of establishing whether or not it has provided 'a proven solution to a business problem' (Plant and Ryan, 1992, p. 22, p. 29).

Finally, let us briefly consider the tension within organizations between two supposedly crucial conditions for effective production or service delivery: collaborative 'teamwork' (Senge, 1990, Chapter 12); and 'competition'. The principle of competition operates at two levels in modern organizations: individual/group relations and corporate relations. Concerning the former, Deming's criticism of the effects of competition is precisely that they have a negative impact on teamwork:

> *Stifling Teamwork*: Evaluation of [individual] performance explains, I believe, why it is difficult for staff areas to work together for the good of the company . . . Result: every man for himself.
> I am afraid to contribute my best efforts to a partner or a team because someone else, because of my contribution, may get a higher rating than I get [Quotation from a member of staff]. (Deming, 1986, p. 107; p. 60)

This highlights the problems created by the tension between the 'meritocratic' and individualistic principle of reward which is generally characteristic of western society and the desire to create a 'collective' identification on the part of their staff with organizational values, styles and objectives. We have already noted typically 'western' attempts to resolve this tension within organizational life by attempting to harness the notion of 'citizenship', i.e., a contractual exchange of rights and obligations (see, in particular, Van Dyne *et al.* (1994)). From this point of view Ishikawa may have a rather more secure basis for such an argument, emphasizing that in Japanese organizations rewards do not depend on individual merit but on seniority and that since Japanese organizations conceive themselves as offering lifetime employment they are not competitive bureaucracies but 'family-like' (Ishikawa, 1985, p. 26, p. 28; see also Dore, 1994).

Let us suppose, then, that a single organization could be re-cast as a 'community', in which rewards did not depend on differentiating individual performances, where one's successes were therefore not at the expense of one's colleagues, where, as in the notion of the 'Learning Company' (Pedler *et al.*, 1991), all interactions are on a 'win–win' rather than a 'win–lose' basis (*ibid.*, p. 21). Even accepting these suppositions at the level of a single organization, we need to ask how far they are sustainable in a context of competition *between* organizations. Although inter-organizational competition is often presented as the key motive for establishing the educative workplace (see the quotations from Senge at the beginning of this section and from Peters), competition also poses a direct threat to education in the workplace, simply by creating a permanent drive to increase productivity by reducing costs (i.e., in particular staff *time*), through the transfer of jobs to more 'efficient' rival enterprises and frequently to lower wage economies. On this level, in other words, inter-organizational relationships are clearly and inevitably on a 'win–lose' basis. Hence the intense and unremitting pressure for immediate and short-term 'operational productivity, leading to what Toynbee (1994) calls 'the cult of overwork': 'if you don't work late, you haven't made it; lunch is for wimps.' When we sense a short-term threat to our very livelihood it is difficult to find the confidence to allocate time to the 'educative' processes of long-term planning and analysis, even though we may be well aware of the chorus of Deming, Senge, Peters, Pedler, etc., assuring us that the two are, in the end, *not* alternatives, but, on the contrary, inseparably linked. From this point of view, the coexistence of the widespread ideal of the learning organization with the equally widespread negative features described by Deming suggests that in important respects current organizational life, beset by a permanent sense of external threat, resembles a state of 'panic', i.e., a state where, by definition, behaviour is at variance with understanding, where understanding is not lacking, but *cannot* be implemented in practice.

Prospects

We do not present these problems as theoretically and ultimately insoluble. On the contrary, as we emphasized earlier, to identify contradictions is to identify areas where creative innovation may be expected, because it is required. (See, for example, the conviction in Heckscher and Donnellon (1994) that over the last forty years there has been a gradual (and still incomplete) emergence of a radically new 'Post-Bureaucratic' form of organization.) Where, then, might we look for new forms of organizational life which might ease the establishment of the educative workplace? Where might we find, therefore, new forms of accommodation between power hierarchies and participation, between teamwork and competition, between the need for verifiable accountability and the intangible quality of so much of human behaviour? One might, for example, point to the continuing significance and effectiveness of 'co-operative' forms of organization and production (see Whyte and Whyte, 1991; Thompson, 1994). Alternatively, some might wish to argue that the typically western combination of technical rationality, competitive meritocratic individualism and bureaucratic hierarchy is currently being challenged in interesting ways by the various emergent Asian modes of economic organization, with their differing combinations of religious values, respect for 'tradition', family orientation, state intervention, and nuanced acceptance of 'collectivized' identities (see Kawabe, 1991; Dore, 1994, Gun-Yung Lee, 1994; Wang Gungwu, 1995).[4]

More immediate and more easily interpreted, perhaps (for western organizations, at least) is the opportunity that may be offered by the increasing influence of women in managerial circles and hence in the determination of organizational cultures. It is important not to oversimplify this argument, of course, and we note the warnings in this respect of Yvonne Due Billing (1994), Stella Maile (1995), and, in particular, the emphasis by Collinson and Hearn (1994) that there are various versions of masculinity. However, it is significant that Frederic Swierczek and Georges Hirsch (1994), writing in the *European Management Journal* (not a publication renowned for a radically feminist editorial stance) include masculinity/feminity as one of four key variables in their analysis of management styles.

A number of gender-based differences have been proposed which would be highly significant for the establishment of an educational culture in the workplace. For example, Tannen (1992) suggests that men tend to approach conversational interactions as a negotiation for status and independence, as a 'contest . . . to achieve and maintain the upper hand if they can'; whereas women treat conversation as a negotiation for 'connection' in which 'people try to seek and give confirmation and support and to reach consensus' (pp. 24–5). From this point of view it is interesting to note the difference between Nancy Kline's description of the 'Thinking Environment', with its emphasis on listening, expression of appreciation, encouragement, and recognition of feelings (Kline, 1993, Chapter 2) and the competitive, antagonistic version of 'dialectical' discussion proposed by Mike Pedler and his (male) colleagues in their evocation of 'The Learning Company' (Pedler, *et al.*, 1991, p. 62). That there may be a gender-based cultural difference between 'adversarial' and 'empathetic' modes of collaborative understanding is also suggested by Belenky *et al.* (1986, p. 96, pp. 100–22). Other lines of argument focus on gendered differences in concern for the detail of particular situations, as opposed to universal rules (Gilligan, 1993), and a concern for experiential practicalities as opposed to abstractions (Smith, 1987; Savage and Witz, 1992).

The purpose of our argument is not to 'explain' gender-based differences such as those outlined here, although explanatory arguments have been proposed. Gilligan, for example, argues in her highly influential study of gender differences in socialization and identity formation (Gilligan, 1993 [1982] Chapter 1) that since the vast majority of carers of infants are women, girls do not (unlike boys) spend crucial years asserting their independence *against* their most significant 'Other', and this is the reason why they acquire a different balance between individualistic assertion (*against* others) and empathy (*with* others). Our argument, however, is merely that there are grounds for believing that women may be able to bring into organizational life a significantly new range of abilities, from which organizational staff in general (including men) will be able to benefit. Our basic argument, then, is simply that a more 'feminized' organizational culture might find it easier to follow Deming's urgent advice that 'leadership' must be reconstructed so that it involves, instead of acting as 'a judge' towards one's staff, acting instead in the role of colleague and counsellor, 'learning from them and with them' (Deming, 1986, p. 117).

Conclusion

Thus, finally, we return to the question of how far the educative workplace may be able to rely on the relationships established for its operational purposes and how far separate 'learning groups' may need to be introduced. If most managers were indeed 'counsellors' rather than 'judges' there would be no problem: the model of learning implicit in Kline's evocation of 'The Thinking Environment' (see above) and our earlier presentation of the conditions for effective 'action learning sets' (McGill and Beaty, 1992) which underpin the ASSET Peer Group process are consonant with (and influenced by) counselling approaches. But, we have argued, the pressures of life in many organizations are such that the majority of staff are *not* likely to have the time or the emotional space to act in a counselling role towards their colleagues or their subordinates. Thus, if the workplace is to become an educative environment, other relationships specifically devoted to that purpose are likely to be required. Hence our introduction of the Peer Group process.

This is not an eccentric conclusion: Pedler *et al.* (1991) suggest that for an organization to become a 'learning company' it will 'need to develop special pro-cedures' (p. 19), including 'courses, workshops, seminars, self-learning materials . . . development groups, one-to-one coaching/mentoring, peer-level one-to-one co-counselling' (p. 23). And Clutterbuck (1991), arguing that 'everyone needs a mentor', notes:

> Mentoring frequently works better if the roles of mentor and boss are not confused, not least because the two roles can on occasion be contradictory.
> (Clutterbuck, 1991, p. 6)

Thus, until and unless employment contexts have been transformed beyond current recognition, we are not inclined to see the ASSET Programme peer groups as a regrettable lapse from our wholehearted commitment to the notion of a genu-inely work-based educational process. Rather, we would argue that the ASSET Peer Group process is currently a necessary component in constructing a strong and durable bridge between the world of employment (where harsh actualities must be carefully distinguished from much current optimistic theory) and what Edward Said significantly termed 'the Utopian space' of education (Said, 1994, p. xxix). What we hear from the vast majority of ASSET candidates, and what we also con-clude from our theoretical analysis, is that practitioners engaged in reflecting upon their practice need such a space, a space where (without denying the tensions that can arise even in groups whose ostensible purpose is mutual educative support) the processes of critique, challenge, 're-framing', and the expression of doubt are still likely to receive more unambiguous endorsement than in the average workplace, even where managers may be sincerely committed to some variant of the idea of the 'learning organisation'.

Notes

1 In developing the social work ASSET Programme we also discussed our plans extensively with the local trade union representatives of the staff who would be involved (i.e., UNISON, then NALGO). Again, we found that the various aims and emphases of the ASSET model seemed to be non-controversial, as indeed our reading of the Trades Union Congress policy document on vocational education, *Skills 2000* (TUC, 1989), had led us to anticipate. In particular, the union welcomed the fact that the ASSET Programme seemed likely to give staff greater autonomy in acquiring formal qualifications which would improve their bargaining position on pay and promotion, in that they would be relatively less dependent on being 'picked' by managers to be 'released' for training 'events'. This was spotted (in passing and 'jocularly') by one Social Services senior manager on the Programme Steering Group as not entirely welcome, as a potential undermining of managerial control over staff training. However, this never became a significant issue in managers' response to the development of the programme, although it may well have been an important tacit awareness on the part of candidates.

2 This section is largely based on Maisch, 1996.

3 Our thanks for this information to Peter Stannack of 'Project North East', Newcastle-upon Tyne.

4. Our thanks to Alan Griffiths, Anglia Polytechnic University, for the information on which this point is based.

9 Evaluation 1995: The Social Work ASSET Programme after Five Years

The first group of candidates began work on the pilot phase of the Social Work ASSET Programme in 1991. By the spring of 1995, the Social Work Programme was thus approaching five years of operation and was due for its regular 'revalidation' by the university. So this seemed an appropriate time to carry out an overall review, to provide a 'systematic' check on our thinking and also to help us to answer more simply and with more confidence some of the blunt questions we were being asked. Questions like: 'Does it work?' 'Does it have any advantage over other curriculum formats?' We therefore sent out a questionnaire form to each candidate enrolled on the programme who had completed at least one of the competence-based modules. We also asked the candidates to give a (different) evaluation form to her or his manager. Copies of these forms are included as Appendix H. (NB. The candidates were *not* asked to put their names on the forms, and they did not do so.)

The key issues we had in mind in designing the questionnaire forms were:

- Does the ASSET model lead to an improvement in practice? (questions 5, 6 and 7h; managers question 3)
- How does the ASSET model compare with other forms of professional development? (question 8; managers question 4)
- We also wished to elicit a general sense of candidates' satisfaction or otherwise (questions 1 and 2) and to find out which aspects of the model were particularly significant in this respect (questions 3 and 4).
- In the light of our awareness of the problems identified in the previous chapter, we were also particularly interested in the issue of adequate support and the effectiveness of the workplace as a site for learning (questions 7f and 7g; managers questions 1 and 2).
- Finally, we wanted to give candidates the opportunity to comment on the different 'components' of the model (questions 7b, 7c, 7d, and 7e).

It is under these headings, therefore, that the following summary of the questionnaire responses is organized.

At this time, there were twenty-seven candidates enrolled on the programme who had completed at least one of the competence-based modules (including the fourteen candidates who graduated in 1995). We received completed questionnaire forms from twenty-three of these candidates. Our 'sample' of responses is thus very close to our 'total population' (an 85 per cent response rate), which means that we can provide relatively focused answers to the questions listed above by the use of summarizing percentages in presenting the results. (The 'key results' are asterisked and begin on a separate line.) We received responses from eight managers (out of the possible twenty-seven). Clearly this sample of managers may be biased by precisely the factors with which we are concerned (the degree of support they offer, the 'educativeness' or otherwise of the work context for which they are responsible). The managers' responses are therefore not used directly as a basis for generalization, but as a source of illustrative quotation to supplement our interpretation of the candidates' responses.

Improving Practice?

Candidates were asked: 'Do you feel that the work for the programme required you to *improve* your practice or simply to document what you were already doing?' Some responses suggested that this was something of a false opposition, that greater detail of documentation actually leads to more 'reflection': as one candidate noted, 'Both are inter-related and result in improved casework and recording.'

* Altogether 83 per cent replied that the work had resulted in improvements in their *practice*, often noting that this was due to an improvement in their *understanding* of practice:

> I felt it required me to improve practice as I had to reflect, research, evaluate, and keep up to date with literature.

Three candidates suggested either that the effect of the programme was increased reflection but *not* improvement in practice or that some (but not all) modules had indeed been largely a matter of documentation.

Later in the questionnaire candidates were asked a more open-ended question (7h): 'Please . . . comment . . . concerning . . . the general effect on your work of undertaking the Programme.'

* 30 per cent of candidates made a specific reference to the quality of their practice in their response.

* 33 per cent of candidates referred to increases in awareness, understanding, critical analysis, confidence, etc. but did *not* refer specifically to their practice as such. One candidate simply wrote: 'The Core Assessment Criteria has been a useful paradigm', which ought to be a reference to both awareness and practice but is difficult to interpret with any certainty! 11 per cent made no response and others picked out various different aspects altogether, such as increased stress or willingness to challenge departmental policies.

In order to sharpen up the issue as to whether the effect of the programme was 'merely' increased 'reflectiveness', candidates were asked about the impact of their work on their clients (Question 5).

* 30 per cent made no response on this, often because, as they explained, they were team leaders and thus not in direct contact with clients.

* 33 per cent said that their work had definitely had a beneficial impact on their clients:

> Some clients enjoyed my participation in the programme as they felt it was one way of helping me, rather than the other way round, and made them feel valued.

* In contrast, 22 per cent did not feel that their work had had any discernible impact on clients.

Managers were asked, 'Have you noticed any changes on the part of staff since they began working on the programme?' In general the responses were very positive, but we might have expected this, since we may assume that the managers who replied felt more involved with the programme than those who didn't. One manager did say that her lack of participation as supervisor (due to her own heavy workload) meant that she was regretfully unable to make any comment on the impact of the programme on the candidate's work, but the other seven mentioned various forms of development: improvements in self-awareness, increased professional understanding ('Significant reappraisal of social work issues') and also specific improvements in practice ('Equal opportunities and interview technique').

The ASSET model Compared with Other Formats for Professional Development

In many ways this is a crucial issue, but one which is very difficult to 'get at', since there are always so many factors involved in any given experience of professional development, and any one of them may 'intervene' and thus distort any attempt to make direct comparisons between the formats themselves. Question 8 asks candidates to compare the ASSET model with 'taught courses', 'workshops', and 'projects' in six different dimensions:

    A   the amount of learning achieved;
    B   the relevance of the learning to the candidate's work;
    C   the candidate's level of interest/motivation;
    D   the ease of managing the learning process;
    E   the convenience of the process; and
    F   the 'ratio' of achievement to effort.

The complex form of this question was an attempt to create directly comparative 'hard' data in response to the key question with which we were being challenged: 'Is the ASSET model better than its alternatives, or not?' However, candidates' responses suggest that this complexity may have been self-defeating: in five of the twenty-three responses question 8 was not completed, and those who answered this question used ticks, blanks, crosses and question-marks in ways which did not always seem to follow the instructions given. Hence, the following analysis must be treated with scepticism, in spite of the apparent precision of its format.

Four candidates ticked all six boxes (i.e., factors A–F above) in the ASSET model column, indicating, as it were, complete 'satisfaction' with the ASSET model. But of these, two candidates also ticked all the boxes in the 'taught course' column and two ticked all boxes in the 'project' column, thus apparently indicating equal satisfaction with other formats. One candidate only ticked boxes in the ASSET column, so again this did not produce any comparative data.

A rather simple indication of which format was preferred could be obtained merely by adding together the ticks placed in the various boxes, ignoring crosses, question-marks and blanks, as being of indeterminate meaning. However, this would not be a valid comparison, because some candidates may not tick any boxes in, say, the project column simply because they had no recent experience of that format, not because they were less than satisfied with it. So in the following grid, the total number of ticks in each box is divided by the number of candidates who ticked *any* box in that column. Thus, the 'ASSET' boxes have all been divided by 18 (since all candidates who answered the question filled in the ASSET column) but the totals in the 'workshop' boxes have been divided by 12, the number of candidates filling in that column. Similarly, the 'project' totals have been divided by 6 and the 'taught course' totals by 14. In the following grid, then, the highest score possible for a given box is 1, meaning that all candidates who considered this model of learning (i.e., this column) picked out this aspect (A–F), along with others, as being a positive feature.

Document 11

Comparison of the ASSET model with Other Learning Formats

		ASSET	Workshop	Project	Taught Course
A	Amount of learning achieved	0.78	0.58	0.83	0.64
B	Relevance of learning to work	0.94	0.41	0.50	0.57
C	Level of interest/ motivation	0.88	0.58	0.67	0.71
D	Ease of managing the learning process	0.44	0.75	0.50	0.71
E	'Convenience' of the learning process	0.50	0.58	0.50	0.57
F	The 'ratio' of learning achieved to the effort involved	0.55	0.25	0.67	0.57
Column Average		0.68	0.52	0.61	0.62

For example, fourteen out of eighteen candidates who made ticks in the 'ASSET' column placed a tick in row A ('Amount of learning achieved') giving a 'score' for that box of 14 divided by 18, i.e., 0.78. Similarly, of the fourteen candidates who put ticks in the 'taught course' column, 9 placed a tick in row A, giving a score for that box of 9 divided by 14, i.e., 0.64. And so on.

The finding that the ASSET model scores well for relevance and level of motivation and relatively low for ease, 'convenience', and ratio of achievement-to-effort comes as no surprise, although it is unclear what meaning candidates attached to some of the terms. That it scored higher than taught courses for 'amount of learning' is surprising, pleasing, and intriguing. That it scored overall higher than the other learning formats is also pleasing, but this, along with the other results on the grid, needs to be treated with caution: since candidates found the form of the question hard to interpret, we must acknowledge that the meaning of their answers is equally so. All we would wish to claim at this stage is that when candidates were given an opportunity to indicate that they preferred other more familiar modes of learning, they apparently did not do so.

Managers were asked: 'What is your view on the relative effectiveness of the ASSET model of professional training and other more conventional forms of training provision in which there is a greater "taught" element?' All of the eight managers' responses to this question endorsed the relative advantage of the ASSET model. For example, one of them replied:

> It seems to me that people develop at their own speed and according to their previous knowledge of the subject, which has to be an advantage.

Expectations, Pleasures and Difficulties

Candidates were asked about their expectations of the programme and how far they had been realized. Some responses concentrated on candidates' worries and hopes concerning the *process* of the work, while others indicated their motives and purposes for enrolling. Of the latter, the responses were evenly balanced between: wanting to obtain a degree qualification, wanting to update their knowledge, wanting to improve their practice, wanting a challenge, and wanting to engage in a form of learning that would be both individualized and work-based:

> To be able to study particular areas of interest which also relate to my work experience and specialism; to be able to structure the workload and timing to suit my own needs and demands on my time.

* 65 per cent of the candidates made very positive statements concerning how far their various expectations had been realized, but several referred to the problem of finding enough time for the work, which will be discussed later.

Question 3 asked candidates to indicate aspects of their work for the programme which had seemed 'particularly enjoyable/interesting/stimulating/valuable'. Responses were varied and predictable: two or three candidates mentioned, respectively: returning to study, particular modules or workshop sessions, the amount of individual choice, the effectiveness of the programme administration, tutorial support, the sense of increasing knowledge and skill in reflection. One candidate picked out the use of the Core Assessment Criteria and four candidates noted the process of demonstrating the competences.

* What was particularly significant, in the light of the argument in the previous chapter is that 50 per cent of all candidates mentioned the value of the Peer Group process in their response to this question. For example:

> Being a member of a Peer Group; this was shared learning, supportive, and a good experience.

* From this point of view it is also significant that by far the most commonly mentioned 'area of difficulty' mentioned in response to question 4 concerned the problem of finding or taking sufficient time to undertake the work. 52 per cent of candidates picked out this issue, although they were divided more or less equally as to whether they blamed the lack of available time on the pressures of the workplace or on their own ability to 'manage' their time. Three candidates specifically referred to a 'conflict' between the programme and the time constraints of the work context, and it seems particularly significant that they picked out this aspect in response to this very general question. All this leads us on directly to the theme of the next section.

Support for Learning in the Workplace

Question 7g asks candidates to comment on 'the suitability of the workplace as a learning context'. Two candidates did not respond to this question. Of the remainder:

* 38 per cent were enthusiastic. Comments included:

> Unparalleled!
> Good; it makes you examine and learn from your practice.

* 19 per cent were negative. For example:

> The pressure of work is not conducive to the learning process. Time out is needed for me to evaluate and think.

* 43 per cent referred to difficulties and drawbacks without implying a rejection of the *principle* that the workplace was an appropriate learning context:

> It would be beneficial to have constructive support in the workplace.
> More involvement and understanding by the line manager would have been useful.
> Good, but also subject to interruption/distraction.
> Overall it has worked well, but it has put additional work onto my colleagues.
> Easier in private practice than with the County Council.

When asked a general question about the adequacy of support/resources (question 7f) candidates' responses were interesting. 25 per cent of the responses were very general but positive (e.g., 'fine', 'satisfactory'). 7 per cent of the responses focused on the adequacy of library provision (positive). 54 per cent focused on tutorial and peer group support (all but one positive). Only 14 per cent made a reference to support in the workplace. This percentage figure represents four responses, and three of these were negative. For example:

> No support in the workplace from supervisor, through no fault of her own.

Thus, we have further confirmation of the argument of the previous chapter, that candidates are not experiencing strong support in the workplace, so that the term 'support' is likely to be interpreted as meaning: support from the tutor-led peer groups.

It is fortunate, therefore, that the Peer Group process received largely favourable comment.

* 55 per cent of the responses simply expressed appreciation, and a further 20 per cent mixed praise with criticism:

> Works well, but not enough time for each student to discuss individual work.
>
> This worked well for me (Distances sometimes problematic).

In 25 per cent of the responses, criticism dominated. There were a variety of complaints, e.g., lack of committment from fellow members, leading to the group being too small, lack of sufficient focus, and a desire for *specialist* tutorial assistance.

Clearly, the Peer Group process is sensitive to the vagaries of personality, circumstances, and individual learning styles. In the ASSET model it is the main 'bridge' between the workplace and the learning process, and as such it has to bear a heavy and complex load (see Chapter 8).

Other Components of the Model

Candidates were asked to comment on 'module content' (Question 7b) although not all did so.

* Of the nineteen candidates who did respond, twelve were unambiguously positive, using terms such as 'relevant', 'appropriate', 'wide ranging', and 'always searching and made you think'. One candidate simply wrote, 'Competences are complex', which may or may not have been intended as appreciative! Another candidate differentiated sharply between two of the general modules (on which the comment was very favourable) and one of the specialist modules, which was described as 'vague' (and which the programme team were already in process of reworking).

This left five candidates (out of nineteen) whose comments were critical. Of these, two found the wording ambiguous, one found the modules 'rigid', one complained that the elements were not always comparable in complexity and difficulty, and one (who had only recently completed her qualifying award) was taken aback by the unfamiliarity of the format.

Concerning the Module Action Plan (Question 7c).

* 50 per cent of the candidates who responded found the process unambiguously helpful and a further 20 per cent found it helpful but also the cause of some anxiety and delay: 30 per cent found it not sufficiently flexible to be fully worthwhile.

Question 7d, concerning 'assessment procedures' was answered on fewer than half of the questionnaire forms returned.

* Of the eleven candidates who did respond, eight were wholly positive, referring variously to the value of discussion with the tutor before submission of the port-folio, to the clarity of the explanations, to the promptness of tutorial response to work, and to the value of peer observation. One candidate used the gratifying phrase: 'rigorous yet supportive', which captures precisely our aims in this respect.

Another candidate commented wryly:

> I like to be able to work at my own pace but would prefer quicker feed-back; but perhaps I can't have it both ways!

The other two responses were critical. One candidate had found the final report on her portfolio 'rather vague', and the other commented that the process seemed 'very variable' and dependent on individual tutors' expectations and prior experience of the ASSET Programme, a timely reminder of the issue discussed in Chapter 6.

The meaning of a set of questionnaire returns is always a matter of interpreta-tion, but our task in this case was made a little easier by the very high response rate. On the whole we are encouraged that a large majority of candidates find the various aspects of the ASSET model to be, on the whole, satisfactory, and that they (and their managers — insofar as they are involved) find the work for the programme to be both intellectually stimulating and relevant to their practice. As a result of analysing these responses, our belief in the viability of the ASSET model is con-firmed, but we are also confirmed in our awareness of the difficulties entailed in establishing an innovative mode of learning and one which is highly vulnerable to external pressures, as outlined in the previous chapter.

10   Current and Future Developments[1]

The ASSET Programme is currently a fully operational system of post-qualifying professional development within the Essex Social Services Department and groups of practitioners in Cambridgeshire and Suffolk are also beginning to take part in the programme. At the time of writing (July, 1995) there are eighty-nine candidates enrolled altogether, of whom fourteen candidates have already graduated, four with First Class Honours. In the Ford Motor Company a second cohort of engineers is about to begin work following the pilot phase of the Ford ASSET project. Where do we go from here? On the whole, the foregoing chapters have indicated that the main features of the model seem to be effective and appreciated, and our main efforts will be devoted to trying to ensure that these features continue in being. However, a number of issues have arisen which seem to require attention, and in this necessarily brief chapter we describe the current direction of efforts taking place in the Social Work Programme to extend and refine the model as described so far. These efforts are concerned with:

- the issue of *the currency* and *authority* of the competence statements,
- the issue of *staffing* — how to maintain an expert community which is confident in its collective interpretation of an innovatory culture,
- the issue of *flexibility* — how to maintain an individualized learning process within a complex set of potentially prescriptive procedures; and
- Finally we describe how, in response to requests from our ASSET graduates, we are beginning to develop a *postgraduate* version of the ASSET model.

Refining the Competence-based Modules

In preparation for the forthcoming five-yearly review of the ASSET Programme as part of the university's routine quality assurance procedures, the next few months will witness a rigorous rationalization of all the competence-based modules. This will involve us (tutors) working very closely with candidates. To begin with, it has become obvious that some of the modules designated for particular client groups have qualities which could be applied to other client groups. In other words, a number of the 'units of competence' are relevant in more than one context. Some 'specialist' modules could therefore become core modules simply by the removal of references to specialist client groupings. There are several examples of modules available within a specialist field which could be 'released' in this way and offered as a 'core' module. This will obviously extend the range of modules available to candidates.

Secondly, we will spend time refining and (where necessary) reducing the number of competence statements in each module. The experience of working with the candidates, helping them to formulate module action plans and giving formative feedback on their evidence, provides invaluable and continuous evaluation of the relevance of the elements to practice and the appropriateness of the wording. For example, in the module 'Promoting clients' potential for independence' (see Chapter 3, Document 2) competence statement no. 7 (Demonstrate a practical understanding of the theoretical basis for the social worker's roles and responsibilities in work with clients) read until very recently: Demonstrate an *understanding* of the theoretical basis for the social worker's *authority*, responsibilities, and *methods of practice*. This version frequently caused confusion over what was required. On the one hand it was argued that the basis of the social worker's *authority* is legislative rather than 'theoretical'; on the other hand, we want candidates to demonstrate that they understand the role of the State in providing 'welfare' and the implications for their work of the fact that they are acting on behalf of the State. After much discussion, we concluded that it was the term 'authority' that was distracting attention from this otherwise familiar notion, and that by stressing a *practical* understanding of the theoretical basis of the *role*, we would help candidates to link the theory of their professional work to practice evidence. (See Chapter 5 on the 'embeddedness' of social work 'theory'.)

We also intend to concentrate on reducing the number of elements in each module. Where there are more than ten elements in a module, we find that there tends to be a significant amount of overlap, so that a reduction in the number of elements can reduce the amount of work for candidates without impairing the quality of the evidence. Elements will be selected out using criteria such as excessive complexity, duplication of other elements of competence, duplication of the Core Assessment Criteria, or appropriateness (in terms of professional values). As an example of the latter: the element of competence '*Work towards enabling the client to come to terms with their own feelings*' was recently removed from the Generic Module on 'Promoting Clients' Independence' (See Document 2) since it seems to imply a process of emotional *adjustment*, whereas the primary professional purpose of social work concerns *empowerment*.

The process of refining the statements of competence is an on-going activity and one to which candidates and tutors all contribute. The fact that we still envisage an extensive process of revision after five years is an important reinforcement of our argument in the final section of Chapter 3, in which we emphasised that a painstaking and rigorous process of deriving the competence statements does not mean that in the end their authority is absolute. Competence statements are *interpretations* of practice situations, and as such they are both historically situated and fallible. In this, of course, the ASSET competence statements are no different from those of NVQs: the structure and wording of the Training and Development 'national standards' document published in 1991 was entirely transformed in the revised version published in 1995 (see Winter, 1995b, for a critique of part of the text of the earlier version.)

Staffing

We are very aware that the ASSET Programme is relatively new and that its success currently depends on the energy of a small number of dedicated people. Its innovative nature and the specialist understanding and expertise required of the relatively few tutors who lead the programme make it vulnerable to sudden losses of staff with their unique knowledge. This is the achilles heel of the ASSET Programme: it depends at the moment too heavily on the specialist expertise and knowledge of a handful of tutors.

Thus, an immediate priority for the ASSET Programme is to have a greater number of trained tutors who can provide appropriate help and guidance to social workers endeavouring to produce portfolios of evidence. By necessity the requirements of the ASSET Programme are tightly structured and assessment procedures are rigorous with each portfolio marked by two tutors. The processes of the programme are explicitly detailed in the handbook with which tutors need to become entirely familiar. More importantly, tutors need to be sympathetic towards, have a full understanding of, and effectively implement the *philosophy* of the programme, and this requires an advanced understanding of adult learning principles, flexibility, and a commitment to student centred learning and professional values, in relation to the demonstration of competences on a degree level programme. Tutors are *catalysts*, enabling their tutees to become active participants in their own learning.

For the candidates this method of learning is still relatively unfamiliar and therefore unsafe. Many candidates express concern that there is a 'hidden agenda'; there is a suspicion that the tutor has something specific in mind in relation to the evidence for the elements of competence and that in order to pass candidates have to conform to a particular tutor's standards and expectations. (One candidate's evaluation form mentioned this — see Chapter 9.) On the other hand, this wariness on the part of candidates can be a useful means of restraining the enthusiasm of the programme team: occasionally we are tempted to progress too rapidly ideas which would be confusing for candidates still in the early stages of grappling with understanding the academic validity of professional practice.

Staff wishing to become a tutor on the ASSET Programme have to undertake a specific module, already validated within the university at postgraduate level. It involves, more than anything else, successful *experience* of working with the programme procedures, under supervision from an experienced tutor (see Chapter 6). At present the majority of the tutors are from Essex Social Services. This has worked well because, being less bound by the academic traditions of universities, they are more open and responsive to innovative assessment tasks and the value of practice evidence. The culture of social services training sections is one which provides structures for catering for the needs of adult learners and which values experience rather than purely intellectual endeavours. Within this culture, 'theory' is seen as a *social practice*: tutors who are confronted on a regular basis with real practice dilemmas recognize that theory must inform everyday conversation and connect with what happens in practice. Social services tutors are thus in a better position to help candidates make sense of the contradictions, purposes and values of their work. Writing in the context of teacher education, Fish (1995) describes the role of the tutor/mentor as helping practitioners to learn through practice and to (re)construct their own knowledge for themselves and each other by deliberating together.

However it will be important to have more university tutors. There needs to be a continued joint ownership of the programme and a true sense of partnership with equal weight given to the views of both institutions. University tutors may also help to avoid an over-reliance on prescribed outcomes, which risk merely reflecting current political ideologies and neglecting important theoretical disciplines which are increasingly being omitted from social work qualifying programmes. Without tutors from the university the ASSET Programme could inadvertently become entirely employer-led, with a subsequent loss of what is best about educational institutions promoting the cognitive basis of professional practice. Wilkin (1990, pp. 13–16) emphasizes the reciprocal interdependence between educational and employment institutions, and distinguishes between *the partnership of complementarity*, as one in which 'each party might take responsibility for different parts of the course with a balance in overall distribution' and *the partnership of equivalence*, as one where 'both parties share equally in all areas and have no special expertise' (quoted in Fish, 1995, p. 25). The 'partnership of complementarity' may describe the current state of the ASSET Programme but we should be striving for a 'partnership of equivalence' as a more progressive notion of the joint ownership of the ASSET Programme. For this reason, therefore, we have recently begun the active promotion of the tutors' modules for academic staff in the university.

Flexibility (1): Developments in the Peer-group Process

One of the basic premises of the programme philosophy is flexibility and choice (see Chapter 2). This becomes a difficult principle to adhere to with ever increasing numbers and without putting available resources under intolerable strain. We have already explained the importance of the Peer Group process in providing support for candidates undertaking the ASSET Programme. So far, Peer Group members have had to work on the same module, often compromising on individual choice to gain a consensus in the group. Hence, even with nearly a hundred candidates on the programme and an increasing range of modules to choose from, the choice of modules is in practice still severely restricted.

In response to this problem, the way forward we are exploring is to run peer groups in which each candidate undertakes a module of their own choosing, as opposed to a module which has been selected through group consensus, but which may not have the same appeal or relevance for all candidates. This would mean any competence-based module could be undertaken through the Peer Group process even if only one candidate wanted to complete a particular module at a given time. At the time of writing a group of candidates is participating in such a 'mixed module' Peer Group facilitated by an experienced tutor. Between them they are undertaking a variety of modules, drawn from a range of specialisms, including adoption and fostering, working with older people, and working with people with a disability.

Feedback from the group so far has been positive, although we have agreed that candidates must have taken part in at least one Peer Group where the module being undertaken is the same, before participating in a group with different modules being attempted. The first module serves the dual function of enabling candidates to learn about the programme procedures as well as providing shared support in the selection of evidence for the same elements of competence. We felt that participants would be exposed to too many unfamiliar processes at once if their first experience also involved understanding and supporting others working on *different* modules.

Some of the key procedures and skills from McGill and Beaty (1992) described in Chapter 8 have been particularly crucial in the facilitation of this experimental Peer Group. Simple tactics such as ensuring that each member of the group knows what everyone else is working on have proved to be important. At the first meeting, all members made a firm commitment to the life of the group and it was agreed that *everyone* should bring evidence to share with each other at each meeting. Each member of the group was also allocated a certain amount of time in each meeting to use in a way that they felt would be of most benefit to them in completing the module. Adhering to equal opportunity principles and balancing the varying needs of the candidates requires skilful management of the process. An unintended outcome of this way of working is that candidates are exposed to areas of work that they would not normally come into contact with. On the evaluation forms recently submitted they remark on feeling inspired (and surprised) by work that is going on in other specialist areas, and yet also pleased by a sense of the generic unity of their profession.

Flexibility (2): 'Hybrid' and 'Personal' Modules

The ASSET Programme endeavours to ensure that the candidates' practice should be the starting point for the content of the competence based modules. However, we have come to realize that although the range of competence-based modules in the ASSET Programme is comprehensive it is not exhaustive. With social services departments moving towards greater specialism some client groups are not fully represented in the range of currently available modules. More generally, we have had to acknowledge that the range of complex and interesting challenges to which candidates may be responding do not always fall neatly into one of the modules available. Fortunately, our colleagues in the Anglia Polytechnic University Centre

for Accreditation and Negotiated Awards have begun to develop helpful procedures intended to address this potential gap between candidates' experience and
module content, and we have begun to take advantage of these opportunities. There
are two main procedures which we have begun to use: the 'hybrid module' and the
'personal module', which we describe in this section.

Hybrid Modules

This will allow candidates to synthesize competence statements from separate
but related modules drawn together in a way that matches their experience as
a practitioner more precisely than the content of any single module. A candidate
wishing to construct a hybrid module will work with a tutor to identify competence
statements against which they could evidence their learning. The competence
statements selected are taken from existing validated competence-based modules
and therefore the process of gathering evidence in relation to the competence
statements follows exactly the same format as candidates undertaking existing
modules. In agreeing to the construction of hybrid modules, the programme team
will bear in mind both the intellectual and professional *coherence* of the set of
competence statements selected, its *applicability* (as a *set* of competence statements) to other candidates working on the programme, and its relevance within the
employment context from which the practice is derived. Candidates will be able to
complete up to a maximum of two hybrid modules when undertaking the programme
to gain a degree (or graduate diploma), which increases the range and flexibility of
opportunities for candidates without undermining the coherence and structure of the
existing programme.

We do not yet have any candidates undertaking a hybrid module, but we
anticipate that as candidates become more confident in their own ability to produce
portfolios of practice evidence in relation to statements of competence, this option
will gain increasing prominence within the programme.

Personal Modules

To help us accommodate candidates with a type of experience that is not catered
for within the validated modules of the ASSET Programme our colleagues in the
University Centre for Accreditation and Negotiated Awards drew our attention to
what they called an 'open box module'. This allows candidates to construct their
own learning outcomes against which to provide documentary evidence. However,
the 'open box module' pertains only to the accreditation of *prior* experiential
learning, whereas we needed a procedure which would allow candidates, if they
wish, to make equal use of current *and* previous learning, in the same way as the
existing modules on the programme. We therefore made our own adaptation of the
'open box module' procedures, calling it the 'personal module'.

Our first step was to write the general learning outcomes described in Document

'Personal Modules': General Learning Outcomes

On successful completion of this module students will have:

1 Identified a particular area of past, present or planned social work practice or intervention from which learning outcomes can be derived that have coherence within the BSc in Social Work Award Programme.
2 Negotiated specific competence statements in relation to either a planned or completed programme of learning or a combination of both these activities.
3 Provided a portfolio of evidence which demonstrates the specified learning outcomes to the standard specified by the Core Assessment Criteria.
4 Demonstrated independence and autonomy in identifying, designing, implementing and evaluating a personal programme of learning.

12. These general learning outcomes were intended to be both specific and flexible enough to guide ASSET tutors in helping candidates design modules based on their individual experiences. We further stipulated that the 'specific competence statements' referred to would need to have the same design characteristics as the competence statements which make up the existing validated competence-based modules. In considering the appropriateness of the suggested area of practice, the tutor will be mindful of the fact that each personal module may itself become a 'validated' module within the programme and must therefore have coherence within the social work award (or other award) and must be potentially applicable in the future to the practice of other candidates on the programme. Having negotiated the specific competence statements, the candidate will then submit to the tutor a module action plan (in the normal way) which will specify how the general learning outcomes and the specific competence statements are to be demonstrated and how the Core Assessment Criteria will be met.

In order to establish the personal module as a credible extension of the competence-based approach, we have worked with one of the ASSET candidates in using the 'personal module' format and reviewed the effectiveness of the procedure. The student concerned had already successfully completed one of the existing competence-based modules and was therefore familiar with the nature of appropriate evidence, the Core Assessment Criteria, and the 'level' and complexity of the work required. This particular candidate, Christine McMillan, wished to construct a degree-level competence-based module in the area of counselling which would enable her to make use of her current and planned practice experience and the knowledge acquired in a taught course (which had *not* been at degree level).

We began by advising Christine that the format of the existing competence-based modules should be used as a 'model' for her 'personal module', and that she would need to think of a title which was broad enough to encapsulate up to ten elements of competence which would comprise a coherent framework against which she could provide evidence. At our second meeting Christine provided us with a draft of the module title and a list of elements of competence. Initially we were slightly dismayed by this first attempt. It seemed clear that we had underestimated the exacting nature of the competence statements (in terms of appropriate standards of practice, level of complexity, and balance between knowledge, skills and values);

we had thus also underestimated the difficulties involved in asking a practitioner to write their own elements of competence which would need to

- indicate an academic level equivalent to the last year of an honours degree,
- match the format of the statements in the existing competence-based modules,
- form a coherent unit of learning; and
- be demonstrable in terms of practice evidence.

We realized that this was considerably more difficult than merely asking a candidate to write 'learning outcomes', which could be more general and loosely based. It was obvious therefore that Christine's first draft sat very uneasily next to the existing modules, derived from a functional analysis, and that it was not acceptable as a degree-level module.

Fortunately, however, the problem turned out to be largely a difficulty at the level of language and format, since Christine understood the nature of a competence-based module at degree level (from her previous work within the ASSET Programme) and she knew exactly what it was she intended to demonstrate. We spent two hours discussing and amending the draft material. For example, we agreed to abandon her proposed statement 'Identify important psychological issues in work with clients' in favour of 'Work with the client to establish and maintain a framework and boundaries for on-going work'. In this way the same 'important psychological issues' would still need to be addressed (especially when the competence statement was linked with one of the Core Assessment Criteria), but in a way which is focused on the actual work with the client, and thus more easy to demonstrate in terms of evidence from practice. Thus the competence statement became both more 'realistic' and also more in line with the interests of the client.

In this way, working together, we (Christine McMillan, Maire Maisch, and Paula Sobiechowska, an experienced ASSET tutor) derived the following set of competences, which seemed acceptable in terms of the programme requirements and which Christine felt fully reflected the work she had in mind.

Document 13

Example of a 'Personal' Module: Counselling with Clients as a Method of Social Work Practice

1 Evaluate the effectiveness of an intervention in a counselling relationship.
2 Demonstrate the use of particular models of intervention in the counselling process.
3 Give a detailed account of the progress of sessionally sequential work with a client.
4 Evaluate the effects on personal learning in the counselling relationship.
5 Consider the relevance of the agency context in relation to the counselling process.
6 Demonstrate a sensitive response to ethical concerns in counselling.
7 Work with the client to establish and maintain a framework and boundaries for ongoing work.
8 Analyse the significance of the counselling process within the social work profession.
9 Demonstrate the effects of a counselling intervention in direct work with a client.

Eventually Christine McMillan produced an excellent portfolio, in which exemplary use was made of the Core Criteria as an analytical reflective tool. Tutors and external examiners readily agreed that it was of an excellent standard, easily comparable with the best of the work submitted for the existing validated modules.

This work gives us hope that the 'personal module' format can open up further flexibility in the implementation of a competence-based approach to professional education. It suggests, once more, the key role to be played by the Core Assessment Criteria, and this is equally apparent in the following section in which we describe the beginnings of our attempt to devise a version of the ASSET model at postgraduate level.

A Postgraduate Version of the ASSET model

When the first set of candidates were approaching graduation from the programme, they proposed to us that we should devise a version of the ASSET model for use in gaining a postgraduate award, i.e., an M.A./MSc.Degree. As senior professional staff, this was the academic level which would have significance for them, but they also emphasized that they wanted to continue to use a competence-based approach to their work, i.e., to gather and analyse evidence from their practice against a set of specified requirements.

In working towards this new documentation we were fortunate in that the University Centre for Accreditation and Negotiated Awards had developed a set of postgraduate 'generic learning outcomes'. We therefore began with the slightly amended version of these criteria which had been adopted in the Health and Social Work Faculty, as listed below:

All successful Masters (sic) students will be able to:

1 design, implement and evaluate a personal learning programme;
2 generalize, apply and transfer their learning and experience;
3 generate theory from observation, practice and experience;
4 innovate at the level of intellectual synthesis (and, where appropriate, practice);
5 handle complex issues from a variety of standpoints; and
6 demonstrate in depth knowledge of, and an ability to contribute to, intellectual debate in a specialized area.

Our second important resource was the document detailing 'the Requirements for Post Qualifying Education and Training' published by the Central Council for Education and Training in Social Work (CCETSW, 1992), which contains two sections on the characteristics of an 'Advanced' (explicitly postgraduate) professional award (pp. 17–18; pp. 33–8), expressed in terms of professional qualities and aspects of practice. Altogether this is an imaginative model of an 'advanced professional' role, comprising four separate aspects (practice, management, research, and education and training) but also seeming to emphasize an 'integrated' vision of a senior professional role in which all four of these aspects are *linked*. For example on p. 34 the requirements under 'practice' refer to '*developing* systems' and to 'seeking to overcome . . . restrictions and problems' (which we might interpret as 'research'); to 'consultancy, teaching, or supervision' (i.e., 'education and training'); and to '*managing* this process effectively'.

This 'integrated' conception of a professional role which entails management, research, education, and a high level of specialist practice expertise is also embodied in the 'Requirements for All Candidates' (Section 4.4.3, pp. 17–18), which is presented below in shortened form:

All candidates must demonstrate the ability to:

a) analyse practices and policies;
b) research, plan, implement, and evaluate strategies for improvement or change;
c) review and critically evaluate the value base of their work in the light of social and political change;
d) define and develop policies and practices which reflect a high standard of anti-racist and anti-discriminatory awareness and understanding;
e) understand, apply, and critically evaluate an extensive an up-to-date range of knowledge, theoretical models, methods, policies, and law;
f) act skilfully in the role of supervisor and consultant;
g) act and communicate effectively in inter-disciplinary and cross-professional work; and
h) manage innovation.

Working out from these two conceptions of a) postgraduate intellectual activity and b) the integrated responsibilities of a senior professional worker, a group of us gradually synthesized a set of what are intended as Core Assessment Criteria for a postgraduate ASSET model, presented in Document 14. The details remain to be worked out, but at this stage it seems likely that we will begin by trying to use the procedures of the 'personal module' described earlier. The challenge of identifying *post*graduate criteria returns us to the vexed issues surrounding educational levels (see Winter, 1993b; 1994a) and the progress of this development so far throws into sharp relief, once more, the crucial importance and value of Core Assessment Criteria expressing *general* educational and professional roles and processes, as argued at length in Chapter 4.

Conclusion: 'Bridging' Education and Work

We began, in Chapter 1, by situating the ASSET Programme in the context of the long-standing debate concerning the proper relationship between university education and practical life. This debate has two aspects. Firstly, how can educational curricula draw upon the requirements of the world of work in order to achieve practical 'relevance'. This is the aspect which is addressed by formulating educational outcomes in terms of specific vocational competences. But there is another aspect: how can the world of vocational practice draw upon *educational* processes — so that it can facilitate *learning*, so that it encourages a *broad* understanding ('theoretical', 'analytical', 'interdisciplinary', 'informed by' bodies of knowledge), and so

Document 14

The Postgraduate ASSET model: Draft Core Assessment Criteria
(Developed by Julie Bateman, George Booker, Maire Maisch, Anne Murray, Paula
Sobiechowska, and Richard Winter)

1 **Consultancy and leadership**
This involves demonstrating specialist expertise in the candidate's chosen field and acting
as a resource to their own agency/other agencies.
It includes:
- Enabling others to see the work from a range of different (including international)
  practice and organizational perspectives;
- Sharing knowledge and understanding in order to illuminate and influence practice;
- Providing colleagues with support, opportunities, and help with the containment of
  anxiety in relation to professional challenges.

2 **Management of innovative practices**
This involves implementing and sustaining changes resulting from new proposals and ideas.
It includes:
- Clarifying lines of authority and accountability within the agency;
- Influencing debates concerning care and practice policies;
- Involving staff and service users to develop ideas on how services can best be
  delivered and advocating these ideas in appropriate policy arenas;
- Implementing and evaluating the development and operation of equal opportunities
  policies in relation to practice;
- Utilising information technology appropriately, with an understanding of its possibilities and its limitations.

3 **Evaluation of the value base of social work**
This involves using a wide range of professional knowledge to define policies and practices
in relation to anti-racist and anti-oppressive principles and engaging in critical evaluation of
the ethical culture of the agency in order to implement recommended changes.
It includes:
- Reviewing the value base of the agency in the light of socio-political and legal
  changes;
- Addressing serious ethical dilemmas;
- Sustained engagement with the need for equality of opportunity;
- Challenging organizational policies which perpetuate discrimination.

4 **Research, evaluation, and personal learning**
This involves evaluating research findings, theoretical and professional models, legislation,
policies, and methods in order to conceptualise and investigate current and evolving practice,
proposing alternatives to established theory and practice, and generating new theoretical
insights.
It includes:
- Evaluating, monitoring, and assessing their own and others' work in relation to complex issues;
- Evaluating, challenging, modifying, and developing professional theory and practice;
- Promoting a culture in which personal and professional critical feedback is welcomed
  and used constructively;
- Demonstrating an understanding of the international context of social work in order
  to inform their professional practice.

5 **Inter-professional collaboration**
This involves initiating and sustaining collaborative and reciprocal working relationships at
various levels in order to enhance networking and negotiate new ventures.
It includes:
- Understanding the structure of power, responsibility, and decision-making in different
  agencies and working flexibly within authority roles;
- Developing coherent solutions to complex issues arising from the different standpoints of various agencies and professions;
- Appreciating the interdependency of a range of agencies and professions and the
  interconnectedness of a range of relevant bodies of knowledge.

that it encourages staff to develop their capacity for autonomous, critical initiative with respect to their responsibilities?

Perhaps there will always be a tension between these two ways of presenting the question of the social 'relevance' of education — the tension between idealism and pragmatism, between theory and practice, between knowledge 'for its own sake' and knowledge for technical effectiveness, between what *is* and what might be/could be/ought to be. These issues underly the whole of human experience, and it is therefore important that they should be addressed, not only within the walls of educational establishments but throughout the institutions in which we work — producing goods and providing services. The analysis of vocational practice and vocational development in terms of 'competences' is one way of attempting to ensure that such issues are addressed *in practice* (as opposed to be being invoked as conventional pieties) and university staff in the UK therefore stand indebted to the work of the National Council for Vocational Qualifications for forcing us to look afresh at the conventions and assumptions underlying our work as educators.

But the relationship between the values of education and the values of production and service provision must be one of *mutual* influence, and a *closer* relationship between the two sets of values entails building a bridge between education and work which, as it were, starts 'from both ends'. The NCVQ model for competence-based curricula, by building out one half of the bridge (*from* the workplace), has challenged the validity, the credibility, and the equity of traditionally taken-for-granted educational practices. But programmes of vocational *education* can and should also challenge the values, policies, and cultures of the workplace, not merely in terms of 'ivory tower' theories and ideals but in terms of the values and under-standings which workplaces themselves *need*, in order to be effective and tolerable as contexts of human activity. This entails building 'the other half' of the bridge, starting from educational values in order to influence those of the workplace.

Perhaps the image of a bridge (with two ends) is rather simplistic as a metaphor for the subtle and complex processes involved here. But we use it (and not for the first time — see Chapter 8) as a way of presenting our conclusion (as a result of our work) that there are two equally important issues at stake in formulating competence-based educational programmes: not only the validity and credibility of educational qualifications but the humanity and creativity of the workplace. It is our contention that the procedures of the ASSET model are a way of formulating vocational education which allow both issues to be treated as opportunities for progress. With its 'two dimensional' approach to assessment, its opportunities for individualized interpretation and definition of competence statements, and its use of learning groups dedicated to the provision of a specific 'space' for mutual support and critical reflection, the ASSET model of competence-based education seeks to put in place *both* halves of the bridge.

Note

1   This chapter is largely based on Maisch, 1996, with contributions from Christine McMillan and Paula Sobiechowska.

Appendices

Appendix A: Staff Contributing to the Development of the ASSET Programmes

The Social Work Project

The Original Instigators of the Project
Anne Hilton, Anglia Polytechnic University (APU)
Paul Stanton, APU
Joyce Brough, Essex Social Services Department (SSD)
Peter Rudge, Essex SSD

The Social Work Project Team
Maire Maisch (Essex SSD)   Richard Winter (APU)
Christine Probert (APU)   Claire Felton (APU)

Essex Social Services Training Section
George Booker   Stewart Thompson
Leo Bishop

Anglia Polytechnic University Centre for Accreditation and Negotiated Awards
Mike Taylor   Christopher Harris
Lynn Brennan   Mick Betts

The Social Work Programme Tutors
Julie Bateman (Essex SSD)   Anne Murray (Essex SSD)
Jean Houlihan (Essex SSD)   Paula Sobiechowska (Essex SSD)
Lindsay Hill (APU)

Members of the Social Work Project Steering Committee
David Pierce (Employment Department)
Judith Croton (CCETSW)
Norman Evans (Learning From Experience Trust)
Ros Kingston (CCETSW)
Roy Stephens (APU)

Members of the Social Work Programme Development Group
Maureen Bunce (Essex SSD)   Vivien Nice (Essex SSD)
Pat Higham (APU)   Maeja Raicar (Essex SSD)

Specialist Module Development Team

Letitia Collins (Essex SSD)   Sue Gourvish (Norwich City College)
Rita Cheatle (Essex SSD)   Carol Oswick (Essex SSD)
Mark Stables (Norfolk SSD)

Pilot Candidates

Barbara Foster (Family Finders)   Ed Kerr (Cambridgeshire SSD)
Pat Howorth (Family Finders)   Margaret Pearson (Essex SSD)
Anne McKinney (Essex SSD)

External Examiners

Clare Gillies (Oxford Brookes University)
Lilieth Grant (Selly Oaks College, University of Birmingham)

Other Contributors

Don Naik (formerly University of North London)
Lloyd Drake (Essex SSD)   Carole Munn-Giddings (Essex SSD)
Jan Phelan (Essex SSD)   Georgie Powell (Essex SSD)
Andy Quinn (Essex SSD)   Bill Stronach (NALGO -now UNISON)

The Ford (Engineering) Project

Instigators of the Ford ASSET project
Anne Hilton (APU)
Ken Mortimer (Ford Motor Company)
John Bale (APU)
Anne Seaman (APU)

The Ford ASSET Programme Team
Samantha Guise (APU)
Mike Holman (Ford)
Richard Winter (APU)
Helen Bowles (APU)
Ann Chapman (APU)

Members of the Ford ASSET project Steering Committee
David Pierce (Employment Department)
Peter Swindlehurst (Engineering Council)
Norman Evans (LET)
John Griffiths (NCVQ)

Members of the Ford ASSET project Management Group
Bob Jaques (Ford)
Alan Mitchell (Ford)

Roy Williams (Ford)
John Macdonald (APU)
Caroline Strange (APU)
John Lowe (Standing Conference for Engineering Manufacture)

Ford ASSET Tutors
Malcolm McKay   Evan Gough
Ken Hart   Paul Ingle
Andrew Minty   David Steward
Edgar Allan

Ford Motor Company ASSET Supervisors
Nick Peacock   Stan Butler
Peter Lloyd   Adrian Moore
Dave Watson

Ford ASSET Pilot Candidates
Andy Delicata   Richard Best
Robert Burnham   Paul Hodges
Navnit Patel   Jeff Titmus
Terry Whitehouse

Appendix B: Current List of Competence based Modules

Core Modules

1 Implementing and developing anti-oppressive practice in the workplace
2 Sustaining morale, developing practice
3 Working with colleagues and other departments and agencies
4 Planning, delivering and evaluating intervention
5 Establishing and encouraging the continuation of effective working relationships between voluntary, independent and statutory agencies
6 Learning from clients in order to develop and extend professional knowledge and skills

Working with Children and Young People

1 Providing the optimum environment for children/young persons and their families
2 Protecting children/young persons from dangerous situations
3 Fulfilling statutory responsibilities in relation to children/young persons and their families
4 Making plans and decisions concerning long-term therapeutic needs
5 Working with family power relationships and race, age and gender roles
6 Interpersonal skills in child care practice
7 Managing and developing staff members' professional potential
8 Encouraging and maintaining relationships between the child/young person, their families and/or significant others
9 Developing an integrative approach to the work of a unit
10 Managing the financial aspects of a unit

11 Helping children/young persons to realize their potential as individuals in group care settings

12 Recruiting and preparing a variety of prospective foster carers/adopters to meet the differing needs of children/young persons requiring family placements

13 Making assessments concerning the suitability of prospective foster carers/ adopters to care for children/young persons

14 Working with birth parent(s) and other family members to enable them to make informed decisions and act in the best interests of the child/ young person

15 Working with children/young persons to prepare them for placements apart from their birth parent(s) and/or normal carer(s)

16 Supporting foster carers/adopters in their role by providing appropriate services

17 Arranging placements for children/young persons suitable to their needs which take account of race, language, religion and culture

18 Maintaining effective working relationships in situations where the planned placement of a child/young person can no longer continue

Working with Adults

1 Promoting clients' potential for independence

2 Maintaining the client in the community

3 Assessing risk

4 Understanding practice and procedures derived from the Mental Health Act 1983

5 Understanding mental disorder and its treatment

6 Ensuring a multi-disciplinary approach to working with people with mental health difficulties

7 Understanding and working with the relationships between clients and carers

8 Managing staff involved in the assessment and provision of services

9 Promoting the rights of people with learning disabilities

10 Enabling adults with learning disabilities to develop strategies for their empowerment

11 Working with adults with learning disabilities to maintain, develop and extend their skills

12 Working with adults with learning disabilities to enable them to participate in valued experiences and relationships

13 Involving clients and/or their carers in making assessments of their needs

14 Enabling adults with physical disabilities to maintain and develop personal relationships

15 Working with people with physical disabilities to develop strategies to combat oppression and stereotyping

Appendix C: Social Work Module: 'Assessing Risk'

Elements of Competence

In order to demonstrate this unit of competence, candidates need to:

1 Demonstrate an understanding of the principles underlying the concept of risk and apply it to a particular practice situation.
2 Consider and interpret the provisions of relevant legislation, policies, codes of practice, and social work theories in relation to an analysis of clients' needs and rights.
3 Collect and consider the multiplicity of factors (personal, situational, and contextual) relevant to the risks of a particular practice situation.
4 Gain a detailed understanding of the client's interpretation of the situation and ensure that it is fully represented and considered in subsequent decision-making.
5 Collect and analyse information concerning the resources and capabilities of the client and of others in the client's situation, and devise strategies to ensure that such personal resources are utilized and supported.
6 Consult other professionals in order to make and justify decisions arising from conflicting views as to priorities of risk and vulnerability.
7 Consult with clients and relevant members of the client's situation in order to analyse and balance the interests of the client and others.
8 Devise a 'risk plan' which summarizes the key decisions involving the assessment and prioritization of risk in the situation, and the criteria whereby the effectiveness of those decisions will be evaluated.
9 Work with the emotions and ethical issues arising from the complexities and risks inherent in the client's situation.

Note: All Core Assessment Criteria must be *implicitly* fulfilled in the evidence for each element; the evidence for each element must be *explicitly* related to *one* of the Core Assessment Criteria.

Appendix D: Social Work Module: 'Anti-oppressive Practice' in the Workplace

Elements of Competence

In order to demonstrate this unit of competence, candidates need to:

1 Demonstrate an up-to-date general theoretical understanding of the nature of oppressively discriminatory attitudes and practices, including their basis both in social and political power structures and in personal, professional, and political ideologies.

2 Recognize and challenge the power of discriminatory social and institutional pressures upon attitudes and practices (including their own) and work towards changing them.

3 Recognize and challenge the ways in which legislation, regulations, and policies can be used to justify discriminatory judgments in particular cases.

4 Work positively with differences between staff, between staff and clients, and between clients.

5 Demonstrate an understanding of the relationship between personal and professional values concerning the rights and dignity of clients.

6 Work with clients (or help others to work with clients) in understanding the impact of oppressive discrimination upon their life experiences.

7 Advocate, implement, and evaluate principles concerning equality of opportunity in relation to policies, practices, and legislation.

8 Respond receptively to challenges concerning their authority, assumptions and beliefs.

9 Demonstrate an understanding of the need to ensure proper client access to information, records, and complaints procedures.

Note: All Core Assessment Criteria must be *implicitly* fulfilled in the evidence for each element; the evidence for each element must be *explicitly* related to *one* of the Core Assessment Criteria.

Appendix E: A Model of Professional Development through Reflection on Practice

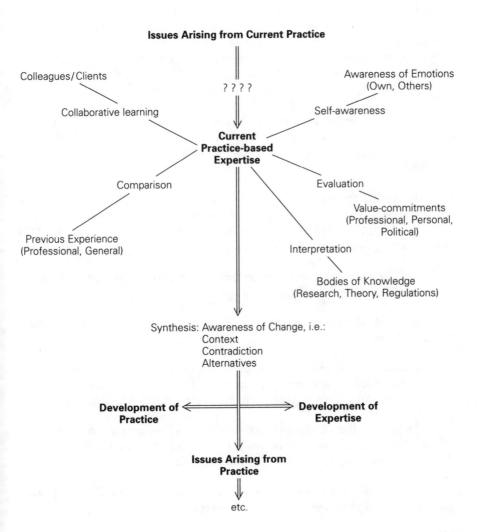

Issues Arising from Current Practice

Colleagues/Clients

? ? ? ?

Awareness of Emotions
(Own, Others)

Collaborative learning

Self-awareness

**Current
Practice-based
Expertise**

Comparison

Evaluation

Value-commitments
(Professional, Personal,
Political)

Previous Experience
(Professional, General)

Interpretation

Bodies of Knowledge
(Research, Theory, Regulations)

Synthesis: Awareness of Change, i.e.:
Context
Contradiction
Alternatives

**Development of
Practice** ⟸ ⟹ **Development of
Expertise**

**Issues Arising from
Practice**

etc.

Appendix F: The ASSET model Format and the NCVQ Format: A Difference of Syntax?

The UK National Council for Vocational Qualifications emphasize that assessment must focus on the outcomes which can be observed in employment practice, not on the activities undertaken by individuals (see Jessup, 1991, p. 33). For this reason, they insist that assessment criteria are presented in 'objective' rather than person-centred terms. In other words, therefore, an NCVQ-style 'performance criterion' takes the form:

> Plans are reviewed, updated and improved at regular intervals after discussion and agreement with the appropriate people. (Management Charter Initiative:(MCI): Management II, Unit II, Element 6.2, Performance Criterion e)

The ASSET Programme, in contrast, focuses on candidates' learning, and so the assessment criteria (the 'elements of competence') are always presented in terms of what the candidates must do. Consequently, if the criterion from the MCI document were used within the ASSET Programme it would be rephrased as follows:

> [Candidates must] review, update and improve their plans at regular intervals after discussion with appropriate people.

All of the 'elements of competence' in the ASSET Programme modules have the latter form:

> [Candidates must] collect and consider the multiplicity of factors (personal, situational, and contextual) relevant to the risks of a particular practice situation. (Social Work ASSET Programme Module — Appendix C)

> [Candidates must] identify and verify root causes of component/system/product failure, by analysing information from various sources. (Ford ASSET Programme, 'Improving Product/Process Quality', Element b)

If the ASSET Programme elements were to be given the NCVQ 'objective' format, the above examples would simply become:

Root causes of component/system/product failure are identified and verified through analysis of information from various sources.

The multiplicity of factors (personal, situational, and contextual) relevant
to the risks of a particular practice situation are collected and considered.

In some ways, this is a rather superficial matter, although it may be symptomatic
of an important difference in emphasis. At one of the ASSET Programme confer-
ences, participants (social work practitioners, managers and educators) were given
examples of competence statements phrased in both of the formats and asked to fill
in a questionnaire indicating their preference. The overwhelming majority preferred
the ASSET format.

Appendix G: The Peer-Group Process

(Extract from the ASSET Programme Handbook — ASSET, 1996)

Outline

The principle underlying the Peer-Group Process is that, given a properly structured sequence of meetings, a group of candidates can provide sufficient support and opportunity for their own mutual learning, so that:

a) The role of Supervisor becomes less crucial, and thus will *not* necessitate prior training;

b) Tutors will only need to provide individual support intermittently, except when it becomes clear that a candidate is having difficulty in meeting the requirements of the process;

c) Observation of practice is undertaken on a mutual basis by the group of candidates (i.e., in a group of five: A observes B, B observes C, C observes D, D observes E, E observes A).

Process

The first step is an orientation meeting for all new candidates on the programme. This will provide for all candidates written details of what exactly is to be required of them at each stage, as described in the Programme Handbook, which will be distributed. Peer groups will also be decided upon at this meeting and candidates will be prepared for their first formal Peer Group Meeting.

For *each module* there will then be a sequence of five meetings. These meetings will be in work time. (It has been agreed that three hours per week of 'release from other duties' are available for candidates.)

The format may be as follows:

The first meeting will involve peer discussion of draft Module Action Plans. (At the end of this meeting, the draft plans will be submitted to the group tutor, who will make any suggestions (if necessary), keep copies, and return originals to the candidates.) Arrangements for the observation of an element of competence will be planned.

The second meeting will involve peer discussion of examples of evidence in relation to competence statements and Core Assessment Criteria, together with commentaries and explanations. (During this meeting, the Group Tutor will try to ensure that he or she sees and comments on material from all candidates.)

The third meeting will involve further discussion of evidence or peer discussion of observation reports (previously sent to the tutor) and of the further evidence required for the element of competence to be demonstrated; tutors will also work with observer/observed couples where the observation report is as yet inadequate.

The fourth meeting may consist largely of individual tutorials.

The fifth meeting will involve peer discussion of draft module portfolios.

Within approximately three weeks of the last meeting, candidates are expected to submit a module portfolio to the Group Tutor. If the Group Tutor is satisfied with the standard, it will be passed to another tutor for final assessment; if the Group Tutor is not satisfied, then she or he will work individually with the candidate to help her or him make the necessary improvements.

Notes and Guidelines on 'Peer Observation'

a) A recording will always be made of peer observation sessions, and this will be available to both parties.

b) The process will be monitored by the Group Tutor, who will receive observers' reports before passing them on to the observed candidate. If the tutor considers that the observation report does not adequately explain how the candidate has demonstrated the element(s) of competence he or she will not pass it on to the observed candidate but will work with the report writer to improve it. Finalizing the assessment may involve the tutor in suggesting to the observer what other evidence (if any) will be required to further demonstrate the element of competence.

c) Immediate verbal feedback from the observer must focus on what the observer has learned professionally from the observation.

d) Written observation reports must focus first on what the observer has learned professionally, before giving an appraisal of the work observed. (This will enable the tutor to evaluate the basis for the appraisal; the recording will be used in case of doubt.)

e) Observation visits arranged mutually between candidates will be an important source of evidence for portfolios. The report written by candidate A upon candidate B's work will be a source of evidence for both B (concerning his or her practice) and could be included in A's portfolio (where it demonstrates his or her understanding).

Appendix H: Evaluation Forms (1995) (NB Spaces Condensed)

MANAGERS FORM

Please would you complete this evaluation form in as much detail as you can, so that the Programme Team can learn from your comments and improve the arrangement for future participating staff.

Please continue your comments overleaf if insufficient space is provided.

Thank you.

Maire Maisch, ASSET Programme Director

Name: **Position:**

Work address:

Names of staff undertaking the programme for whom you are responsible:

1   How far were you aware of the work that your staff were undertaking for the programme?
2   What support and resources were provided for staff during their involvement with the programme?
3   Have you noticed any changes on the part of staff since they began working on the programme? If so, please give details.
4   What is your view on the relative effectiveness of the ASSET model of professional training and other, more conventional forms of training provision in which there is a greater 'taught' element?
5   Further comments. Please continue overleaf if you wish.

Signature: _____ **Date:**

CANDIDATES FORM

Please would you complete this evaluation form in as much detail as you can, so that the Programme Team can learn from your comments and improve the arrangement for future participating staff.

Please continue your comments overleaf if insufficient space is provided.

Thank you.

Maire Maisch, ASSET Programme Director

Name of your tutor:

Approximate date at which you began work on the programme:

Titles of modules already completed:

1 What expectations did you have before you began work on the ASSET Programme?
2 How far have these expectations been achieved?
3 Please indicate any aspects of your work for the ASSET Programme which seemed particularly enjoyable/interesting/stimulating/valuable.
4 Please indicate any areas of difficulty you experienced in your work for the ASSET Programme.
5 Please summarize any comments you were able to obtain from your clients regarding your participation in the programme and your use of material concerning your work with them. Did they feel that your participation in the programme was beneficial to them?
6 Do you feel that the work for the programme required you to *improve* your practice or simply to document what you were already doing? Please give details.
7 Please make any further comment you wish concerning the following aspects of the programme: (Please continue overleaf if you wish)
   a) Preparation/information prior to the programme
   b) Module content
   c) The Module Action Plan
   d) Assessment procedures
   e) The peer group process
   f) Adequacy of support/resources
   g) The suitability of the workplace as a learning context
   h) The general effect on your work of undertaking the programme

Comparing the ASSET Programme process with other forms of training provision, i.e., taught programmes, workshops, workplace project work

- If you have had recent experience of any of these other forms of training provision, please complete the following grid.
- In each box on the grid below place a tick ('satisfactory') or a cross ('unsatisfactory') or a question-mark ('difficult to say').
- If you have had no recent experience of one of the forms of provision then leave the boxes in that column blank.
- Your replies to this section are only intended to provide us with a rough guide, which will alert the Programme Team to issues for further investigation.

For example

If you felt that, by your own standards, you experienced a generally high level of motivation and interest in workshop-based training events, then place a tick; if, in comparison, you felt rather bored and frustrated during your ASSET work, then place a cross. If your feelings about your work for a taught programme were somewhere in between, then place a question-mark; if they were fairly similar to your feelings about the ASSET work, then place another cross.

		ASSET	Workshop	Project	Taught Course
A	The amount of learning you achieved				
B	The relevance of your learning to your work				
C	Your level of interest or motivation				
D	The ease of managing the process				
E	The 'convenience' of the process				
F	The efficiency of the process (i.e., the 'ratio' of your achievement to the effort involved)				

Bibliography

ALLEN, M. (1991) *Improving the Personal Skills of Graduates*, Sheffield, University Personal Skills Unit.

ARGYRIS, C. (1982) *Reasoning, Learning, and Action (Individual and Organisational)*, San Francisco, Jossey-Bass.

ARISTOTLE (1976) *Ethics*, Harmondsworth, Penguin.

ARMSTRONG, P., CARROLL, G., FRAZER, S. and PATEL, K. (1992) *Equal Opportunities and the Development and Assessment of NVQs and SVQs*, Sheffield, Employment Department.

ASHWORTH, P. (1992) 'Being competent and having "competencies"', *Journal of Further and Higher Education*, **16**, 3, pp. 8–17.

ASHWORTH, P. and SAXTON, J. (1990) 'On "competence"', *Journal of Further and Higher Education*, **14**, 2, pp. 3–25.

ASSET PROGRAMME (1996) *Handbook for Candidates, Supervisors, Assessors, Tutors*, Chelmsford, Anglia Polytechnic University/Essex Social Services Department.

ATKINS, M., BEATTIE, J. and DOCKRELL, W. (1993) *Assessment Issues in Higher Education*, Newcastle-upon-Tyne University, School of Education/Employment Department.

BALL, C. (1990) *More Means Different: Widening Access to Higher Education*, London, RSA.

BARNES, D. (1976) *From Communication to Curriculum*, Harmondsworth, Penguin.

BARNETT, R. (1990) *The Idea of Higher Education*, Buckingham, SRHE/Open University Press.

BARNETT, R. (1992) *Improving Higher Education*, Buckingham, SRHE/Open University Press.

BARNETT, R. (1994) *The Limits of Competence*, Buckingham, SRHE/Open University Press.

BECHER, T. (1989) *Academic Tribes and Territories*, Buckingham, SRHE/Open University Press.

BECKER, H., GEER, B. and HUGHES, E. (1958) 'Student culture and academic effort', *Harvard Educational Review*, **28**, pp. 70–80.

BECKER, H., GEER, B. and HUGHES, E. (1968) *Making the Grade*, New York, John Wiley.

BELENKY, M., CLINCHY, B., GOLDBEERGER, N. and TARULE, J. (1986) *Women's Ways of Knowing*, New York, Basic Books.

BELSEY, C. (1980) *Critical Practice*, London, Methuen.

BENNER, P. (1984) *From Novice to Expert*, Menlo Park, Addison-Wesley.

BENNETT, J. (1971) *Rationality: An Essay Towards Analysis*, London, Routledge and Kegan Paul.

BETTELHEIM, B. (1987) *A Good Enough Parent*, London, Thames and Hudson.

BISSELL, C. (1992) 'Shifting into higher gear', *Times Higher Educational Supplement*, 31 January, p. 17.

BLAGG, N., BALLINGER, M. and LEWIS, R. (1993) *Development of Transferable Skills in Learners*, Sheffield, Employment Department.

BLISS, J. (1983) *Qualitative Data Analysis for Educational Research*, Beckenham, Croom Helm.

BLOOM, B. (1975) 'Mastery learning and its implications for curriculum development', in GOLBY, M., GREENWALD, J. and WEST, R. (Eds) *Curriculum Design*, London, Croom Helm, pp. 334–50.

BOYNE, N., FOREMAN-PECK, L. and TALLANTYRE, F. (1992) *Enterprise Education; A Re-evaluation through Six Case Studies of Higher Education's Task in Preparing Students for Work*, Sheffield, Department of Employment.

BRAVERMAN, H. (1974) *Labour and Monopoly Capital*, New York, Monthly Review Press.

BRODIE, I. and WHITTAKER, R. (1996) 'Pathways in practice: Implementing CCETSW's post qualifying framework', *Issues in Social Work Education*, (forthcoming).

BROWN, A. (1995) *Organisational Culture*, London, Pitman.

BRUNER, J. (1966) *The Process of Education*, 2nd ed., Cambridge, MA, Harvard University Press.

BTEC (1991) *Common Skills, General Guidelines, Interim Document*, London, Business and Technician Education Council.

BTEC (1992) *Implementing BTEC GNVQs: An Interim Guide for BTEC Centres*, Issue No. 1.

BTEC (1993) *BTEC GNVQ Bulletin, No. 2*, London, Business and Technician Education Council.

BUZAN, T. (1993) *The Mind Map Book*, London, BBC Publications.

CALLENDER, C. (1992) *Will National Vocational Qualifications Work? (Evidence From The Construction Industry)*, Brighton, Institute of Manpower Studies.

CARE SECTOR CONSORTIUM (1990) *Residential, Domiciliary, and Day Care Project, National Standards*, London, Care Sector Consortium.

CARE SECTOR CONSORTIUM (1991a) *Integration Project, Second Phase Consultation Document*, London, Care Sector Consortium.

CARE SECTOR CONSORTIUM (1991b) *Social Care, Draft National Standards*, London, Care Sector Consortium.

CARR, W. (Ed) (1989) *Quality in Teaching*, Lewes, Falmer Press.

CCETSW (1992) *The Requirements for Post Qualifying Education and Training (Paper 31)*, (2nd ed.; original edition 1990), London, Central Council for Education and Training in Social Work.

CLUTTERBUCK, D. (1991) *Everyone Needs a Mentor*, 2nd ed., London, Institute of Personnel Management.

COBBAN, A. (1975) *The Medieval Universities*, London, Methuen.

COLLINSON, D. and HEARN, J. (1994) 'Naming men as men: Implications for work, organisation and management', *Gender, Work and Organisation*, **1**, 1, pp. 2–22.

CONFEDERATION OF BRITISH INDUSTRY (1989) *Towards a Skills Revolution*, London, CBI.

COUNCIL FOR INDUSTRY and HIGHER EDUCATION (1987) *Towards a Partnership: Higher Education, Government, Industry*, London, CIHE.

COUNCIL FOR INDUSTRY and HIGHER EDUCATION (1995) *A Wider Spectrum of Opportunities*, London, CIHE.

COUNCIL FOR NATIONAL ACADEMIC AWARDS (CNAA) (1989) *Credit Accumulation and Transfer Scheme Regulations*, London, CNAA.

COUNCIL FOR NATIONAL ACADEMIC AWARDS (CNAA) (1991) *Handbook 1991–2*, London, CNAA.

CRYSTAL (1989) *Newsletter*, Issue No. 5, April.

CVCP (1994) *Strategy Paper on Vocational Higher Education*, London, Committee of Vice Chancellors and Principals.

DEARDEN, G. (1989) *Learning While Earning*, London, HMSO.

DEBLING, G. (1990) 'The importance of knowledge and understanding', in FENNELL, E. (Ed) *Competence and Assessment Compendium No. 1*, Sheffield, Employment Department, p. 22.

DELUGA, R. (1994) 'Supervisor trust building, leader-member exchange and organisational citizenship behaviour', *Journal of Occupational and Organisational Psychology*, **67**, pp. 315–26.

DEMING, W.E. (1986) *Out of the Crisis*, Cambridge, Cambridge University Press.

DOUGLAS, J. (1990) 'The wholeness of care', *Community Care*, 5 April.

DORE, R. (1994) 'Japanese capitalism, Anglo-Saxon capitalism: How will the Darwinian contest turn out?', in CAMPBELL, N. and BURTON, F. (Eds) *Japanese Multinationals*, London, Routledge.

DREW, S. and ANDERSON, V. (1995) *Principles of Assessment; Putting Principles into Practice*, Assessment Issues Group, Open Learning Foundation.

DREYFUS, H. (1979) *What Computers Can't Do*, New York, Harper and Row.

DREYFUS, S. (1981) 'Formal models vs human situational understanding', Schloss Laxenburg, Austria, International Institute for Applied Systems Analysis.

DRUCKER, P. (1974, reprinted 1991) *Management*, Oxford, Butterworth/Heineman.

DUCKENFIELD, M. and STIRNER, P. (1992) *Learning through Work*, Sheffield, Employment Department.

DUE BILLING, Y. (1994) 'Gender and bureaucracies: A critique of Ferguson's "The feminist case against bureaucracy"', *Gender, Work and Organisation*, **1**, 4, pp. 179–93.

EISNER, E. (1975) 'Instructional and expressive objectives', in GOLBY, M., GREENWALD, J. and WEST, R. (Eds) *Curriculum Design*, London, Croom Helm/Open University Press, pp. 351–4.

ELLIOTT, J. (1991) 'Competence-based training and the education of the professions: Is a happy marriage possible?', in *Action Research for Educational Change*, Buckingham, Open University Press, pp. 118–34.

EMPLOYMENT DEPARTMENT (1990) *Higher Education Developments: The Skills Link*, Sheffield, Employment Department.

EMPLOYMENT DEPARTMENT (1993) *Knowledge and Understanding: Its Place in Relation to NVQs and SVQs (Competence and Assessment Briefing Series, No. 9)*, Sheffield, Employment Department.

ENGESTROM, Y. (1994) *Training for Change*, Geneva, International Labour Office.

ENNIS, C., LLOYD, N. and PATTERSON, R. (1993) *Construction Industry Standing Conference Professional Competence Project Report*, London, Engineering Occupations Standards Group.

ERAUT, M. (1993) *Assessing Competence in the Professions*, Sheffield, Employment Department.

ERAUT, M. (1994a) *Ethics in Occupational Standards, NVQs and SVQs*, Sheffield, Employment Department.

ERAUT, M. (1994b) *Developing Professional Knowledge and Competence*, London, Falmer Press.

EVANS, N. (1981) *The Knowledge Revolution*, London, Grant McIntyre.

EVANS, N. (1990) 'Systematic reflections', *Times Educational Supplement*, 23 March.

FENNELL, E. (1989) 'TAG guidance note number 2: Developing standards by reference to functions', *Competence and Assessment*, **8**, pp. 2–6.

FIELD, J. (1991) 'Competency and the pedagogy of labour', *Studies in the Education of Adults*, **23**, 1, pp. 41–52.

FINEGOLD, D., KEEP, E., MILIBAND, D., RAFFE, D., SPOURS, K. and YOUNG, M. (1990) *A British 'Baccalauréat' — Ending the Division between Education and Training*, London, Institute for Public Policy, Research.

FISH, D. (1995) *Quality Mentoring for Student Teachers*, London, David Fulton.

FLEMING, D. (1991) 'The concept of meta-competence', in *Competence and Assessment*, **16**, pp. 9–12.

FOWLER, B. (1994) *Management Charter Initiative Personal Competence Model: Use and Implementation*, Sheffield, Employment Department.

FREIDSON, E. (1994) *Professionalism Reborn: Theory, Prophecy, and Policy*, Cambridge, Polity Press.

GADAMER, H.-G. (1975) *Truth and Method*, London, Sheed and Ward.

GARFINKEL, H. (1984) [1976] *Studies in Ethnomethodology*, Cambridge, Policy Press.

GILLIGAN, C. (1993) [1982] *In a Different Voice*, Cambridge, MA, Harvard University Press.

GLASGOW CALEDONIAN UNIVERSITY (1994) *BA in Post Qualifying Social Work, Validation Document*, Glasgow, Caledonian University.

GOFFMAN, E. (1968) *Stigma*, Harmondsworth, Penguin.

GOODLAD, S. (1995) 'Building the ideal engineer', *Times Higher Education Supplement*, 7 July, p. 23.

GOODMAN, C. (1987) 'The Delphi technique: A critique', *Journal of Advanced Nursing*, **12**.

GUNGWU, W. (1995) 'Asia to turn Japanese', *Times Higher Education Supplement*, 9 June, p. 16.

GUISE, S., HOLMAN, M. and WINTER, R. (1994) *Ford ASSET Programme Pilot Stage Evaluation Report*, Chelmsford, Anglia Polytechnic University.

HABERMAS, J. (1976) *Legitimation Crisis*, London, Heinemann.

HABERMAS, J. (1978) *Knowledge and Human Interests*, 2nd ed., London, Heinemann.

HAKES, C. (1991) *Total Quality Management: The Key to Business Improvement*, London, Chapman and Hall.

HANDY, C. (1985) *Understanding Organisations*, London, Penguin Books.

HANDY, C. (1991) *The Age of Unreason*, London, Arrow Books.

HARDING, S. (Ed) (1987) *Feminism and Epistemology*, Milton Keynes, Open University Press; Bloomington, Indiana University Press.

HARRIS, T. (1973) *I'm OK, You're OK*, London, Pan Books.

HECKSCHER, C. and DONNELLON, A. (Eds) (1994) *The Post-bureaucratic Organization*, London, Sage Publications.

HEYWOOD, J. (1989) *Assessment in Higher Education*, 2nd ed., Chichester, John Wiley.

HEYWOOD, J. (1994) *Enterprise Learning and its Assessment in Higher Education*, Sheffield, Employment Department.

HOGG, B., JONES, G., MORICE, P., PREECE, P., SPARKES, J. and SWANSON, S. (1993) 'Developments in first degree courses in engineering', *Engineering Professors Conference, Working paper, No. 6*, University of Sheffield, Engineering Professors Conference.

HOLSTI, O. (1969) *Content Analysis for the Social Sciences and Humanities*, Reading, MA, Addison Wesley.

HOPPER, B. (1987) *Co-operative Learning: An Overview*, Nottingham, University of Nottingham School of Education.

HOSKIN, K. and MACVE, R. (1993) 'Accounting as discipline', in MESSER-DAVIDOW, E., SHUMWAY, D. and SYLVAN, D. (Eds) *Knowledges: Historical and Critical Studies in Disciplinarity*, Charlottesville, University Press of Virginia.

HOUGHTON, V. and RICHARDSON, K. (Eds) (1974) *Recurrent Education*, London, Ward Lock Educational.

HUTCHINS, D. (1988) *Just in Time*, Aldershot, Gower.

ILLICH, I. (1975) *Medical Nemesis: The Expropriation of Health*, London, Calder and Boyars.

INSTITUTE OF DIRECTORS (1991) *Performance and Potential: Education and Training for a Market Economy*, London, IOD.

ISHIKAWA, K. (1985) *What is Total Quality Control?: The Japanese Way*, London, Prentice Hall International.

JESSUP, G. (1990a) 'The evidence required to demonstrate competence', in BLACK, H. and WOLF, A. (Eds) *Knowledge and Competence*, London, Careers and Occupational Information Centre/HMSO, pp. 39–42.

JESSUP, G. (1990b) 'The role of knowledge and understanding in NVQs', in FENNELL, E. (Ed) *Competence and Assessment, Compendium No. 1*, Sheffield, Employment Department, p. 23.

JESSUP, G. (1991) *Outcomes*, Lewes, Falmer Press.

KAWABE, N. (1991) 'Problems of and perspectives on Japanese management in Malaysia', in YAMASHITA, S. (Ed) *Transfer of Japanese Technology and Management to the ASEAN Countries*, Tokyo, University of Tokyo Press, pp. 239–66.

KELLY, D., PAYNE, C. and WARWICK, J. (1990) *Making National Vocational Qualifications Work*, London, National Institute for Social Work.

KELLY, G. (1955) *The Psychology of Personal Constructs*, New York, Norton.

KITSON, A. (1990) *Quality Patient Care: The Dynamic Standard Setting System*, Harrow, Royal College of Nursing/Scutari Projects.

KLINE, N. (1993) *Women and Power*, London, BBC Books.

KNASEL, E. and MEED, J. (1994) *Becoming Competent: Effective Learning for Occupational Competence*, (Technical Report, No. 17), Sheffield, Employment Department.

KOLB, D. (1984) *Experiential Learning*, Englewood Cliffs, Prentice Hall.

LEARNING FROM EXPERIENCE TRUST (1993) *Work Based Learning for Academic Credit*, London, HMSO.

LEE, G. (1994) *Different Impacts of Confucianism on Corporate-Society Formation in Japan and Korea*, Nagoya, Nagoya Shoka University Economic Research Centre.

LINDEMAN, C. (1975) 'Delphi survey of priorities in clinical nursing research', *Nursing Research*, **24**, 6.

MACDONALD-ROSS, M. (1975) 'Behavioural objectives: A critical review', in GOLBY, M., GREENWALD, J. and WEST, R. (Eds) *Curriculum Design*, London, Croom Helm/Open University Press, pp. 355–86.

MAILE, S. (1995) 'The gendered nature of managerial discourse', *Gender, Work and Organisation*, **2**, 2, pp. 76–87.

MAISCH, M. (1996) A critical evaluation of a competence- and work-based degree level award in social work with some general implications for work-based learning in higher education, Chelmsford, Anglia Polytechnic University, Unpublished MA Dissertation.

MAISCH, M. and WINTER, R. (1992) *The ASSET Programme Final Report*, Chelmsford, Anglia Polytechnic University.

MANSFIELD, B. (1989) 'Functional analysis: A personal approach', *Competence and Assessment*, Special Issue No. 1.

MANSFIELD, B. (1990) 'Knowledge, evidence and assessment', in BLACK, H. and WOLF, A. (Eds) *Knowledge and Competence*, London, Careers and Occupational Information Centre/HMSO.

McGILL, I. and BEATY, L. (1992) *Action Learning: A Practitioner's Guide*, London, Kogan Page.

McGREGOR, D. (1960) *The Human Side of Enterprise*, New York, McGraw-Hill.

McINTYRE, D. and HUSTLER, D. (Eds) (1996) *Developing Competent Teachers: Case Studies in Specifying, Assessing, and Reporting on Competences in Initial Teacher Education*, London, David Fulton.

McNair, S. (1993) *An Adult Higher Education: A Vision*, Leicester, National Institute for Adult Continuing Education.

Messer-Davidow, E., Shumway, D. and Sylvan, D. (Eds) (1993) *Knowledges: Historical and Critical Studies in Disciplinarity*, Charlottesville, University Press of Virginia.

Miller, C. (1989) 'Iteration, loops, and brainstorming', *Competence and Assessment*, Special Issue No. 1, pp. 10–13.

Mitchell, L. (1989) 'The definition of standards and their assessment', in Burke, J. (Ed) *Competency Based Education and Training*, Lewes, Falmer Press.

Mitchell, L. (1990) 'The identification of knowledge', in Fennell, E. (Ed) *Competence and Assessment, Compendium No. 1*, Sheffield, Employment Department, pp. 24–6.

Mitchell, L. (1993) *NVQs/SVQs at Higher Levels, Competence and Assessment Briefing Series No. 8*, Sheffield, Employment Department.

Mitchell, L. and Bartram, D. (1994) *The Place of Knowledge and Understanding in the Development of NVQs and SVQs (Competence and Assessment Briefing Series, No. 10)*, Sheffield, Employment Department.

Montebello, A. and Haga, M. (1994) 'To justify training, test, test again', *Personnel Journal*, January, pp. 83–7.

Moon, B. and Mayes, A. (1995) 'Integrating values into the assessment of teachers in initial education and training', in Kerry, T. and Mayes, A. (Eds) *Issues in Mentoring*, London, Routledge, pp. 232–42.

Moonie, N. (1992) 'Knowledge bases and frameworks', *Educational and Training Technology International*, **29**, 3, pp. 216–25.

Morgan, D. (1988) *Focus Groups as Qualitative Research*, Newbury Park, California, Sage Publications.

Morris, W. (1994) [1884] *A Factory as It Might Be*, Nottingham, Mushroom Bookshop.

NCVQ (1989) *Delivering NVQs*, Milton Keynes, Open University Press.

NCVQ (1991) *Guide to National Vocational Qualifications*, London, National Council for Vocational Qualifications.

NCVQ (1995a) *NVQ Criteria and Guidance*, London, National Council for Vocational Qualifications.

NCVQ (1995b) *GNVQs at Higher Levels*, London, National Council for Vocational Qualifications.

NCVQ, BTEC, City and Guilds, and RSA (1995) *GNVQ Quality Framework*, London, National Council for Vocational Qualifications.

Newman, J. (1994) 'Marking schemes are for dullards', *Times Higher Educational Supplement*, 8 July, p. 11.

Newman, J.H. (1982) [1873] *The Idea of a University*, Indiana, University of Notre Dame Press.

Norris, N. (1991) 'The trouble with competence', *Cambridge Journal of Education*, **21**, 3, pp. 331–42.

NZQA (1993) *Guidelines, Criteria and Regulations for the Registration of Units and Qualifications for National Certificates and National Diplomas*, Wellington, New Zealand Qualifications Authority.

OATES, T. (1992) *Developing and Piloting the NCVQ Core Skills Units*, London, National Council for Vocational Qualifications.

OATES, T. (1994) 'Taking care to look where you're going: Caution and credit framework developments', in YOUNG, M.F.D., WILSON, P., OATES, T. and HODGSON, A. *Building a Credit Framework: Opportunities and Problems*, London, Post-16 Centre, University of London Institute of Education.

O'NEIL, M. and JACKSON, L. (1983) 'Nominal group technique: A process for initiating curriculum development in higher education', *Studies in Higher Education*, **8**, 2, pp. 129–38.

OTTER, S. (1992) *Learning Outcomes in Higher Education*, London, Unit for the Development of Adult Continuing Education/Further Education Unit.

OXMAN, R. and GERO, J. (1987) 'Using an expert system for design diagnosis and design synthesis', *Expert Systems*, **4**, 1.

PARSONS, T. (1954) 'The professions and social structure', in *Essays in Sociological Theory*, New York, Collier-Macmillan.

PEDLER, M., BURGOYNE, J. and BOYDELL, T. (1991) *The Learning Company*, London, McGraw Hill.

PELIKAN, J. (1992) *The Idea of the University*, New Haven, Yale University Press.

PETERS, T. (1987) *Thriving on Chaos*, London, Pan Books.

PLANT, R. and RYAN, R. (1992) 'Training evaluation: A procedure for validating an organisation's investment in training', *Journal of European Industrial Training*, **16**, 10, pp. 22–38.

POLYANI, M. (1962) *Personal Knowledge*, London, Routledge.

POSDAKOFF, P. and MACKENZIE, S. (1994) 'Organisational citizenship behaviours and sales unit effectiveness', *Journal of Marketing Research*, **31**, pp. 351–63.

PRING, R. (1992) 'Standards and quality in education', *British Journal of Educational Studies*, **40**, 1, pp. 4–22.

RADCLIFFE-BROWN, A. (1964) [1935] 'Structure and function in primitive society', reprinted in COSER, L. and ROSENBERG, B. (Eds) *Sociological Theory*, 2nd ed., New York, Macmillan, pp. 629–36.

RORTY, R. (1979) *Philosophy and the Mirror of Nature*, Princeton, Princeton University Press.

ROSS, G., PARRY, J. and COHEN, M. (1993) *Philosophy and Enterprise: The Implications for Philosophy of the Enterprise in Higher Education Initiative*, Leeds, University of Leeds Department of Philosophy.

RYLE, G. (1963) [1949] *The Concept of Mind*, Harmondsworth, Penguin.

SAID, E. (1994) *Culture and Imperialism*, London, Vintage.

SALT, D. (1995) 'Cunning humans, selfless machines', *The Times Higher Education Supplement*, 28 April, p. 17.

SALZBERGER-WITTENBERG, I., HENRY, G. and OSBORNE, E. (1983) *The Emotional Experience of Learning and Teaching*, London, RKP.

SAVAGE, M. and WITZ, A. (1992) *Gender and Bureaucracy*, Oxford, Basil Blackwell.

SCHON, D. (1983) *The Reflective Practitioner*, New York, Basic Books.

SENGE, P. (1990) *The Fifth Discipline: The Art and Practice of the Learning Organisation*, London, Century Business.

SHAPIN, S. (1994) *A Social History of Truth: Civility and Science in Seventeenth Century England*, Chicago, University of Chicago Press.

SIMON, H. (1982) 'From substantive to procedural rationality', in McGREW, A. and WILSON, M. (Eds) *Decision-making: Approaches and Analysis*, Manchester, University Press.

SMITH, D. (1987) 'Women's perspective as a radical critique of sociology', in HARDING, S. (Ed) *Feminism and Methodology*, Bloomington, University of Indiana Press.

SMITHERS, A. (1993) *All Our Futures*, London, Channel 4 TV.

SODEN, R. (1993) *Teaching Thinking Skills in Vocational Education*, Sheffield, Employment Department.

SPENCER, L. (1983) *Soft Skill Competencies*, Edinburgh, Scottish Council for Research in Education.

SUTHERLAND, R. and POZZI, S. (1995) *The Changing Mathematical Background of Undergraduate Engineers*, London, The Engineering Council.

SWIERCZEK, F. and HIRSCH, G. (1994) 'Joint ventures in Asia and multicultural management', *European Management Journal*, **12**, 2, pp. 197–209.

TAKENOUCHI, H. and IWASHITA, Y. (1987) 'An integrated knowledge representation scheme for expert systems', *Expert Systems*, **4**, 1.

TANNEN, D. (1992) *You Just Don't Understand: Women and Men in Conversation*, London, Virago.

THOMPSON, D. (1994) *A Day in the Life of Co-operative America*, Washington, National Co-operative Bank.

TOYNBEE, P. (1994) 'The cult of overwork has seized every organisation', *The Radio Times*, London, BBC, 26 November, p. 16.

TRADES UNION CONGRESS (1989) *Skills 2000*, London, TUC.

TRAINING AGENCY (1988/9) *Development of Assessable Standards for National Certification: Guidance Notes*, Sheffield, Employment Department.

TRAINING and DEVELOPMENT LEAD BODY (1995) *National Standards for Training and Development: Learning Development*, Rotherham, Employment Department/Cambertown Ltd.

TUXWORTH, E. (1989) 'Competence-based education and training: Background and origins', in BURKE, J. (Ed) *Competency Based Education and Training*, Lewes, Falmer Press, pp. 10–25.

TYLER, R. (1949) *Basic Principles of Curriculum and Instruction*, Chicago, University Press.

VAN DYNE, L., GRAHAM, J. and DIENESCH, R. (1994) 'Organisational citizenship behaviour: Construct redefinition, measurement, and validation', *Academy of Management Journal*, **37**, 4, pp. 765–802.

VYGOTSKY, L. (1962) *Thought and Language*, New York, John Wiley.

WEBB, J. and MAUGHAN, C. (Eds) (1996) *Teaching Lawyers Skills*, London, Butterworths.

WEBER, M. (1971) [1904] 'The ideal type', in THOMPSON, K. and TUNSTALL, J. (Eds) *Sociological Perspectives*, Harmondsworth, Penguin, pp. 63–7.

WEBER, R. (1985) *Basic Content Analysis*, Beverly Hills, Sage Publications.

WHYTE, W. and WHYTE, K. (1991) *Making Mondragon*, Ithaca, NY, ILR Press.

WILKIN, M. (1990) 'The development of partnership in the United Kingdom', in FURLONG, V., BOOTH, M. and WILKIN, M. (Eds) *Partnership in Initial Teacher Training*, London, Cassell, pp. 3–23.

WINNICOTT, D. (1965) *The Family and Individual Development*, London, Tavistock.

WINTER, R. (1989) *Learning from Experience: Principles and Practice in Action-Research*, Lewes, Falmer Press.

WINTER, R. (1992) ' "Quality management" or "The educative workplace": Alternative versions of competence-based education', *Journal of Further and Higher Education*, **16**, 3.

WINTER, R. (1993a) 'Education or grading?: Arguments for a non-subdivided honours degree', *Studies in Higher Education*, **18**, 3, pp. 363–77.

WINTER, R. (1993b) 'The problem of educational levels' (Part 1), *Journal of Further and Higher Education*, 17, 3, pp. 90–104.

WINTER, R. (1994a) 'The problem of educational levels' (Part 2), *Journal of Further and Higher Education*, **18**, 1, pp. 92–106.

WINTER, R. (1994b) 'Work-based learning and quality assurance in higher education', *Assessment and Evaluation in Higher Education*, **19**, 3, pp. 247–57.

WINTER, R. (1995a) 'The University of Life plc: The "industrialisation of higher education?" ', in SMYTH, J. (Ed) *Academic Work*, Buckingham, Open University Press.

WINTER, R. (1995b) 'The assessment of professional competences: The importance of general criteria', in EDWARDS, A. and KNIGHT, P. (Eds) *Assessing Competence in Higher Education*, London, Kogan Page, pp. 65–78.

WINTER, R. and MAISCH, M. (1992) *The ASSET Programme, Volume 1*, Chelmsford, Anglia Polytechnic University.

WITTGENSTEIN, L. (1967) [1953] *Philosophical Investigations*, Oxford, Basil Blackwell.

WOLF, A. (1990) 'Unwrapping knowledge and understanding from standards of competence', in BLACK, H. and WOLF, A. (Eds) *Knowledge and Competence*, London, Careers and Occupational Information centre/HMSO, pp. 31–8.

WOLF, A. (1994) 'Assessing broad skills within occupational competence', *Competence and Assessment*, **25**, pp. 3–6.

WOLF, A. (1995) *Competence-based Assessment*, Buckingham, Open University Press.

WOLF, A., BURGESS, R., STOTT, H. and VEASEY, J. (1994) *GNVQ Assessment Review Project Report*, Sheffield, Department of Employment.

YOUNG, M.F.D. and GUILE, D. (1994) *Work-based Learning for the Teacher/Trainer of the Future*, London, Post-16 Education Centre, Institute of Education.

Index